Marshall W. Mount

AFRICAN ART

The Years Since 1920

New introduction by the author

A DA CAPO PAPERBACK

Library of Congress Cataloging in Publication Data

Mount, Marshall W. (Marshall Ward)
  African art.

  (A Da Capo Press paperback)
  Reprint. Originally published: Bloomington: Indiana
University Press, 1973.
  Bibliography: p.
  1. Art, Black—Africa, Sub-Saharan. 2. Art, Primitive—
Africa, Sub-Saharan. I. Title.
N7391.65.M68 1989   709.67   89-11818
ISBN 0-306-80373-9

Published by Da Capo Press, Inc.
A Subsidiary of Plenum Publishing Corporation
233 Spring Street, New York, New York 10013

INTRODUCTION TO THE
DA CAPO EDITION

AFRICA has continued to experience political and social upheavals during the sixteen years since the original publication of this book, yet African art and the continent's artistic activity in general proceed very much along the lines described in the earlier edition. Most of the art schools and workshops in both the French- and English-speaking areas still train and have on their faculties interesting, inspiring artists. And although some of the painters and sculptors independent of art schools have died, many others are still active and working in the same style.

Organized according to the chapters of the book, the following are some comments on developments in African art since 1973. A list of name-changes, death dates, and other information supplementing or updating the original edition appears at the end of this introduction.

Mission-Inspired Art in Nigeria

The influence of Father Carroll's workshop style continues unabated in southwestern Nigeria. Father Carroll, himself, has settled outside of Yorubaland in New Bussa, a town on the Niger River. Many younger sculptors, such as Bisi Onawale of Lagos, Israel Ola Taiwo and B. Akin Fakeye of Ibadan, E. Ola and Michael Odekunle of Oyo, and Joseph Imale of

Osi-Illorin are working in this style.[1] Like their famous role model, Lamidi Fakeye, they carve both Yoruba and Christian subjects in traditional Yoruba sculptural forms, such as figures, bowls, and doors. Lamidi, still active, now teaches the techniques and aesthetics of traditional Yoruba sculpture as a full-time faculty member of the University of Ife, one of Nigeria's most prestigious schools.[2]

Souvenir Art in Nigeria

Thorn carvings are still extremely popular in southwestern Nigeria but the originator of this unusual style, Justus Akeredolu, unfortunately died in 1983. During a visit with him in his house at Owo, in 1979, I was surprised to see — in addition to thorn carvings — his carvings of houseposts, ivory bracelets, hip masks, and fan handles. Willett, in his article on the artist and on thorn carvings in general, illustrates a well-carved wood panel with a naturalistic representation of a Yoruba drummer by Akeredolu.[3] For about 15 years before his death, the artist also designed and executed jewelry in a heavy, bold, and extremely imaginative style. Unlike most souvenir artists, Akeredolu was truly gifted and worked well in a wide range of styles and media.

Art Schools in English-Speaking East and Central Africa

Because of the troubled conditions that prevailed in Uganda for most of the last two decades, it has been impossible to obtain information about the present status of the School of Fine Arts at Uganda's Makerere University College, formerly the most influential art school in East Africa. The school's former director, Cecil Todd, under whose leadership it once flourished, left in 1974 to direct the newly established Department of Creative Arts at the University of Benin in Nigeria. In 1976 he returned to England. The painter, Sam Ntiro, who had taught at Makerere, became a professor at the University of Dar Es Salaam and retired in the mid-1980s. Another Makerere faculty member, Teresa Musoke, now has a studio in Nairobi.

[1] Examples of Imale's work may be seen in Joan B. Waite, "The African Art Museum of the S.M.A. Fathers," *African Arts*, XVI, no. 1 (November 1987), 64-67, Plates 2,5.
[2] A fascinating article, based on a videotape of Lamidi carving a figure, is Frank Willett's "An African Sculptor at Work," *African Arts*, XI, no. 2 (January 1978), 28-33.
[3] See Frank Willett, "Nigerian Thorn Carvings, A Living Monument to Justus Akeredolu," *African Arts*, XX, no. 1 (November 1986), 48-53, Plate 22.

Excellent work continues to come out of the Zimbabwean workshop school Frank McEwen established at the museum in Harare almost thirty years ago. This material is now called Shona sculpture since most of it nowadays is, indeed, sculpture and much of it is produced by members of the Shona, Zimbabwe's largest ethnic group.

Following the departure of McEwen, the Shona sculptors found a new patron in Tom Blomfield. He started a workshop on his large farm at Tengenenge, near Sipolilo, for workers unemployed because of the economic sanctions leveled against Zimbabwe before independence in 1980. Although these sculptors turned out important work, exhibited in Europe and America, the movement later collapsed during Zimbabwe's long civil war. Fortunately it was revived in the 1980s and there are now some 70 sculptors carving again at Tengenenge and others working in Harare.[4] Their sculptural material has been exhibited widely at shows in Europe, New Zealand, and Australia. New York City also has a gallery specializing in the finest examples of this school.[5]

Thomas Mukarobgwa. *The Family,* serpentine. Collection of Contemporary African Art gallery, New York.

A representative example of recent Shona sculpture is a work by the first participant in McEwen's original workshop, Thomas Mukarobgwa. Entitled *The Family,* it was carved in serpentine in 1987. Typical of Mukarobgwa's sculptural style, the work is made up of stacked intertwined figures. In *The Family* the father is the uppermost figure; underneath him are the heads of the mother and child. Thomas's fine sense of humor surfaces in this work, where we note the complacent, satisfied mien of the dominant father and the grimacing expressions on the lower two heads. The strong patriarchal bias of many African households is powerfully, albeit comically, portrayed here.[6]

Art Schools in English-Speaking West Africa

In addition to the two Nigerian art schools discussed in the original edition, i.e., Ahmadu Bello University in Zaria and Yaba Technical Institute in Lagos, three more schools gained prominence in the 1970s and 1980s. They are the art departments at the University of Ife, the University of Nigeria at Nsukka, and the University of Benin in Benin City. Fine work is being produced at Ife, where the faculty includes the Oshogbo painter, Muraina Oyelami and the Yoruba sculptor, Lamidi Fakeye.[7]

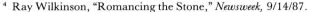

[4] Ray Wilkinson, "Romancing the Stone," *Newsweek,* 9/14/87.
[5] William Karg's gallery, Contemporary African Art, 330 West 108th Street, New York, N.Y.
[6] Conversation with William Karg, February 15, 1989.
[7] John Rowland Oluwasemi Ojo is Head of the Department of Fine Arts at the University of Ife. Conversation with Roland Abiodun, February 3, 1989.

Under the leadership of the outstanding Nigerian artists, Solomon Irein Wangboje at Benin and C. Uche Okeke at Nsukka, these two schools, together with Ife, have challenged the former pre-eminence of Zaria in art training and education in Nigeria.[8]

Benin's program offers a wide range of specialties including painting, sculpture, graphic arts, jewelry, and ceramics, as well as art history and art education. Two fine sculptors, Josiah Onemu and Emmanuel Ifeta, are on the faculty. The former Head, Solomon Irein Wangboje, a noted art educator and graphic artist, both administered the department and conducted several Mbari-type workshops in Benin City similar to those he had led at Ife in the late 1960s.

Unaffiliated with any university, the Mbari-type workshop at Oshogbo continues, although not with the same vigor and creativity of fifteen years ago. The artist, Twins Seven-Seven, only occasionally produces new paintings. Asiru continues to turn out aluminum plaques from time to time and in these he repeats themes and compositions from his earlier work. Jimoh Buraimoh is still, however, extremely active, creating his beaded paintings and executing large mosaics, such as the one on the facade of the new museum in Benin City. In the late 1970s, he took courses in etching at Ahmadu Bello University, Zaria. He has become skilled and prolific in this medium.

Since the original edition, several new Oshogbo artists have appeared. Z. K. Oloruntoba's painting style is similar to that of Twins Seven-Seven although broader and more decorative.[9] Also similar to Twins is a very recent painter, Sam Babarinsa. Isaac Ojo Fajana has pioneered a new technique in his works of stitched, brilliantly colored threads on black cotton backgrounds. His subjects are the spirits and ghosts much beloved by the Oshogbo group.[10] Most interesting of these new artists is Nike Olaniyi, the second of Twins Seven-Seven's seven wives. She, too, works in cloth doing embroidery and, more importantly, batik. Eschewing the traditional Yoruba cassava-resist dyeing, she employs the more versatile wax-resist method. The results are extremely detailed and creative.[11]

[8] Wangboje is now Deputy Vice Chancellor and Emmanuel Ifeta is Head of the Department of Fine Arts at the University of Benin. C. Uche Okeke has retired from Nsukka and is heading a Cultural Center in his hometown of Nimo. The new Head at Nsukka is S. Okeke. *Ibid.*

[9] See Michael Peplow and Z. K. Oloruntoba, "King Marapaka's Dream," *African Arts,* VIII, no. 4 (Summer 1975), 48.

[10] See "Competition 1974," *African Arts,* VIII, no. 2 (winter 1975), 13, back cover.

[11] See Victoria Scott, "Nike Olaniyi," *African Arts,* XVI, no. 2 (February 1983), 46-47.

Artists Independent of African Art Schools

Malangatana of Mozambique, possibly Africa's most expressive painter, has continued to develop. He was active in Mozambique's struggle for independence in the mid 1970s. Since then he has worked for the government in various capacities. At present he is Director of the Craft Department for the state.[12] Added to his earlier themes of both aberrant and elemental aspects of life, are powerful subjects drawn from his imprisonment by the former Portuguese authorities as well as from his experiences during the revolution and independence.

The Senegalese painter N'Diaye, now permanently settled in Paris, has devoted himself exclusively to his art. He has participated frequently in exhibitions including an important retrospective at the Musée Dynamique in Dakar in 1977 and a solo exhibit in New York at the African-American Institute in 1982.[13]

The Nigerian sculptor, Felix Idubor, has not been active for some time. He has moved back to his birthplace, Benin City, where he operates a large art gallery.

A number of independent artists have emerged in recent years, two of whom have already had solo exhibitions in the United States. They are the Sudanese graphic artist Mohamed Omer Bushara, who exhibited at the African-American Institute in 1981, and the Nigerian sculptor Sokari Douglas Camp, who exhibited at the National Museum of African Art in Washington, D.C. in late 1988 and early 1989.[14]

Clearly, then, contemporary African art continues to flourish in a variety of media and styles throughout the continent. It is gratifying to note, too, that this work is steadily gaining international recognition.

[12] Elizabeth Ann Schneider, "Malangatana: Artist of the Revolution," *African Arts,* XXI, no. 3 (May 1988), 58-63.

[13] See catalogue of this exhibition: Lowery S. Sims, *Iba N'diaye: Evolution of a Style* (New York: The African-American Institute, 1982).

[14] See "Competition 1974," *African Arts,* VIII, no. 2 (Winter 1975), 9-11, front cover and *Echoes of the Kalabari: Sculpture by Sokari Douglas Camp* (Washington: National Museum of African Art, 1989).

Name Changes

Countries:

Dahomey to Benin
Rhodesia to Zimbabwe

Cities:

Lourenço Marques, Mozambique to Maputo; Luluabourg, Zaire to Mubuji-May; Salisbury, Zimbabwe to Harare

Peoples:

Today most Africanists drop the prefixes BA and WA. Therefore names in the text should read, for example, Yaka instead of Bayaka, Kamba instead of Wakamba.

Birth and Death Dates

Dr. Paul S. Wingert, d. 1974
Justus Akeredolu, b. 1915, d. 1984
Jimo Akolo, b. 1935
Bamgboye, d. 1978
Yemi Bisiri, d. early 1970s
Osei Bonsu, d. 1977
Erhabor Emokpae, d. 1984
Palmer Erguavo, d. unknown
Vincent Akwete Kofi, d. early 1970s
Gregoire Massengo, d. 1978
Ibrayima Njoya, d. unknown
Simon Okeke, d. 1967

Miscellaneous Information

The painter, Mode, is also known as Mode Muntu.

The African Mission Society should be referred to as the Society of African Missions, cf. page 31.

The Christian Mission Society should be referred to as the Church Missionary Society, cf. page 49.

Since 1973, Makonde carvings have been widely sold throughout Africa by itinerant dealers and souvenir shop owners, cf. page 56.

Mbari clubs, workshops, or centers, other than the original Mbari Club in Ibadan, should be referred to as Mbari-type clubs, workshops, or centers, cf. pages 65-66, 147-58.

Vincent Kofi's Drummer is now at the University of Ghana, Legon, cf. page 128.

Twins Seven-Seven's painting, "Inspiration. . ." was painted in 1969 and purchased by Sean Kelly for the Collection of the Voice of America Bureau, Lagos, Nigeria, cf. pages 149-150.

CONTENTS

Introduction to the Da Capo Edition   v

Foreword by Paul S. Wingert   xvii

Preface   xix

I: Survivals of Traditional Styles   3

II: Mission-Inspired Art   22

III: Souvenir Art   39

IV: The Emergence of a New Art: Introduction   62

V: Art Schools in French-Speaking Africa   74

VI: Art Schools in English-Speaking East and
Central Africa   95

VII: Art Schools in English-Speaking West Africa   124

VIII: Artists Independent of African Art Schools   160

IX: Summary   187

Appendix: Autobiographies of Two African Artists   194

Glossary of Names   199

Bibliography   204

Notes   211

Index   231

PLATES

Map of Africa   2

1. Bayaka tribe, composite mask   8
2. Bapende tribe, mask   8
3. Chief Omoregbe Inneh, plaque commemorating visit of Queen Elizabeth II   11
4. Chief Osdaye Inneh, plaque commemorating the sacrifice of an elephant   13
5. Chief Omoregbe Inneh, *Portrait of Oba Eweka II*   13
6. Osei Bonsu, akua-ba figures   14
7. Yèmadjê, appliqué cloth hanging   16
8. Vincent Lanmandoucelo, *Leopard Attacking a Man*   18
9. Yemi Bisiri, *Female Figure with Attendants*   18
10. Areogun, house post   21
11. Bamgboye, house post   21
12. Lower Congo crucifix   24
13. Lazarus Kumalo, *Mother and Child*   24

14. Sam Songo, *Mashona Legend*   27
15. Cyrene Mission Chapel, *Expulsion from Paradise*   29
16. Étienne Honutondji, *St. Christopher*   29
17. Lamidi Fakeye, doors for church in Oke-Padi, Ibadan   34, 35
18. Lamidi Fakeye, house post   37
19. Afro-Portuguese cup   42
20. Grégoire Massengo, male head   47
21. Anonymous, head   47
22. Cotton tree thorn genre figures   49
23. Donvidé family, lion armchair   50
24. Donvidé family, *Dog*   50
25. Anonymous, *Antelopes*   53
26. Anonymous, *Roaring Lion*   53
27. Anonymous, *Fertility Spirit*   58
28. Anonymous, *Spirit*   58
29. Anonymous, *Spirit Group*   59
30. Pilipili Mulongoya, *Crocodiles and Fish*   78

31. Mwenze Kibwanga, *Devouring of an Antelope*   78

32. Jean-Bosco Kamba, *Serpent and Birds*   80

33. Mode, *Figures*   80

34. D. Bakala, effigy cup   82

35. Ondongo, *Drummers*   86

36. Zigoma, *Figures*   86

37. Zigoma, *Masks*   88

38. Thango, *Composition*   88

39. Papa Ibra Tall, *The Stride of the Champion*   91

40. Papa Ibra Tall, *Peace Will Come*   91

41. Christian Lattier, *The Chicken Thief*   93

42. Gregory Maloba, *Ham Mukasa*   97

43. Sam Ntiro, *Drawing Water*   99

44. Elimo Njau, *Nativity*   101

45. George Kakooza, *Thinkers*   103

46. Teresa Musoke, *Symbols of Birth and New Life*   104

47. Ahmed Mohamed Shibrain, *Calligraphic Abstraction*   107

48. Ahmed Mohamed Shibrain, *Message 40*   107

49. Ibrahim el Salahi, *Allah and the Wall of Confrontation*   109

50. Ibrahim el Salahi, *Funeral and Crescent*   109

51. Ibrahim el Salahi, *Poor Women Carry Empty Baskets*   112

52. Ibrahim el Salahi, *The Embryo*   112

53. Skunder Boghossian, *Yin and Yang*   112

54. Skunder Boghossian, *Explosion of the World Egg*   115

55. Skunder Boghossian, *Cosmological Explosion*   115

56. Gebre Kristos Desta, *Green Abstract*   118

57. Gebre Kristos Desta, *Tin Cans*   118

58. Thomas Mukarobgwa, *View You See in the Middle of a Tree*   121

59. Bernard Manyandure, *Strong Man*   122

60. Boira Mteki, *Granite Head*   122

61. Kofi Antubam, *Paramount Chief and Attendant*   126

62. Kofi Antubam, carved door for the Assembly Hall, Accra   128

63. Vincent Kofi, *Drummer*   128

64. Vincent Kofi, *Pregnant Mother and Child*   131

65. Vincent Kofi, *Awakening Africa*   131

66. Yusuf Grillo, *Yoruba Woman*   134

67. Simon Okeke, *Girl Who Was Turned into a Calabash*   134

68. Bruce Onobrakpeya, *Quarrel between Ahwaire the Tortoise and Erhako the Dog*   137

69. Bruce Onobrakpeya, *Three Spirits*   137

70. C. Uche Okeke, *Fabled Brute*   139

71. C. Uche Okeke, *Maiden's Cry*   139

72. Demas Nwoko, *Nigeria in 1959*   141

73. Demas Nwoko, *Beggars*   141

74. Demas Nwoko, *The Leopard*   143

75. Festus Idehen, *Seated Man*   143

76. Festus Idehen and Paul Mount, relief for Standard Bank of West Africa, Lagos   145

77. Twins Seven-Seven, *Inspiration of Mr. Kelly and Twins Seven-Seven and the Ghost of the Voice of America*   150

LIST OF ILLUSTRATIONS

78. Jimoh Buraimoh, *Obatala and the Devil*   152

79. Jimoh Buraimoh, *Flute Player*   152

80. Asiru Olatunde, *Elephant*   154

81. Asiru Olatunde, *Pigs Cavorting around a Tree*   154

82. Adebisi Akanji, screen for Esso Service Station, Oshogbo   157

83. Valente Malangatana, *Rape*   162

84. Valente Malangatana, *Last Judgment*   162

85. Ibrayima Njoya, *Sultan Njoya Teaches the First Letters of His Alphabet to His Nobles*   164

86. Ibrayima Njoya, *The Battle*   164

87. Ibrahim N'Diaye, *Market*   166

88. Gerard Sekoto, *Mother and Child*   170

89. Gerard Sekoto, *Negro Clarinetist*   170

90. Afewerk Tekle, stained glass window, Africa Hall, Addis Ababa   172

91. Oku Ampofo, *Puberty*   175

92. Oku Ampofo, *To the Sky God*   175

93. Ben Enwonwu, *Risen Christ*   178

94. Ben Enwonwu, *Ibo Dancers*   178

95. Felix Idubor, carved doors for the National Hall, Lagos   182,183

96. Erhabor Emokpae, *Mother and Child*   185

97. Erhabor Emokpae, *The Seeker*   185

FOREWORD

GREAT transformations have taken place during the past fifty years in Black Africa. Changes in the political, economic, social, and, to an extent, in the religious institutions have been investigated considerably by various "on-the-spot groups" from both Europe and America. Their researches have led to the publication of numerous books and articles, and, as a result, some knowledge of these aspects of Black African culture is widely dispersed.

Humanistic studies of the emerging transformations have, however, lagged behind those of the political, economic, and socioreligious aspects. This is not to say that the humanities have been entirely neglected—far from it. Various treatises have been written about the plastic, graphic, and performing arts, and on the literary arts of poetry, the essay, and the novel. An important listing of many of these publications appears in the catalog *Africana,* issued annually by International University Booksellers, Inc. Important contributions on the plastic, graphic, and literary arts are published by the quarterly *African Arts,* which is brought out with copious and handsome illustrations by the African Studies Center at the University of California, Los Angeles.

The majority of books and articles written on the arts of Black Africa have, however, been concerned largely with the traditional tribal arts of the nineteenth and early twentieth centuries. In all too many instances the greatest importance of these publications has been their corpora of illustrations and their occasional documentation of single pieces. For several decades the importance and quality of traditional African art have been recognized, but this art belongs to the precolonial or the colonial periods. More information and careful consideration of the art since the colonial period are badly needed, for the new Black African art did not emerge suddenly after Independence from a limp background. It is necessary to follow clues back to the colonial period in order to understand the current emergence of important artists and the presence of a valid, significant art.

Marshall Ward Mount's *African Art: The Years Since 1920* is important for many reasons, but particularly because it gives a continuity to the study of the traditional, the colonial, and the developing new art. The inception of this study dates to 1961, and the decade of research that has elapsed between its beginning and its completion has produced a very careful investigation of what has transpired throughout sub-Saharan Africa between the introduction of new materials and the emergence of a truly new and creative art. The book is in fact a compendium of personalities and events involved in the development of contemporary African art and an important reference work on this emergent period.

African Art: The Years Since 1920 is a much-needed survey of what has been taking place from the colonial period to the present. While it makes no pretence of being a final evaluation of contemporary African art, it presents the historically important factors relative to this new art and to its present-day setting.

Columbia University   PAUL S. WINGERT, *Professor Emeritus*
December 1972   ART HISTORY AND ARCHAEOLOGY

PREFACE

AFRICA, as the world is aware, is currently undergoing transformation at a speed unequaled in the history of civilization. Changes that took centuries in Western Europe are being telescoped into a few short decades. Perhaps never again will people move so quickly from tribal societies to modern nations whose power and influence are so quickly felt throughout the world.

Details of the political evolution of Africa are well known. New nations have been created despite traditional boundaries, loyalties, and animosities. Traditions already weakened by long contact with Western ways have been broken down further by the goals of independence and nationalism.

It is nevertheless surprising that until recently little attention has been paid to the cultural changes that are an inextricable part of Africa's emergence into the modern world. With the disappearance of traditions so fundamental to life, the cultural environment as well as the political structures of new nations are changing rapidly. Insofar as possible, this study constitutes a detailed investigation of a vital component of any culture, namely, its art. Art must be considered one of the most important African cultural elements. Sculpture, and to a lesser degree, painting, often served in tribal Africa as a kind of cultural mirror, since it was largely produced in response to religious and social needs and consequently reflected and gave visual expression to certain fundamental aspects of life. It is obvious, therefore, that a changing culture must give rise to new art forms.

It was to investigate these changes that the author conducted research throughout sub-Saharan Africa for nineteen months during 1961 and 1962. He returned to that continent in 1966 and again in 1968, 1969, and 1972 for the purpose of updating his original findings. To examine the varieties of art produced on a continent as huge and diverse as Africa was a formidable task.* Although both articles and books concerning artistic developments during recent decades were used in this research, reliance for the most part was placed on information gathered in the field, primarily from artists, patrons, and school and museum personnel. Government officials, church dignitaries, and even interested observers also provided aid.

Four distinctive categories of art have been produced in Africa in recent decades. One of them, art done in traditional styles, is now almost a thing of the past. Traditional styles have continued, however, in a few isolated areas, and an effort was made to investigate some of these survivals.

Shortly after European contact, as early as the fifteenth and sixteenth centuries, an art of strong European influence appeared at the mouth of the Congo River. During this period sculptures, consisting largely of bronze crucifixes and saints, were created by Congolese most likely working under the direct influence of Christian missionaries. After a hiatus of several centuries, the past few decades have seen a revival of art encouraged by Christian missions in Africa, called in this study, mission-inspired art.

A third category, one which can be considered art only in the broadest sense and which is important in present-day Africa primarily because of its economic significance, is work designed for sale to tourists. Like mission-inspired work, souvenir art has had a revival during this century after an early historical precedent. The Afro-Portuguese ivories, created in the sixteenth century for sale as souvenirs to the Portuguese, are the earliest-known examples of this work.

By far the most important type of art in modern Africa is largely one of new media and techniques and personal expression. Often produced by educated and/or acculturated individuals, this art frequently reflects an African-*cum*-Western art school background. The artists work either independently or, more often, in conjunction with art schools.

Many diverse styles of this new art have developed in modern Africa. Most of them are an amalgam of traditional African art and modern Western influences. A major concern of this study is with the themes and techniques of this new art and its influences from the past and present. The African artists involved in this contemporary expression fall into several overlapping generations. Although a good portion of the study will be concerned with very young artists, the older

* Fieldwork was conducted in the following countries: Burundi, Cameroun, Chad, Dahomey, Ethiopia, Gabon, Ghana, Guinea, Ivory Coast, Kenya, Liberia, Mali, Nigeria, People's Republic of Congo, Republic of Zaïre, Rhodesia, Rwanda, Senegal, Sierra Leone, Tanzania, Togo, Uganda, Republic of South Africa, the Sudan, and Zambia.

men, although only ten to twenty years their senior, have also made significant contributions.

Because it would be impossible to discuss the production of every artist working in Africa today, this study makes no pretense at being all-inclusive. To those artists who may have been omitted because of the exigencies of space, I apologize.

I would like to thank the Rockefeller Foundation for providing the support for the research on which this book is based. I owe a particular debt of gratitude to Dr. Robert W. July, now of Hunter College, but formerly of the Foundation staff, whose vast knowledge of and interest in all things African provided the original impetus for this project. But for his aid this book would never have been written.

I am most grateful, too, to Dr. Paul S. Wingert, Professor Emeritus at Columbia University, who was responsible 25 years ago for my initial interest in African art. Since then I have learned much from him, and his assistance, editorial advice, and wide knowledge of African art have contributed a great deal to this work. Other scholars whose suggestions have been incorporated are Drs. Hans Himmelheber, William Hance, Elliot Skinner, and Graham Irwin.

Dr. Joseph Black of the Rockefeller Foundation was responsible for helping provide supplemental support for research carried out in Africa in 1968. President Rodney O. Felder of Finch College and that institution's Faculty Research Fund have also played a role in this study's completion.

I also wish to thank the artists, collectors, institutions, publications, and photographers who have helped make available the material illustrating this book. The collections credited are those in which the works were found at the time I studied and photographed them.

I am especially grateful to the following: for plates 1, 2, 8, 9, 14, 21, 22, 23, 25, James M. Coxe; 4, Western Nigeria Information Service; 7, Dahomey Information Service; 12, 16, *Liturgical Arts;* 18, Frank Speed; 19, B. and W. Forman, Batchworth Press; 26, Kenya Information Service; 27, 28, 29, J. Anthony Stout; 35, Rolf Italiaander; 42, Uganda Information Service; 45, George Kakooza; 47, Ahmed Mohamed Shibrain; 49, 50, 52, Ibrahim el Salahi; 53, Skunder Boghossian; 54, 55, Dennis Duerden, Paul Hamlyn; 56, 57, Sidney Head; 58, The Museum of Modern Art, New York; 59, 60, Frank McEwen; 63, Walter E. Marten, Ghana Information Service; 69, Juliet Highet; 71, Mbari Publications, Ibadan; 76, *Nigeria Magazine* Archives; 80, 83, Ulli Beier; 85, Musée National, Douala, Cameroun; 86, Cameroun Information Service; 93, 94, 95, Nigerian Information Service. The assistance of *African Arts,* in which several of these photographs first appeared, is also gratefully acknowledged. All other photographs are by the author. The map of Africa is by Helen Kirkpatrick.

To the many other people who freely offered information and advice—librarians in the U.S., Europe, and Africa, museum personnel, art school directors, private collectors, and of course, the artists themselves—I also wish to say thank you. Finally, I must thank my wife, Isabel, whose skills as researcher, editor, and secretary and whose encouragement and good advice have all helped make this book possible.

Finch College
February 1973

Marshall W. Mount

African Art: *The Years Since 1920*

Dakar • • Thiès
SENEGAL

Zaria
NIGERIA
Oshogbo
• Ibadan • Foumban
CAMEROUN

LIBERIA
IVORY COAST • Kumasi GHANA
BENIN

Abidjan
Accra
Abomey
Lagos
Benin City

CONGO
GABON
M'Bigou
Brazzaville
Kinshasa

ZAIRE

Lubumbashi

Khartoum •
SUDAN

Addis Ababa
ETHIOPIA

UGANDA
Kampala
KENYA
Nairobi

TANZANIA
Dar es Salaam

MOZAMBIQUE

Harare •
ZIMBABWE
Bulawayo

Maputo

Johannesburg

SOUTH AFRICA

I: Survivals of Traditional Styles

ART IN sub-Saharan Africa has a long heritage. Excavations in the plateau region of Nigeria have uncovered evidence that sculpture was done there perhaps as early as 500 B.C. The terra cotta heads and figures that have been found in that area are among the oldest known examples of traditional art. They have been attributed to the Nok culture, a society that may have been contemporary with the great age of Greek art. But because archeology is a science new to Africa below the Sahara, so far we have only isolated examples of the arts of other early cultures. The few surviving examples known, however, all in materials such as bronze, stone, and terra cotta and so preserved from the ravages of tropical insects and climate, show a high degree of technical excellence that could only have been achieved after considerable development and experience. That would indicate that art has held a continuously important place in the societies of at least part of the continent for several thousand years.

The great bulk of traditional African art known to us, however, is sculpture made of wood. Because of the perishable nature of the material most of this work is not very old, having been made within the last 100 years or so. This sculpture was until recently done in a wide variety of styles and techniques, all along the West Coast of the continent and in the Congo, as well as by a few scattered tribes in the East, such as the Makonde. The masks, figures, heads, and ceremonial and utilitarian objects created by the many societies of these areas are as varied as the peoples that produced them.

But there is one major similarity most traditional African sculpture shared for all its stylistic variation. Unlike recent Western art it often had a social function in addition to an aesthetic purpose. African artists made most carvings and castings to be used, often in religious ritual. But museums and private collections also hold numerous weaving pulleys, food bowls, weapons, and other objects that had a secular function. In either case, the sculpture was used as an integral part of the culture that produced it, and was created in response to specific religious or social needs.

Today the religious and social traditions of Africa are in a state of flux. In many places they have already almost completely disintegrated. As a result, it is now exceedingly difficult to find artists who work expertly in the styles of their ancestors. Often the last skilled craftsman, if still alive, is too old to work, or his successors are so inept that their works are crude and worthless parodies of the fine traditional sculpture. Only in a very few areas are artists who work in the traditional styles continuing their work with little loss in quality. It is impossible to be optimistic about the continued survival of traditional art, for when the few older artists still producing good work die, it is likely that this art will die with them.

The breakdown of African traditions began with the advent of the European colonial powers that ruled the continent for generations. These countries introduced through trade, even before colonization, their own long-established customs. Under the influence of these new ideas every sphere of African life—economic, political, social, and religious—began to change. The newly independent African nations largely base their economies on either European capitalist or socialist systems; have governments patterned after the legislative, executive, and judicial bodies found in Europe; and have, in large part, adopted the dress, speech, and even religion of the former ruling nations.

The breakdown of traditional religions has been one of the most important of the changes in that it has had the most devastating effect on traditional art. Christian missionaries, permanently established in Africa by the mid-nineteenth century, sought to supplant the prevailing religious practices by establishing their own churches and schools. At times they actually destroyed publicly, sometimes in dramatic bonfires, objects associated with African religious beliefs. Thus missionaries often almost completely destroyed native religious practices, thereby eliminating one of the strong raisons d'être for most traditional African art.[1]

As a result of generations of indoctrination the attitude of today's African "elite" sometimes contributes to, rather than arrests, this disappearance of traditional sculpture.[2] The majority of Africans of this group received their earliest training at mission schools, the only education available on most of the continent, and their ideas, particularly among the older generation, often reflect this early Western-inspired training.

This attitude was at times expressed in the writings of one of Ghana's best-known contemporary artists, the late Kofi Antubam:

> It will therefore be illogical for the Ghanaian in the twentieth century to be expected to go and produce the grave and ethnological museum art pieces of his ancestors. The argument that he should continue to do so because of the unfortunate influence of African traditional art on the meaningless abstractionists' modern art of Europe, is not sufficient to dupe him into being complacent. He is determined to paint, sculpt, and write using such methods as are used in the older nations of the world, and basing his work on subjects selected from the meaningful and realistic aspect of his way of life. The glad thing about him is that he is well aware that in art, what is important is not the kind of medium used, but what one expressed with the medium. And what the Ghanaian expresses in art today needs not necessarily continue to be featured by disproportions and distortions which undoubtedly are the greatest quality of the sort of art expected of him by the world outside Africa.[3]

Furthermore, in conversations with Antubam, his suspicion of the motives for Western interest in traditional art were at times also evident. The African "elite" sometimes believe that Westerners, by their enthusiasm for the continuance of traditional art, are attempting to "keep Africans in their place," "hold them back," and perpetuate Western domination.

This negative attitude toward the old art is beginning to shift, however, particularly among younger African artists, many of whom incorporate older elements into their work. Several governments of the new African nations, too, have become concerned with the problem and are trying to revive interest in traditional art by commissioning carvers to produce works in this vein for their government buildings, for example, in Nigeria and Dahomey.[4]

Another effort to preserve Africa's artistic heritage is centered in the museums of the continent. In this respect African nations are continuing to support and enlarge museums of traditional art established by colonial powers.[5]

Found in almost every country, these museums collect and exhibit old, traditional pieces. They are of extreme importance in inculcating respect for this art.[6] Several of these institutions have, in fact, sought to buy back masterpieces from overseas museums and private collections. Some have also been instrumental in persuading their governments to enact laws to prohibit the export of traditional works or "antiquities." However, in the future, African museums might take an even more active role in maintaining, if not possibly improving, the quality of this art by finding patrons for the few artists who are still active.

Some of the traditional work still being produced continues to be used in time-honored ways, but many examples of this art are also being made for sale to Europeans.* For instance, akua-ba figures carved by excellent Ashanti sculptors are sold both to Europeans and to those local women desiring them. It was impossible in most cases, however, to determine what proportion of objects of a specific style type are sold for traditional purposes. Consequently, work done in the traditional style by authentic artists of the original tribe or kingdom will be discussed in this chapter. In contrast, there are copies of traditional African art which are made by artists of other tribes or kingdoms, often thousands of miles away from the site of the style's origin. These works, never used for traditional purposes, are sold exclusively to Europeans. Moreover, these copies frequently incorporate deviations from the original traditional style in materials, subject matter, and formal qualities. Such examples, which are wholly souvenir works, will be discussed in chapter 3.

Two factors determined the examples herein discussed. The first consideration was that the grant from the Rockefeller Foundation that made this investigation possible was for the study of the new arts of Africa: souvenir art, mission-inspired art, and most important, the newly emerging twentieth-century art. Consequently, the major research carried out in Africa was done in those areas where those new arts flourished. It was considered important, however, also to examine work being done in the traditional styles in these regions. By the same token, it was impracticable to spend much time in those

* The term "European" is used throughout this study in the same sense that it is used in Africa, to denote persons of the Caucasian race whether from Europe or America.

areas of sub-Saharan Africa where the new arts were apparently either non-existent or unimportant. As a result, several former traditional art-producing areas, such as the Ivory Coast, Liberia, Mali, Gabon, Upper Volta, and Angola, were not included in this study. The purpose of this chapter, then, is to indicate what has happened to traditional art in several selected regions of sub-Saharan Africa. It is not meant to be a thorough investigation of the subject, a study which in itself would have required much more time than was available.

The second factor determining the traditional styles examined was the extent to which political conditions limited travel within various regions. For example, Zaïre and, to a lesser extent, Cameroun, both formerly significant traditional art areas, were at that time in political turmoil. Although it was possible, if not always safe, to visit certain major cities in those two countries, extensive travel throughout the countryside was impossible. It was therefore difficult to determine the amount and quality of their traditional-style art at that time.

In this regard working in Zaïre was particularly frustrating because the country was then torn by civil strife which prevented investigation in those areas where surviving traditional work had most recently been reported. It was possible, however, to visit Luluabourg as well as Kinshasa and Lubumbashi.

In some of these cities, an examination of recently created examples of traditional-style art shows that they retained some of the earlier style qualities. For example, a composite Bayaka mask (Plate 1) purchased in Kinshasa reflects much of the quality of the traditional initiation masks of these people. No information was available as to whether it had ever been used by the tribe: such use, however, is doubtful, since the interior of the mask and its handle are very new indeed in appearance. Unlike another example, seen in a local souvenir shop, it is made in the traditional composite technique of this style. Its colors are not of the garish hues found in the more commercialized version of this mask. On the other hand, its recent manufacture is indicated by the relative crudeness of the carving of the inside of the mask, which is roughly blocked out with only one eye slit corresponding with the eye of the mask; the other eye slit punctures the forehead.

At the same time a number of recently carved masks from the Bapende tribe were purchased. Plate 2 illustrates one of those of good quality, showing only a minimum of degeneration. Like the Bayaka mask, however, it

1. Anonymous. Composite mask, wood and raffia, Bayaka tribe. Collection of the author.

2. Anonymous. Mask, wood and raffia, Bapende tribe. Collection of the author.

evidences little sign of use. A handwritten inscription inside gives a provenance and a date, August 12, 1956. It is not as finely carved as the earlier masks from the same tribe, for roughly carved areas above and below the eyebrows and surrounding the mouth tend to vitiate the traditional style. Most of the typical style traits of old Bapende masks are, however, retained in this example.

In Luluabourg, capital of Kasai Province, I interviewed Paul Timmermans, a young Belgian artist in charge of the local museum. He directed the museum from 1959 until his return to Belgium in 1961, when the museum was permanently closed. He was an enthusiastic supporter of art using traditional forms and had regularly purchased objects from Bakuba and Badjokwe craftsmen for exhibition and sale at the museum. Timmermans asserted that as a result of the chaos after Independence all such work among these peoples had ceased.

An example of the work sold at the museum in Luluabourg was a Bakuba cup that showed much more deterioration in quality and style than the masks discussed above. It was thick and heavy when compared with traditional cups. Its shape, too, was different from most older vessels, and was an adaptation of the chalice used in Christian worship. The cup was, however, decorated with a typical Bakuba interlace design, although the design was carved without the technical control evident in earlier examples.

Cameroun presented like difficulties for research. Foumban, the capital of the Bamoun tribe, where a civil war raged at the time, was a center for much of the brass work made in that country. Again travel throughout the countryside was restricted. Numerous examples of brass work were seen although the tourist trade in the Bamoun city was then nonexistent. The pieces included several small genre figures, some of erotic subjects, and many brass masks.[7] The style retained much of its former quality, although technically the work was not as fine as in the older masks and the casting seemed cruder.

The kingdom of Benin in Nigeria, formerly a center for a strong traditional art style, evidenced the poorest quality of work of all the areas investigated. The traditional-style wood carvers in Benin City were the late Idah and the four sons of Ine Igbesamwa, head of the carvers guild. Igbesamwa's sons still occasionally carve crude and simplified versions of the traditional stools, altar heads, rattles, food bowls, and boxes formerly found in the kingdom and used primarily by the chiefs. They are only nominally traditional craftsmen, however, since most of their time is spent carving the ebony portrait busts that are so popular with Europeans (see below, pp. 46–48).

The brass casters of Benin are more numerous and active. They work, as did their predecessors, in a special quarter of the city. The most important among them are Chief Omoregbe Inneh, Chief Ihama, J. N. Omodamwven, David Ihama, and Palmer Erguavo.

Chief Inneh, the head of the brass casters guild, is the most skilled. He was born in Benin City about 1903 and learned his trade from his father, Chief Osdaye Inneh. About 1926 he began working in the palace of Oba Eweka II, joining eight other casters, among whom he was second in rank. Here he made small pieces such as bells and a few plaques. In 1938 the colonial administration sent him to Achimota College in Accra, Ghana, for two years, to study as well as to teach the traditional Benin cire perdue method of brass casting. At Achimota he learned to prepare gelatin and plaster of Paris molds, techniques he has since discarded. On his return he was placed in charge of brass casting at the Arts and Crafts School in Benin City, where he remained. Here he worked along with Omodamwven, lecturing to schoolchildren and training apprentices.

Inneh's best-known work is probably the plaque displayed in the reception room of the Oba's palace (Plate 3). Produced on his own initiative to commemorate the visit of Queen Elizabeth II to Benin City in 1956, it memorializes, in traditional fashion, an important event occurring during the Oba's reign. As in ancient Benin plaques, the Oba is attired in ceremonial dress and in traditional hierarchical fashion is the larger figure.

There all similarity with traditional work ends. The plaque is of brass rather than bronze and its format is horizontal rather than square or vertical. It is framed with a ropelike design. Unlike earlier examples, its background is not decorated with foliate or circle designs, but carries instead a raised inscription. The Oba is shown in profile rather than in the traditional frontal pose. Elizabeth's image, on the other hand, is a composite one. Her frontal torso is combined with profile legs, arms, and head, a convention found in earlier relief arts, such as the Egyptian, Mesopotamian, and archaic Greek, but not in Benin. Moreover, both figures occupy a specific position in space defined by a ground line. The informality of the pose, an Oba shaking hands, and the crude casting are further departures from the original Benin relief style. As a work of art the relief is crude, naive, and relatively without merit.[8]

It is revealing to compare this work with a plaque made by Chief Inneh's

3. Chief Omoregbe Inneh. Plaque commemorating visit of Queen Elizabeth II, brass, Benin Kingdom. Collection of Oba Akenzua II, Benin City, Nigeria.

father, representing the sacrifice of an elephant in 1936 in honor of the Oba (Plate 4). A much more successful work, the earlier brass continues many more features of the traditional Benin style. It, too, however, shows departures from ancient Benin plaques. The material is brass, the casting is relatively crude, and the background is undecorated. The composition, although bearing a closer resemblance to the earlier work than does Chief Inneh's plaque, is somewhat disorganized. This plaque is the only one ever commissioned by Oba Akenzua II during his long reign, and, significantly, it is kept in the museum rather than the palace. It is interesting to speculate how the relief style might have developed if more commissions had been forthcoming.

Chief Inneh's work in the round is seen in his portrait of the deceased Oba Eweka II (Plate 5). It is one of the few recent works executed in the traditional bronze. Modern castings are done in brass because, according to Inneh, it is cheaper and people prefer it because it more closely resembles gold. The casting is cruder than the ancient works and the filing of surfaces and details is considerably more inept.

In this work the sculptor departs radically from the classical Oba portrait, an important traditional subject. The head is expanded into a European-style bust. The face is more naturalistic or, as the artist said, "more correct." Most disturbing are the more lifelike eyes, which, in contrast to the time-honored, dramatic, staring eyes, are narrowed, with the pupils directed downward. Because of its increased naturalism the portrait no longer conveys the tremendous power and the absolute authority of the Benin Oba. None of these new portraits has yet been purchased by the present Oba for use on the royal ancestral altars.[9]

The kingdom of Ashanti in Ghana is also still producing art in the traditional style. Brass gold weights are being cast although they are no longer used in the conventional manner, for weighing gold dust, but instead are sold to Europeans. According to Chief Inneh, knowledge of the cire perdue technique of casting, the method by which these weights were made, had already disappeared in this area by the late 1930s. He maintained it was he who was partly responsible for reviving the art, having retaught some Ashanti the technique while he was at Achimota College. Nowadays it is possible to buy these new weights readily in Ghana in shops and hotels or from the ubiquitous Hausa traders (see below pp. 40–41).

The present-day weights consist of single or double figures engaged in

5. Chief Omoregbe Inneh. *Portrait of Oba Eweka II,* bronze, Benin Kingdom. Collection of the artist.

4. Chief Osdaye Inneh. Plaque commemorating the sacrifice of an elephant, brass, Benin Kingdom. Collection of Oba Akenzua II, Benin City, Nigeria.

6. Osei Bonsu. Akua-ba figures, wood, Ashanti Kingdom. Asante Cultural Center, Kumasi, Ghana.

genre activities or acting out proverbs. They are uniform in size, approximately two inches high. The figures are typically Ashanti in proportions and details, but they are simpler than the older examples and the casting is cruder.

It is in woodcarving that the Ashanti excel today. Undoubtedly the leading carver in recent years has been Osei Bonsu, who was for many years court carver to the deceased king or Asantehene, Otumfuo Nana Sir Agyeman Prempeh II. Bonsu, grandson of an Asantehene, was born in Kumasi in 1900. He learned carving from his father and in turn taught the craft at Achimota College from 1937 to 1945 and at Adisadel College from 1947 to 1956. Returning to Kumasi after 1956, he resumed his duties as the Asantehene's carver and continued to work with the next Asantehene, Opoku Ware II.[10]

Bonsu specialized in the carving of royal paraphernalia—objects such as linguist staffs, umbrella tops, state sword handles, and drums. He has also carved a number of stools.[11] In both categories his work is completely traditional in style and of high quality.

The artist has carved as well many traditional-style Ashanti "fertility dolls" or akuaba figures for local women and for Europeans. Two of them (Plate 6) are exhibited in the museum of the Asante Cultural Center in Kumasi. In the left figure especially, Bonsu attempts to break away from the traditional style. The result is much greater naturalism, akin to that introduced into the earlier akuaba figures by the same sculptor and illustrated in Rattray's pioneer work on the Ashanti, published in 1927.[12] Unlike the Rattray figure, where the naturalism is introduced into the body, here, with the exception of a slight bulge in the cylindrical torso, Bonsu has concentrated the naturalism in the head. The head is teardrop shaped with ears, and the facial features, too, are lifelike. The new akuaba figure is not, however, as aesthetically successful as the more geometric and highly stylized traditional ones.

Osei Bonsu's eldest son, named Kojo Bonsu, served as the Asantehene's carver during his father's imprisonment for political activities against the Nkrumah regime. He was trained by his father, and his style, which appears in a comparable array of objects, is very similar to his father's, although not quite as refined.

Both traditional brass casters and appliqué cloth makers are still at work in Abomey, capital of the Fon kingdom of Dahomey. The cloth workers, as is customary, are members of the Yèmadjê clan living in the Hechilito quarter near the palace. A recent hanging, shown in Plate 7, is similar in technique,

7. Yèmadjê. Appliqué cloth hanging, cotton, Fon
Kingdom. Collection of the artist.

subject matter, and composition to the older examples exhibited in the nearby palace of past Fon kings. Certain departures, however, have been made from the earlier style. Forms appliqued to the neutral background, usually symbols of past kings and their exploits, are often crowded together, emphasizing the lack of compositional unity found in the older hangings. These forms are now bright red, yellow, blue, and green, as opposed to the more subtle vegetable-dye colors of the works displayed at the palace. Yèmadjê also makes the appliqued cloths used in the umbrellas and hats formerly fashionable among the Dahomean nobility.

Brass work is the outstanding traditional Fon art still practiced. Vincent Lanmandoucelo, born in Abomey in 1898, was not only the most important artist but the head of the brass casters as well. His family has always worked in this medium and his sons are continuing the craft. Hundreds of pieces are offered for sale in his house; they mostly portray such traditional themes as the hunter and the elephant lifting a man on his trunk. A group composition depicting a leopard attacking a man (Plate 8) makes it clear that there has been minimal loss in quality in recent work. Characteristics of the older Fon style are evidenced by such elements as the fineness of the casting, the proportions of the figures, the shaping of facial features, and the chased surface designs.

Lanmandoucelo has, however, in response to European demands, experimented with new themes. He has, for example, created a series of earthy and erotic brasses representing the taking of enemas and the different positions of sexual intercourse. One of his most popular recent subjects is an acrobat holding aloft a pole surmounted by a platform on which a separately cast pair of figures is so carefully balanced that the platform rests, and will even spin, on its small, pointed base. This subject is readily obtainable anywhere in Dahomey, and it is often hawked by Hausa traders in the neighboring countries of Nigeria and Ghana.

Among the Yoruba tribe in Western Nigeria, some of the most important traditional-style art is being created. Traditional brasses for the highly secret Ogboni society and other Yoruba cults are still being made. Yemi Bisiri, a brass caster who lives in the village of Ilobu near the important Yoruba town of Oshogbo, frequently makes objects for the Ogboni society. His fame is demonstrated by sales of his brasses not only to local society members but to others scattered throughout Nigeria, Ghana, and Cameroun as well. He sells, too, to European collectors of traditional art.

8. Vincent Lanmandoucelo. *Leopard Attacking a Man,* brass, Fon Kingdom. Collection of the author.

9. Yemi Bisiri. *Female Figure with Attendants,* brass, Ogboni society, Yoruba tribe. Collection of the author.

Bisiri, using the cire perdue technique, casts such traditional Yoruba subjects as the mother and child with flanking figures illustrated in Plate 9. These works share many style traits common to Yoruba figures and masks, for example, the proportional relationships of figures in a group and the treatment of large, bulging eyes.

Although Bisiri's style has been called that of Obo-Ekiti, a comparison of an individual figure from Plate 9 with equestrian figures in the Obo style illustrated by Willett indicates that in addition to his cruder casting Bisiri has made significant stylistic departures from the traditional style.[13] Although his elongated and schematic figure is similar to the Obo work, the head deviates radically. It is represented by a small volume to which an enormous protruding open mouth and spherical eyes are attached. The large, spherical eyes, occasionally separated by a median split, reappear as shapes so often that they constitute a clear style trait. His fascination with this form is evident in his frequent use of spheres to decorate figure supports. In this figure, as in his other sculpture, an over-sized, flattened headdress is a crowning feature.

It appears that Bisiri "has found a highly personal style. . . . His figures look rough at first sight, but they have a wonderful vitality about them that is comparable to any ancient work."[14] He is one of the few traditional artists who have developed a style that is not a weaker copy of earlier work. He has taken the traditional art forms and used them as the basis for his own exciting new ideas.

In most Yoruba areas traditional woodcarving has degenerated, but among the Ekiti Yoruba in the northeastern part of Western Nigeria it remains relatively strong. Several important carvers have worked in recent decades among the Ekiti. They are Areogun, Bamgboye, Bandele, and Lamidi Fakeye, sculptors who have carved bowls, house posts, doors, and the many Epa masks required for use in this region.

The late Areogun, the earliest carver about whom there is sufficient information, was born about 1880 in Osi, a village north of the border between the present Ekiti and Ilorin provinces. Areogun (a nickname meaning literally "he who gains money in the service of Ogun," the god of craftsmen who work with iron tools) enjoyed great fame, and his work may be seen in villages many miles from Osi. He apparently produced a great quantity of work, carving until his death in 1954.[15]

Two years before his death Areogun carved the house post with an equestrian Oba and his followers on exhibit in the museum of the University of

Ibadan (Plate 10). In contrast to the house posts with superimposed figures typical in other Yoruba areas, Areogun follows the format used in the Epa masks of the Ekiti area. As in most traditional Yoruba work, scale relationships are based on conceptual rather than optical reality.

Bamgboye is the Ekiti carver best known to Europeans. Bamgboye Alogbonnikubioyimbo (the latter name meaning "wise like a European") has lived his long life in the remote village of Odo-Owa at the northern limits of Western Nigeria. Here he produced works on commission for local people and expatriates and for some time taught carving in a local school.

A house post Bamgboye carved in 1931, now in the Lagos Museum, is illustrated in Plate 11. Its style is close to that of Areogun, although it shows less interest in surface decoration. Bamgboye, unlike his predecessor, has developed new sculptural types, such as coffee tables, breadboards, and letter openers specifically created for sale to Europeans. In these works the figure style and even the geometric decorations have lost vitality and expressiveness and have become hard and slick.

Areogun's son Bandele has a style practically identical with his father's. He has carved doors, drums, and posts for palaces and Ogboni society houses among the Ekiti Yoruba. In 1947 he joined the workshop at Oye-Ekiti at the invitation of its director, Father Kevin Carroll, and remained there for seven years.[16] During this period he trained the youngest of the traditional Yoruba carvers considered in this study. Lamidi Fakeye (see below, pp. 33–38). In later years, because sculpture commissions were scarce, Bandele worked as a sawyer in the Ekiti village of Ifaki, but he has returned to work with Father Carroll.[17]

Those, then, are some of the survivals of African art in the traditional styles. Research done for this study, within the already mentioned limitations, has found this art survives most strongly among the Benin, Ashanti, and Fon Kingdoms and the Yoruba tribe of the West Coast. Although in most instances, the media and technique have continued practically unchanged, by and large the quantity and particularly the quality of production have diminished greatly in recent years. The Yoruba have maintained the highest quality of work, while the art of their neighbors in Benin has suffered considerable degeneration in style. In the traditional-style art that remains, numerous other changes in style have taken place. While many of them have been regrettable, the exciting and original brasses of Yemi Bisiri are the result of a change that has had positive results.

10. Areogun. House post, wood, Yoruba tribe. Museum of the University of Ibadan, Ibadan, Nigeria.

11. Bamgboye. House post, wood, Yoruba tribe. National Museum, Lagos, Nigeria.

II : Mission-Inspired Art

MISSION-INSPIRED art is still being produced throughout Africa largely under the guidance of Christian missions. Although Christian themes are usually portrayed in this work, commissions are sometimes accepted from outside the church when secular subject matter may be represented. In either case styles are at times adaptations derived from European art.[1] In other instances, comparable adaptations come from traditional art; occasionally, however, mission-inspired art bears little relationship to either of these sources.

The primary aim of most of this art is to promulgate the concepts of Christianity, that is, for the education of mission parishioners. To further this end, the works usually embellish the walls, altars, and portals of mission churches. They are also at times sold to Europeans, thereby providing additional, much-needed revenue for the missions. A corollary result, obviously, is the training of craftsmen and artists; some of them have, in the course of time, successfully established themselves in workshops independent of the mission and consequently are free to sell to whomever they choose.

Mission-inspired art has had a long history in sub-Saharan Africa. It began at the end of the fifteenth century, when there appeared in the Lower Congo region (the mouth of the Congo River) reproductions of Christian liturgical objects produced by Congolese artisans. They included copper and brass crucifixes called Nkangi, statues of St. Anthony, bells, and staffs.[2] Beginning in the seventeenth century, these works were no longer made and the old pieces lost their Christian meaning. They remained valued objects, however, serving either as chiefs' insignia or playing an important, although non-Christian, role in African ceremonies and rites.

Crucifixes, like the one illustrated in Plate 12, are particularly interesting, and suggest by their variety origins in a number of local Congolese workshops. Such variation appears especially in the treatment of details in the representation of Christ. An enlarged navel, so prevalent in African sculpture, may or may not be present, arms and legs may be thin or heavy, and hands and feet may at times be nailed to the cross. The head is always treated differently and lacks the crown of thorns.[3]

Certain generalizations may nevertheless be made about these crucifixes. The faces are always African, while the figure style often bears a striking resemblance to the early Romanesque sculpture of Europe. Figures are stiff and flat and the heads are too large for the body. These characteristics may represent a simplification and reduction of models the Portuguese brought with them, since at that date Portuguese crucifixes expressed the more naturalistic styles of the late Gothic and early Renaissance periods.

The Lower Congo works are the earliest extant examples in the history of mission-inspired art. There is no evidence of any other body of work of this kind until the present century, but that does not exclude the possibility that a quantity of work in one style, probably in a less permanent medium such as wood, might have been produced sometime in the past several centuries. All that remains, however, are some unrelated old pieces, such as carved saints, which in the absence of other evidence appear to be individual, unrepeated efforts.

But during the past fifty years there has been an increase in the production of mission-inspired art. Stimulated by outstanding individuals within the churches, several Protestant and Catholic missions have either commissioned objects from traditional craftsmen or have founded their own art schools and workshops.

The Protestant church has begun only one such school worthy of mention, the well-known art workshop of the Cyrene Mission outside Bulawayo in Rhodesia. The mission was established in 1936 and was operated by the Church of England for the first three years as a school for delinquent English boys. In 1939 it was converted into a school for Africans. The Reverend Edward Paterson, minister and part-time artist, directed the school until his retirement in 1953.

12. Anonymous. Lower Congo crucifix, brass. Collection unknown.

13. Lazarus Kumalo. *Mother and Child,* sandstone. Collection of Rowena Burrell.

While Paterson was director, instruction in painting and sculpture was stressed, although Cyrene is a typical mission school with primary- and secondary-school divisions. All students practiced art one afternoon a week. Those showing promise, as well as several cripples who could not perform the daily tasks in carpentry, agriculture, and crafts, were given extra time and attention.

Paterson's mode of instruction is well known. After an interview with him Glencross reported:

> He has never tried to force the hands of his pupils, put ideas into their heads or hold up models for their imitation. As far as possible he keeps his hands off their work. Suggestions and criticisms are thrown out, encouragement is given where it is needed and praise where it is deserved. He doesn't give tidy little lectures on the history of European art, nor does he show them El Greco or Dürer. He has complete faith in the power of their own imagination to create forms and objectify them in whatever way they please. . . . Sometimes Paterson has suggested the original design for a piece of work, but more often pupils work out their own ideas.[4]

Paterson's "laissez-faire" approach was complicated by the students' tribal backgrounds, coming as they did from Malawi, Zambia, Rhodesia, and Botswana—areas lacking, in large part, a vital art tradition.

Lazarus Kumalo, born in 1930 near Bulawayo and a former Paterson student, has become a sculptor of note. Crippled from birth, he went from the hospital directly to Cyrene in 1950. In the mid-1960s he spent a year studying at Makerere University College in Uganda. He has exhibited in several annual Federal Exhibitions at the Rhodesian National Gallery in Salisbury, and has been carving and teaching art in Bulawayo.

Kumalo's *Mother and Child* (Plate 13), carved from a rich red sandstone, the sculptor's favorite material, typifies his style. Like most of his figures, it is large (more than four feet tall) and massive, with bulky limbs and elephantine feet; facial features are large and coarse. Enhancing this massiveness is the figure's compactness; only rarely are parts detached from the core. Above all, his carvings have a power and monumentality reminiscent of some early Romanesque works from provincial European centers.

One of Paterson's own works, placed at the entrance to Cyrene's chapel, is close in style to that of Kumalo and would seem to belie Paterson's claim of no instruction. It is a stone font in the shape of an African flour milling mortar. Like Kumalo's works, it resembles early Romanesque sculpture.

Sam Songo, one of Paterson's most talented students, is undoubtedly the best-known Cyrene graduate. His enrollment at the school in 1946 and subsequent progress were recalled by Paterson:

> Mr. Steward, our Divisional Inspector, brought this boy who lay on the ground seemingly barely alive. Two withered legs protruded but clearly his hands were not normal. I asked Mr. Steward, 'What is right about this boy?' to which he replied, 'I think his left hand is no sae bad.' . . . [H]e was put to drawing . . . and he made rapid progress. One day he claimed that he could carve and to our amazement he has turned out to be quite excellent. He was one of the carvers of the kist for the Princess Elizabeth.[5]

After finishing his studies Songo remained at the school, serving as a part-time art instructor.

Unlike Kumalo, Songo is both a sculptor and a painter. He has executed many commissions in Rhodesia and Zambia. In recent years there has been great demand for his work, partly as a result of sanctions which prevented importation of foreign works of art. He has carved a number of rather dull representations of Madonnas and bishops in wood and in slate. More impressive are his sets of wooden doors decorated with carved relief panels for the Colliery General Office in Wankie, Rhodesia, and for a mining company in Kitwe, Zambia. The panels depict, respectively, the animals of Rhodesia and the history of mining in Zambia.

It is in painting, however, that Songo has done most of his work. His watercolor *Mashona Legend* (Plate 14), painted in 1960, has figures placed in a believable, spacious landscape. Many varieties of plants and trees are set among rock formations suggesting the nearby Matopos region. The landscape and especially the foliage are painted in great detail. (There are often as many as 4,000 separate leaves in a Songo painting.) Figures and objects are outlined and tend to be flat, although there is a rudimentary use of light and shade. The colors blue and green predominate. This work represents a tribal legend, but Songo has also painted historical episodes, such as scenes with Livingstone, pure landscapes, and Bible stories.

Mashona Legend is not only typical of Songo's style but is characteristic of Cyrene painting in general. It is related in many ways to Indian and

14. Sam Songo. *Mashona Legend,* watercolor. Collection of the author.

Persian miniatures and to the works of the Douanier Rousseau. Despite Paterson's disclaimer it seems likely that his students had contact with material illustrating these other paintings.

The Cyrene Mission style is most comprehensively represented in the mission's chapel. Between 1945 and 1947, under Paterson's close supervision, a number of young Cyrene artists[6] painted large murals on both the inside and the outside walls.[7] The chapel is a small rectangular building (about 60' x 20') with a semicircular apse and a pitched roof. Its exterior and interior walls are almost entirely covered by tempora-on-plaster paintings. Both the quality and the quantity of the work create an impressive effect.

The exterior scenes, many of which are considerably larger than life-size, are taken primarily from the New Testament.[8] Flanking the entrance at the southwest corner is the *Expulsion from Paradise* (Plate 15). The composition is obviously derived from Western art, recalling particularly Massaccio's fifteenth-century "Expulsion" fresco in the Brancacci Chapel, Santa Maria del Carmine, Florence. Adam and Eve, obviously African figures, standing side by side, fill a large part of the mural. Their placement in space is on a line diagonal to the plane of the picture.

The program and placement of the interior scenes are in the manner of many Christian churches. The apse is decorated with a central Christ flanked by martyrs; on the side walls are narrative scenes, predominantly parables; above the entrance on the west wall is a Last Judgment.[9] All the apse figures, including Christ, are portrayed as Africans. With one exception, Simon of Cyrene, all the apse figures were drawn by Paterson. Again, as in much of Paterson's work, there is a close relationship to Romanesque art.[10]

With the exception of those in the apse, all the paintings, interior and exterior, were executed by students. An excellent example from the interior is *The Stoning of St. Stephen* from the north wall. Besides the Cyrene style attributes already mentioned, certain additional elements are present, such as vertical perspective and a crowded composition. The scene is framed with a zigzag design commonly used traditionally throughout Africa in sculpture and the decorative arts. Other chapel scenes are bordered with similar traditional designs, such as the interlace found on Benin bronzes, Bakuba "velvets," and elsewhere and the almost ubiquitous stylized cowrie shell motives.

An excellent example of Cyrene's typical Africanization of biblical figures and narratives is found in another painting on the same wall, *The Good*

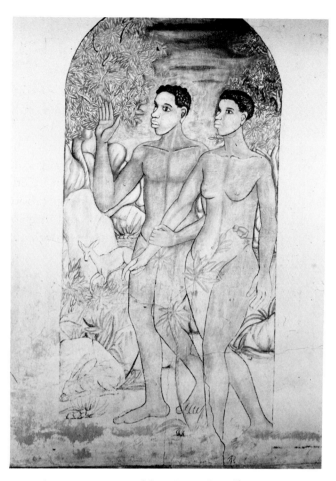

15. Anonymous. *Expulsion from Paradise,* tempera. Southwest exterior wall, Cyrene Mission Chapel, Bulawayo, Rhodesia.

16. Étienne Honutondji. *St. Christopher,* brass. Collection unknown.

Samaritan, in which Jerusalem and Jericho are represented as African villages. The traveler is attacked by a band of *tsotsis,* the term widely used in this part of the continent for young African hoodlums. He is then carried by the Good Samaritan to an African hotel, "Hotel La Bantu." The priest who refused aid is an obese African country preacher, who rides jammed into a small donkey cart. The Levite becomes an African schoolteacher in a long white dustcoat.

The atmosphere that produced this art changed abruptly when Paterson left Cyrene. Intensive art instruction ceased, and if it were not for the part-time teaching done by Sam Songo, the Cyrene style might have ended. As it was, the few remaining students working with Songo frequently resorted to sterile imitations of earlier works.[11]

Full-time art instruction was reestablished at Cyrene in 1961 by William Ainslie, a young white South African artist who left two years later. Instruction has continued since then and, according to the present rector, it is no longer possible to speak of a "Cyrene style" among most of the mission's students. That style, however, continues in the work of several students who are taught informally by Sam Songo as well as in the work of Songo himself.

Unlike the Protestant mission at Cyrene, the Catholic church, in its attempts at art instruction, has turned to traditional African art styles. Encouragement to do so has come from the highest Church authorities. Pope John XXIII told the *Présence Africaine*–sponsored Second International Congress of Negro Artists and Writers:

> Wherever there are authentic values of art and science that can enrich the human family, the Church is ready to favour such efforts of the spirit. She, as you know, does not identify herself with any particular culture, not even with Western Culture to which her history is so closely bound. . . . The Church is ever ready to recognize, to welcome and indeed to encourage all things that honour the human mind and heart.[12]

Even more specific are two encyclical letters. The earlier one, *Evangelii Praecones,* issued by Pope Pius XII in 1951, has several pages on the adaptation of native cultures. *Princeps Pastorum,* issued by Pope John, reaffirms the previous pope's ideas on adaptation and requires, in addition, that bishops establish centers of local culture in their areas and that the clergy be taught about these cultures in the seminaries.[13]

The Catholic church has frequently exhibited as well as made permanent collections of its mission-inspired art, largely to promote interest among both clergy and public. Collections are displayed in special museums in Aix-La-Chapelle and the Lateran in Rome, for example. A comprehensive exposition, with many African examples, was held at the Vatican during the Holy Year 1950. Pope Pius XII thought the exhibition significant enough to comment on it at length in *Evangelii Praecones.*

Despite this official encouragement, there have been only two significant Catholic experiments in Africa. One produced only a small number of works over a short period of time, some brasses with Christian themes made in Dahomey in the late 1940s. They were commissioned by Mlle. Marie Barranger, leader of the group called Art et Louange in Paris, from a traditional Fon brass worker in Abomey. Étienne Honutondji. Even though the finished works were never used in any of the Dahomean churches, they were nevertheless taken to Europe and exhibited in the Vatican's Holy Year exhibition of mission-inspired art. The production of these few brasses, however, cannot be considered as an effort to establish any lasting program for this type of art.

Moreover, Mlle. Barranger supplied the subject matter and the brasses were then cast in the cire perdue technique traditional among the Fon. The results of this collaboration can be seen in *St. Christopher* (Plate 16).[14] The figures adopt poses standard in Christian iconography. Although dressed in modified European fashion and carrying Western symbols and objects, they are characteristic of the lively and animated traditional brass Fon figures. The Fon style is seen particularly in their elongation, with large, spatula-shaped hands and feet and typical Dahomean facial features. Furthermore, the artist often chased traditional Fon designs on the European garments.

The Catholic church itself established several workshops in Western Nigeria that produced a quantity of aesthetically important work. Unlike the Dahomean brasses, some of this material has been utilized by Nigerian churches.

The first of these workshops, begun under the aegis of Father P. M. Kelly of the African Mission Society, was established in 1947 in the town of Oye-Ekiti in northeastern Yorubaland. Fathers Kevin Carroll and Ṣean O'Mahoney ran the workshop jointly.[15] It is important to note that there were gathered together here a small group of traditional Yoruba craftsmen who were for the most part non-Christians. They included carvers, weavers, embroiderers, bead workers, and a single leather worker, who made liturgical objects for use in local Catholic churches. (These craftsmen, however, were not kept from executing commissions for their traditional patrons—the village chiefs and priests.)

The Oyo-Ekiti center closed after a new provincial superior took over from Father Kelly. Two smaller workshops, still operating, were then established in Yorubaland by Father O'Mahoney at Ondo and Father Carroll at Ijebu-Igbo. Contrary to the Oye-Ekiti workshop situation, both new centers have concentrated on carving, although some contracts were given to other craftsmen and musicians.

Since the work created in these centers was under the direct supervision of the two Fathers, there resulted to a certain extent, as in the Dahomean brasses, a combination of European ideas and African forms. The themes here are again Christian but the techniques and formal elements are now Yoruba. Unlike the Dahomean brasses, some of the less important Christian figures, such as the Magi and Pilate, wear African garments. Major figures, Mary and Christ especially, are usually represented in European clerical robes.

Concerning the nature of the relationship between the priests and the craftsmen, Father Carroll has recorded the following:

> We are often asked 'how do you get the carvers to do what you want?' They are told in general what is required, and the matter is discussed and everyone round makes suggestions (especially the bead-worker). For example we discuss 'can our Lady be carved with a head-tie (gele).' After we have come to a conclusion, more technical details, such as composition, relating the work to its surroundings, etc., are decided with the carver. When the work is finished or in progress obvious mistakes, like a forearm bent in the middle or a thumb on the wrong side of a hand are criticized.
>
> There are a few unpleasant features in our school of carving, e.g. the beak-like shape of the mouth (this is not obvious when the face is bearded). Sooner or later we will suggest a changeover to another more pleasing way of carving a mouth (e.g., the Effon style). But it is dangerous to change such things too quickly—it is a matter of years not months. If we draw the carver's attention too much to anatomical details he will lose the firm grasp of design which all good woodcarvers have. They themselves however often refer to the human body and do not work rigidly according to the method taught them.[16]

European models were never shown to the artists, although Father Carroll has stated that in one case a carver was familiar with Western-style crucifixes.[17]

Lamidi Fakeye is the best-known artist to have been associated with all of these Nigerian Catholic workshops. He served his apprenticeship and continued to develop as a sculptor within this environment. Born about 1925 in Illa Orangun near Oshogbo, he is the son of a traditional Yoruba carver.[18] In his youth he viewed carving as "useless work." This attitude was frequently entertained by the sons of traditional Yoruba artists. Instead of studying intensively with his father, Fakeye went to school, although he always did some carving.

In 1948 he asked to be admitted to the Oye-Ekiti center, although he had recently been converted to Islam. Concerning his first meeting with him, Father Carroll has said: "I found his work quite imperfect, but decided to apprentice him to Bandele, son of Areogun, who was working for me. I was glad to meet an educated boy who had some skill as a carver and who was interested in carving as a career."[19] Between 1948 and 1951, under the combined influence of Bandele and Father Carroll, Lamidi completely changed his style.[20]

Lamidi transferred in 1955 to Father O'Mahoney's workshop at Ondo, where he was carving when he was first interviewed for this study. Here he was assisted by several apprentices—his brothers and cousins—two of whom were skilled carvers. He left the workshop in the early 1960s, however, in order to establish (following the example of the successful Nigerian sculptor Felix Idubor) an independent studio in Ibadan, where he has a wider audience and is able to deal directly with his clients.[21]

In 1962–63, on a scholarship from the French government, Lamidi studied stone carving and cement sculpture at the Cité Université in Besançon and at the École des Beaux-Arts in Paris. Leaving France, he paid brief visits to England and the United States. After returning to Nigeria he did no work in stone, for he maintains it is difficult to obtain stone in that country.

In 1966 he returned to the United States, where he served as artist-in-residence at Western Michigan University in Kalamazoo, lecturing and demonstrating techniques of Yoruba carving. Foreign travel and study have not appreciably changed Lamidi's style.

Lamidi has executed a great many important commissions, of which the most numerous are his carved doors. He has made them for churches in

AFRICAN
34 ART

17. Lamidi Fakeye. Doors for church in Oke-Padi, Ibadan, Nigeria, wood. Single panel enlarged, *Christ among the Elders.*

Ondo (1961), Oke-Padi, Ibadan (1956–57), Ebute-Metta, and Lagos (1961), and for the Catholic Chapel at the University of Ibadan (1954–55). He has also carved doors with secular themes for the University Hospital and for the Executive Council Chamber in Ibadan (both 1961), and for the U.S.I.S. office in Ibadan (1967). He was commissioned to carve house posts for the Edena gatehouse of the Oni's palace at Ife (1953),[22] for the Federal Pavilion at the Independence Exhibition held in Lagos in 1960, and for Africa House at Northwestern University, Evanston, Illinois. Among his important works are the speaker's table and the chairs in the Western Region House of Chiefs and the House of Assembly at Ibadan (1955).[23]

Among Lamidi's most memorable relief carvings are the panels on the three sets of double doors for the church in Oke-Padi. The center and most elaborate set, containing six carved panels separated by traditional Yoruba interlace designs (Plate 17a), represents scenes from the life of Christ, from The Presentation in the Temple to The Entombment.

The panel *Christ Among the Elders* (Plate 17b), illustrates the combination of Yoruba and Christian concepts. The composition and some obvious details, such as the halos and Mary's veil, are European. Other elements, however, are Yoruba. Other common Yoruba style traits include the facial features with bulging eyes, Joseph's slab-like beard, and receding chins. Mary's conical hairdress and the agbadas, or robes, and caps of the men are present-day fashions favored in the region.

Beier, speaking of a similar door, makes several valid criticisms of Lamidi's style that are applicable here:

> The door . . . is a charming work depicting the life of Christ in a series of panels. The basic forms employed are Yoruba, but the proportions show a tendency to become more naturalistic and the general sense of form lacks the boldness of a traditional carving.
>
> As a result, it could be held that the carving had suffered. It is pleasant; but a little dull and vague. It lacks the big sweep and power of traditional art and loses itself in a lot of detail. This is only to be expected. A moslem carver (a contradiction in terms?) who grew up as a pagan and now works for the Roman church in alliance with a modern architect, must obviously take some time to find his way.
>
> What is important is not the absolute merit of the door, but that the process of adaptation and integration is actually taking place; and that from this new process there may eventually come a style of carving that will express the mind of the new African.[24]

18. Lamidi Fakeye. House post, wood. Nigerian Antiquities Service.

Lamidi has been more successful in his free-standing works using tribal iconography, for example, the large house post shown at the Independence Exhibition (Plate 18). These posts represent traditional Yoruba figure types of the local Ekiti style that Lamidi learned from Bandele. They have a vigor and expressiveness as well as a monumentality lacking in the figures represented on the doors.

Lamidi's career demonstrates the success of Catholic mission workshops in Nigeria. They provided instruction and practice for him as a young and inexperienced carver and secured many important commissions for him over a period of fifteen years. Lamidi, therefore, has had the opportunity to carve full-time and to train young assistants. Moreover, as a consequence of his private commissions from individuals and the government, he has been able to continue, if only to a certain degree, the style of his ancestors. Lamidi is certainly one of the most skilled of today's Yoruba carvers.

It is evident that mission stimuli in Rhodesia, Dahomey, and Nigeria have often produced a mission-inspired art in a modified African-European style. In Rhodesia, as has been shown, a new art was created, while in Dahomey and Nigeria traditional styles were adapted to Christian purposes. The Rhodesian and Nigerian mission workshops have, moreover, enjoyed considerable local success.

Protestant and Catholic missions could very well establish and support in other parts of sub-Saharan Africa small art workshops or schools comparable to those in Rhodesia and Nigeria. Such centers could not only provide employment for traditional craftsmen but could also discover and encourage new artists. Of benefit to the church, these schools and workshops could produce works that would add richness and beauty to the bare, and often depressing, African churches. Furthermore, these works would, like many art objects used by traditional African religions, have a valuable instructional purpose.

III : Souvenir Art

PERHAPS the best-known category of present-day African art is souvenir art. Involving both painting and sculpture, it is created primarily for sale to Westerners eager to own a piece of "genuine" African art but who are either unaware or unappreciative of traditional work. The raison d'être for this work was forthrightly verbalized by an East African souvenir carver, "We find out what they [Westerners] like. We make what they like when we are hungry."[1]

An entirely new art expression has therefore evolved, an art depicting for the most part the Africa known to the visitor and ignoring the subjects and styles of traditional art. For example, exotic and picturesque flora and fauna that appeal most to the European are realistically represented. Subjects and styles that have proved commercially successful are usually then repeated without variation. Examples of this work, it is important to note, have recently been exported in large quantities as well as sold to Europeans visiting Africa. As a commercial enterprise, souvenir art must be considered an important factor in the economy of many new African states. It is to be found, in fact, throughout the new African nations, even though they are not specifically referred to here, although the present account of this important mercantile adventure certainly embraces the major centers.

Craftsmen producing souvenir work are found all over sub-Saharan Africa, but they are concentrated in the large cities of those countries that either attract many Western visitors or have a large permanent white population. Numerous souvenir craftsmen work in Kenya, Tanzania, Zaïre, Nigeria, Ghana, the Ivory Coast, and Senegal, although there is probably no African country that does not have at least some artisans producing sculpture and painting solely for the European market.

These craftsmen work as individuals or in family or tribal groups. Occasionally a number of craftsmen, commonly of the same tribe or kingdom, band together and form an association such as the Benin Carvers Association or the Akamba Industries Co-operative Society. These groups are often independent and self-supporting, operating as small businesses. There is little or no difference in the style of their work, and it is almost impossible to pick out the hand of any individual craftsman.

Sometimes a man merely frequents a workshop or "studio" owned or subsidized by someone else. The materials and tools are then supplied by the owner, who retains the product and pays the craftsman a salary. These workshops are sometimes subsidized by businessmen, like M. Alhadeff in Kinshasa, or by Wakamba traders in several large East African cities. Sometimes, however, they are indirectly subsidized by the government through craftsmen attached to museums, as in Abidjan in the Ivory Coast.

Various methods have been evolved for the sale of souvenir objects. Some craftsmen hawk their goods in cafes and hotels frequented by Westerners in the large cities. In some instances, where craftsmen have formed an association, goods may be displayed in a showroom. The most usual method is for the individual or association to sell to a dealer who specializes in selling works of this sort. He often sets up a small display showing a variety of goods, frequently spreading it out on the ground near an airport terminal or a hotel catering to Europeans.[2] There are sometimes only one or two dealers at a location, but occasionally there are many more. In the square opposite the Hotel du Parc in Abidjan, up to twenty-five dealers, established in semi-permanent covered stalls rented from the city, sell souvenir works as well as traditional works of poor quality.

The majority of these dealers come from a few African tribes: the Hausa and the Wolof of West Africa, who control the extensive markets of that part of the continent, and the Wakamba from Kenya, who dominate the lucrative markets of East Africa. Both the Hausa and the Wakamba, however, operate in the Republic of Zaïre. To sell their wares these men travel hundreds and even thousands of miles on foot, by bicycle and bus, and even by jet plane. If they are successful enough to afford an assistant it is usually a young boy, who carries the heavy sacks of goods.

In the largest cities craftsmen may often sell to European-owned souvenir shops. In tourist-frequented East and South Africa many such shops sell these souvenirs by means of tastefully arranged and even dramatically lighted displays at the highest possible prices.

Some African governments operate or indirectly subsidize the shops selling souvenir goods. Countries on the west coast of Africa, such as Nigeria, Dahomey, Ghana, and Senegal, have sponsored shops of this kind for some time. The oldest of these establishments is the Ghana Industrial Development Corporation, founded in 1951. The IDC sells varied Ghanaian souvenir work in a large salesroom in the capital city of Accra. The corporation has also helped arrange exhibitions of this art within Ghana and overseas. IDC occasionally advances money to local craftsmen to enable them to buy materials.

In 1961 the Nigerian government opened Galerie Labac in Lagos, where the best of Nigeria's souvenir art as well as some examples of the new contemporary painting and sculpture are available at moderate prices. In recent years shops have been established on the East Coast; for example, the government of Uganda has opened a crafts shop in Kampala, and with government help the World Crafts Council has established a branch in Dar es Salaam, Tanzania.

Europeans are the principal purchasers of souvenir art. They may be tourists or businessmen visiting Africa briefly or missionaries or other expatriates going home on leave. But Africans, too, occasionally buy these objects; political leaders, for example, sometimes select souvenir work as gifts for their overseas hosts. During the administration of President Franklin Delano Roosevelt, African leaders brought him gifts such as souvenir-style ebony elephants, and the late Chief S. L. Akintola, while Premier of Western Nigeria, visited Washington in 1961 and presented a gift of "modern ebony carvings" to President and Mrs. Kennedy.

Art designed to please a European rather than a tribal patron had its origin in the early sixteenth century with the so-called Afro-Portuguese ivories (Plate 19). The earliest-known examples of African souvenir art, these ivories were brought back to Europe from the west coast of Africa by Portuguese sailors as early as 1505.[3] Although these objects show strong individual design elements of tribal origin, they were carved for European

19. Anonymous. Afro-Portuguese cup, ivory. British Museum, London.

use. Such untraditional forms as pedestal cups, forks and spoons, dagger handles, and hunting horns are recorded in the account book of the Casa de Guinée as having been taken through customs by sailors and officials returning to Portugal from Guinea. Among these objects the cups are the most impressive.

Both the provenance and function of the Afro-Portuguese ivories have been problematical for some years. In the past they were thought to have been carved by Africans for use as chalices in the Portuguese mission churches. These assertions were based on the fact that the cup shapes, never found in traditional African art, resemble Christian chalices. More recently, however, these objects have been generally accepted as salt cellars.[4]

William Fagg originally narrowed the site of manufacture of these ivories to one of three possible locations: Sierra Leone near Freetown, the Lower Congo region, and Nigeria-Dahomey between the cities of Lagos and Ouidah.[5] Later, however, he changed some of his ideas regarding the provenance of these works. He seems to have reached conclusions similar to those expressed by Ryder.[6] Fagg states:

> It can now be said that, while the great majority of these curious and beautiful hybrid works were made by carvers from the Sherbro area of Sierra Leone, a much smaller number, perhaps a quarter of the hundred or so known pieces, were carved by Bini trained in the style of the Igbesamwan; there is internal evidence to show that the Portuguese recruited fine carvers from these two tribes and set them to work together somewhere on the West Coast, or more probably in Portugal itself, in the late sixteenth century. . . . The Bini examples are distinguished by the characteristic all-over decoration and by simple decorative motives which are still in use by the Igbesamwan in this century on large tusks for the ancestor altars in the palace at Benin and on wooden idegobo and uhumwelao for the cults of the kingdom at large.[7]

In accord with these conclusions, Fagg now divides the old, so-called Afro-Portuguese ivories into two distinct styles: Bini-Portuguese and Sherbro-Portuguese.[8]

Souvenir painting and sculpture produced during the last fifty years encompass a wide range of styles. They include in some instances the open and frankly admitted copying of traditional African sculpture (in contrast to the faking or covert copying of traditional African art, a vast subject beyond the scope of this study), occasionally incorporating stylistic innovations. They are more commonly executed, however, in entirely new styles, and vary from extremely realistic representations of human figures and busts to stylized, almost schematic, treatments of people and animals. In these new styles, as in mission-inspired work, influences from European art and traditional objects are at times apparent.

The making of admitted copies of traditional art is, with a few exceptions, a function of museums, so that it is relatively easy to trace the history of this work. The origin of many of the new souvenir-art styles is often, however, puzzling. While in a few cases data as to their origins do exist, the beginnings are more usually obscure. But it is known that in one instance a colonial administrator directed the creation of a new sculptural style (see below, p. 48). Although documentation is lacking, Protestant and Catholic missions may have played an important role in starting and developing new souvenir styles. In agreement with the missions' aim to provide Africans with useful skills, students were taught in some mission workshops to become proficient in popular souvenir-art styles, such as ebony busts.[9] This role of the missions is independent of that discussed in the previous chapter, where the primary aim was to provide Christian art for use in Christian churches in Africa.

Admitted copies of traditional sculpture are made in several areas of Africa. They are not carved by traditional artists but they are produced instead in workshops or museums usually under the supervision of Europeans. Sculpture thus produced is never bought by Africans for traditional use.

The Alhadeff workshop in Kinshasa, Republic of Zaïre, produces many copies as well as other souvenir art. The director, M. Alhadeff, is a highly successful businessman who has been interested in art as a hobby and a business since 1949. He also operates a souvenir shop as an outlet for the workshop's production, and some of this material has been exhibited in New York.

The several dozen craftsmen employed by Alhadeff create countless works ranging in quality from competent examples of the new art to mediocre souvenir material. Alhadeff's loose direction is responsible for the varied quality of the work. He lacks art training himself, and he believes, like his artist friend, the late Pierre Romain-Desfossés, that African artists should not be given instruction or direction.[10]

The most interesting Alhadeff-produced souvenir works are copies of traditional sculpture. Carving with modern European tools, craftsmen often copy works illustrated in books on African sculpture, sometimes reproducing objects that originated thousands of miles from their area.[11] While most of these copies show adequate technical ability, they are dull and lifeless. Some carvers, with Alhadeff's encouragement, have introduced variations into traditional styles. In one such variant, a Bakuba royal portrait figure served as the inspiration. The tailorlike pose, the flexed arms, and the small square base with geometric designs were traditional, but the portrayal of a figure holding a musical instrument (a sanza) and the more realistic face, with wrinkles and open mouth, were innovations. Alhadeff asserted, incorrectly, it would seem, that in a work such as this the old style had been improved and enlivened.

Several museum workshops and schools also specialize in copying traditional art. Students at the Maison des Artisanats, a school allied with the museum in Bamako, Mali, are taught to copy some of the old sculpture styles of former French West Africa. These reproductions include Baoulé figures, Senufo bowls, and Bambara tji-wara masks. They are generally fairly accurate, but occasionally, as with the Alhadeff workshop Bakuba figure, realistic effects are introduced.

The finest copies of traditional African art are those produced at the museum in Abidjan. Sculptors employed there will reproduce a fine copy of any carving a visitor selects from the museum's excellent and extensive collection of traditional Ivory Coast material. Irrespective of their tribal affiliations, these carvers are adept at copying the diverse styles represented in the collection. They use traditional materials and techniques in an attempt to simulate the form and finish of the original objects. In common with all copyists, however skillful, these craftsmen find it difficult to reproduce the signs of age and usage.

One of the most ambitious museum projects in Africa is the Rhodes-Livingstone Museum Craft Village in Livingstone, Zambia, just a few miles from tourist-frequented Victoria Falls. Not only are reproductions of the country's traditional objects made there, but typical dwellings, granaries, and shrines have been reconstructed for inspection by visitors. Within this "village," built on an acre of land, various craftsmen, including Barotse carvers, Balunda Makishi mask makers, and blacksmiths, are seen at work and their products may be purchased for a nominal price.

Admitted copying of traditional objects is an important category of souvenir art, but a more frequently encountered tourist art is based on nontraditional forms. Such work is found everywhere; some examples are diffused over wide areas, others are available within a small, restricted zone.

For example, a style spread throughout West Africa has been dubbed by Michael Crowder, a British scholar who has written extensively on Africa, "the canoe and palm tree school of painting." Executed in Western fashion in oil on cardboard or canvas, this work is produced in the major coastal cities by numerous craftsmen with limited training. The prices of the paintings usually range from several dollars to $25, depending on their size, media, and the purchaser's bargaining ability. The frame is often included in the price, having already been painted as part of the picture. The paintings illustrate typical river or lagoon scenes, always containing, in different arrangements, canoes, palm trees, and huts. In the best of these works there is a naiveté which is surprisingly similar in some respects to the paintings of the turn-of-the-century French artist, the Douanier Rousseau. They resemble one another in the bright color, the detailed and decorative handling of the foliage, and the calmness and tranquility of the scenes.

The idealized portrait bust, a European-inspired type unknown in traditional African art, is one of the most commonly found souvenir styles in sculpture.[12] Although there are regional variations, examples of these busts with many elements in common may be bought everywhere from Senegal to South Africa. Usually carved in black ebony, sanded, and highly waxed, they are almost always somewhat smaller than life-size.[13] The models for these portraits are the various physical types of sub-Saharan Africa, and although scarification marks are often ignored, hairdresses, jewelry, and individual dress are usually accurately indicated. It is largely a pedestrian style, which rarely achieves any real aesthetic quality.

But the busts carved by Grégoire Massengo are worthy of mention. Massengo, like the majority of the ebony carvers, never formally studied art; instead he learned his craft as an apprentice in a workshop comparable to the one he operates several miles outside Brazzaville in the People's Republic of Congo. He has achieved a considerable local reputation, largely because of commissions in Brazzaville and exhibitions there and in Paris. Although he ordinarily carves conventional ebony busts, Massengo departs in at least some of his works from this dull tradition. For example, the impressive large head, almost four feet high, before the main entrance of Brazzaville's Hotel Relais is carved in a richly grained, deep brown ironwood rather than in ebony. Another of his large heads of approximately the same size (Plate 20) perhaps

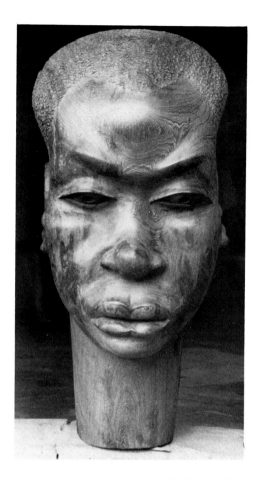

20. Grégoire Massengo. Male head,
    ironwood. Collection of the artist.

21. Anonymous. Head, steatite. Collection of Dr.
    George I. Lythcott, New York.

shows his particular style of souvenir art at its best. In this work he achieves a degree of quality through emphasis on bold, sculptural forms and the elimination of all small-scale descriptive detail.

Aside from the widespread styles just discussed, a considerable amount of souvenir art is produced by members of particular tribes within restricted areas. One such localized style is that of the M'Bigou steatite carving of Gabon, perhaps the least known of all souvenir material. In the late 1920s, in the village of M'Bigou in southeastern Gabon near the Congolese border, seven men who had for sometime cut pipes from steatite were encouraged by the local French administrator to expand their repertoire to encourage tourist trade. As a consequence, such objects as figures, heads, animals, and vases are made in this village.

The steatite, obtained from a site several days' journey by foot from M'Bigou, is first carved with a small adze and a knife and is then heated and colored with palm oil. The finished works, whether grey or red-brown, have, therefore, a rich, lustrous finish.[14] A great variety of subjects appears within the M'Bigou repertoire, but they are rarely identical.[15] In most examples, as in the head illustrated in Plate 21, there is an emphasis on volume; the full, rounded head has, in typical M'Bigou style, the facial features cut in a fairly marked, incisive style. The treatment of the eyes, half ellipsoids cut by a deeply incised median line, is typical of most M'Bigou carvings. Sometimes, as in Plate 21, this work seems derived from traditional sculpture, in this instance from an Ogowe River style mask.

In Western Nigeria, miniature carvings made from cotton tree thorns constitute an extremely popular, localized souvenir art (Plate 22). In Africa they are carved only in Nigeria. The thorns are two to four inches in height, and vary in color from light tan to dark brown and pink. Figures are carved from them with a sharp knife and then sanded. Projections from the figures, such as arms and legs and implements, are sculptured separately and attached with glue.

Picturesque genre aspects of village life are chosen as subject matter: palm wine tappers climbing trees, acrobats, and women pounding cassava. Usually represented in casual poses, these figures have a momentary, almost impressionistic character comparable to that appearing in traditional Fon brasses of Dahomey and Ashanti gold weights of Ghana. In the 1960s more ambitious subjects, such as chess sets and nativity scenes, were added to the repertoire.[16] The small carvings, however, have little relationship in their proportions and modeling to traditional West African art. Most of the figures

22. Anonymous. Genre figures, cotton tree thorns. Collection of the author.

show realistically proportioned muscles and bone structure enhanced by descriptive details, frequently carved of thorns of a different color and attached.

The thorn-carving style was created in the early 1930s by Justus Akeredolu, a chief born in the town of Owo. From 1933 to 1938 he taught his new technique to students at the Owo Government School. He has had many imitators, and thorn carvings have become one of the most popular souvenir styles in Nigeria.[17] Since 1949 Akeredolu has been painting in descriptive details, a technique his imitators have not yet adopted.

Because of their small, fragile nature, thorn carvings are rarely hawked like other souvenir goods. They may be obtained either from the carvers directly or from the highly respected Christian Mission Society bookshops, Nigeria's leading bookstore chain.[18] Many have also been sold at the numerous exhibitions of thorn carvings that are held throughout Nigeria, as well as in London and New York.

Another kind of important souvenir art is that found in the wood carvings of the Donvidé family in Dahomey. While many of their sculptures are strictly utilitarian, for example, chairs, tables, and stools, they also include human and animal figures, masks, and occasionally figures joined by chains and made from one piece of wood.

23. Donvidé family. Lion armchair, wood. Collection
of Mr. and Mrs. Irwin Hersey, New York.

24. Donvidé family. *Dog,* wood. Collection of the late
Justin Aho, Abomey, Dahomey.

They are made in Gbanamé, a small village approximately fifty miles east of the ancient Fon capital of Abomey, but most of the works are sold in a shop operated by a member of the family on the main coastal road in Dahomey between Porto-Novo and Cotonou. Most varieties of Donvidé carvings are usually displayed here but others not in stock may be ordered from a photographically illustrated catalog.

Articles of furniture, such as armchairs and stools, are among the family's most notable works. The armchairs, carved in characteristic monoxyle African fashion, are often supported by paired lions, with another pair appearing as armrests (Plate 23). Human figures are often used as supports for the stools. European prototypes certainly inspired the armchair design, since traditional Fon seats are either simple three-legged stools or seats related stylistically to the typical Ashanti stool.[19] Conversely, however, many details are traditionally Fon. The lion, for example, was the symbol of Glèlè, one of the Fon kingdom's most revered rulers, who reigned from 1858 to 1889. In traditional Fon fashion lions are represented in a striking pose, often open-mouthed with bared teeth and with a large, chunky head. Although quite different in style from the locally carved traditional bochio,[20] the human figures represented on this furniture have many traits in common with the figure-carving style of the neighboring Yoruba tribe. For example, legs are short, thick cylinders, feet are large and flattened at the base, while shoulders and arms often form a wide continuous arc reminiscent of the Oyo ibeji style of Yoruba carving. As in Yoruba sculpture, the clothing is boldly and simply handled.

The large (approximately three feet tall) Donvidé free-standing bird and animal figures (Plate 24 shows one example) are expressed in a strongly sculptural style, achieved by large, simple, voluminous shapes and a concentration of surface detail in small, clearly defined areas. This impressive, often dynamic, style is to a degree reminiscent of traditional Fon brass-covered animals.

The Donvidé style of wood carving practiced by the family since 1909, was originated by Aqueminon Donvidé. Although since the beginning these carvings have been sold almost entirely to Europeans, in one instance they have been purchased by a Fon noble family. The father of the late Fon paramount chief, Justin Aho, made a large purchase of Donvidé carvings in the 1920s for personal use. Justin Aho himself also purchased many pieces in the 1930s.

By far the most popular and the most commercially successful of souvenir-art products are the sculptures of the Wakamba tribe of East Africa. Produced in the relatively small tribal area between Kitui and Machakos in Kenya, Wakamba carvings are sold widely throughout the continent. They can be purchased, in fact, in every East, Central, and South African city, and can be secured as readily in such cities as London and New York.[21]

Wakamba carvings, ranging in size from approximately six to sixteen inches, are usually made from a very hard, dense, two-toned wood called muvuvuu, which is readily available in Kenya. Dark brown with a very light brown outer layer, muvuvuu enables the carver to create dramatic color contrasts. The Wakamba have begun using ebony imported from Tanzania, a two-toned wood that is black with an outer white layer, largely because of the preferences of American buyers.[22] The traditional wood-carving tools, the adze and the knife, are employed and the surfaces are sandpapered and then highly polished with floor or shoe wax.

Tribal peoples of Kenya are frequently represented in this style. These carvings are similar to the ebony portrait busts in their emphasis on such details as hairdress, jewelry, and costume. Perhaps the oldest and most popular of the Wakamba subjects is the one that portrays their picturesque Masai neighbors. The Masai, wearing traditional metal neck rings, are represented as standing or kneeling figures which often serve as handles of salad spoons and forks.

Among the most successful of Wakamba commercial sculptures are those portraying East Africa's varied and abundant wild animals. A veritable Noah's Ark is represented. Elephants, rhinoceroses, and antelopes in varying positions, sometimes standing alone or as decorative bookends, have proved popular (Plate 25). Wakamba-style animals and figures are fairly realistic in their modeling of form, although the heads, as in traditional sculpture, are large in proportion to the body. Smooth, highly polished surfaces are extremely important, and consequently details are minimized. Facial expression is rare. In some instances, however, decorative treatment gives way to an expressive, and sometimes dramatic, presentation of form, such as in the roaring lion shown in Plate 26.

Periodically, new subjects are introduced into the Wakamba repertoire.[23] There is, however, a distressing, almost machine-made, uniformity in all examples of each subject type.[24] It is commonly heard in East Africa that

25. Anonymous. *Antelopes,* wood. Collection of the author.

26. Anonymous. *Roaring Lion,* wood. Collection unknown.

these carvings are produced on lathes in expatriate-owned factories in Kenya, or are even imported from New York or Tokyo. This statement is completely false, although Western-derived mass-production techniques are occasionally utilized in their creation. It has been reported, for example, that "a group of village carvers carry out the first stages. When the blocks of wood have been roughly shaped they are taken to an Indian or Goan shopkeeper who keeps another group of carvers in his shop. The shopkeeper's job is to finish them off, polish them and paint them as required."[25]

To a greater extent than in most other souvenir styles, knowledge of the origins and development of Wakamba carving is readily available. The work is still largely produced within the restricted area of its origin, namely, Kenya, while its considerable commercial success has stimulated numerous articles about its history in African publications.[26]

It is important to note that before intensive European contact, the Wakamba carved no sculpture.[27] Their only art work consisted of metal wire ornamentation inlaid on the seats of wooden stools. Such complex and Arab-inspired designs bear no relation to the present-day commercial work.[28]

Mutisya Munge was the first Wakamba souvenir sculptor.[29] Stationed at Dar es Salaam during the First World War, he apparently learned to carve, perhaps from other African tribesmen, while serving with the British army. Returning to Kenya, he began to carve full-time and taught his sons as well. For many years the craft remained within the family, but gradually other Wakamba learned the skill from them. In 1966 an estimated 3,000 men were earning part or all of their living through carving.[30]

Several historical factors fostered the growth of a Kenya souvenir style.[31] Primary among them perhaps was the influx during the past fifty years of European settlers. During the Second World War British soldiers returning on leave frequently took Wakamba souvenirs to England; while after the War, together with the greater number of visitors, there was a sudden increase in overseas demand for Wakamba carvings, especially in the United States.[32]

The ecology of the Wakamba country contributed considerably to the increase of this souvenir art. While the Wakamba were traditionally a pastoral people, aridity and frequent droughts made grazing precarious. A new and major source of revenue was therefore provided by woodcarvings for tourists.

It is interesting to observe that over the years, as the demand for these sculptures increased spectacularly, the sales methods of the Wakamba changed. The carver originally sold directly to the buyer, often in the streets of Nairobi. After World War II a prohibition against street selling in that city created a problem. The solution was obviously to establish shops where these works could be procured from full-time dealers, often former Wakamba carvers themselves. At first the dealers sold carvings on commission but this procedure soon proved unsatisfactory because the carver was in no position to wait for his money. As a consequence the dealers now buy their goods outright.[33] Some dealers now operate workshops in the large East African cities, employing local or imported Wakamba carvers.[34]

Other traders travel extensively today to sell these carvings. As a result these sculptures are now obtainable throughout East Africa and Zaïre. In 1954, one carver, Mwambetu, a son of the original Mutisya, went to London, where he is reputed to have done very well. More recently Josiah Wambua, a Wakamba, established an office in London which trades under the name of "African and Akamba Handcrafts." His success is apparent, for he soon had five agents throughout Britain.[35]

Earlier, in 1951, both the dealers and the carvers, encouraged by the colonial administration, organized the Akamba Industries Co-operative Society to increase sales of Wakamba carvings. Attempting to operate as a European business, with "printed price lists, headed note-paper and a proper Post Office box address," it failed within a year.[36] Its failure was occasioned by endless arguments over profits between dealers and carvers and because some dealers had their businesses thousands of miles away and communication was difficult.

Elkan gives some idea of the money earned from Wakamba carvings.[37] In 1958, the part-time carvers earned between $11 and $16 a month, those working full-time in workshops, between $31 and $34 a month. Traveling dealers earned anywhere from $21 up, and those dealers owning workshops had monthly incomes of $112 to $140. Since the average monthly wage of regularly employed black Africans in Kenya in 1956 was $15.40, the popularity of carving as a profession is immediately understandable.

The commercial success of Wakamba carvings can be explained only partially by the aggressive selling tactics of the dealers. Probably more important are the aesthetic qualities of this sculpture, which appear to be in close rapport with the taste of the average European buyer. Some Westerners may find Nigerian thorn carvings and ebony portrait heads a little too realistic, perhaps old-fashioned; Donvidé and M'Bigou carvings and "canoe and palm tree" paintings, with their simplifications and stylizations, may appear too "primitive." Wakamba carvings, however, although realistic, lack the fussy and cluttered detail of the ebony heads. The plain, hard, and frequently highly polished surfaces of Wakamba sculptures have a streamlined appearance which is similar to modern decorative objects and consequently blends into many contemporary interiors.

Another souvenir art style has developed in East Africa in recent years, certainly in part as a result of the enormous commercial success of Wakamba carving. This carving is produced by members of the Makonde tribe who have migrated to Dar es Salaam, Tanzania, from their traditional homeland in northeastern Mozambique and southeastern Tanzania.[38] Although souvenir carving is done by other Makonde groups, for example, by those remaining in Mozambique and by craftsmen living on a remote lime estate outside of Mtwara in southern Tanzania, it is only the carvers in and around Dar es Salaam who create work of any aesthetic interest.[39]

Carvers in that city number about one hundred.[40] Half these men work alone in their homes outside Dar es Salaam. A carver may sell his production to several dealers or to only one; in any case his contacts with the customer are negligible. Other Makonde carvers work in groups associated with one "curio" shop dealer, who is usually Indian or European. Sometimes the craftsmen are physically separated from the shop, carving together elsewhere. In other instances they actually work in the shop, occasionally with craftsmen of other tribes or nationalities, such as Indian goldsmiths. When the connection with the dealer is direct the dealer usually supplies the wood and he is committed to buy all the carvings meeting his standards. Unlike the Wakamba, the Makonde seem little interested in becoming dealers. Furthermore, no African itinerant dealers sell Makonde carvings, and few souvenir shop owners in East, Central, and South Africa have shown interest in this work. Hence the carvings are available principally in Dar es Salaam and Nairobi in limited quantities.

Makonde souvenir art is made of ebony, almost always only the black inner core of the log. The carvings may be divided into three basic types: single-figure and group compositions in the round, and reliefs (the reliefs are the least aesthetically interesting of the three types). There is wide variation in size, ranging from eight inches to almost four feet in height, with the majority of pieces standing between 14 and 22 inches high.

The subject matter of new Makonde carving deals largely with the mystical aspects of life. Sorcerers are represented frequently, but by far the most important subjects are human and animal spirits, the latter including fishes, serpents, and birds. Much less often carvings represent elemental themes of life and death. In contrast to Wakamba work, there is no interest in picturesque subjects obviously designed for the tourist. The most popular of all Wakamba subjects, the wild game of East Africa, is totally absent from the Makonde repertoire. Until recently in every category of subject matter each Makonde piece was unique. Under the pressures of commercial success, however, some duplications and similarities have begun to appear. There is still a marked contrast, however, with Wakamba work, where identical salad sets with Masai-figure handles are produced by the thousands.

Representations of spirits may be seen in Plates 27, 28, and 29. Plate 27, a fertility spirit, is one of the most easily identifiable of the spirit subjects, since fertility is obviously indicated by the distended abdomen supported by a pair of widely separated, bowed legs. The bowing of the legs gives the impression they are supporting great weight. Although this figure is one of the more realistic Makonde souvenir-style works, there are certain obvious distortions, such as the extreme slenderness and elongation of the legs and especially the reduction of the arms to stumplike appendages.

Another spirit, probably female but otherwise unidentifiable, may be seen in Plate 28. The upper part of the figure is a large head with facial features carved in rather high relief. A lip plug, worn traditionally by Makonde women and occasionally by men, embellishes the upper lip. Precariously balanced on the head is a stoppered calabash probably meant for carrying water.[41] At this point the effect of a realistic figure ends, and in contrast to Plate 27, where the overall impression was of realism, this figure becomes fantastic. Joined to the left side of the face, which is missing an eye, is an elongated, carved leg. Two other gracefully formed attenuated legs meet other parts of the head. No explanation for the strange iconography of this piece is given by the carver.

It is in work such as this that Makonde souvenir sculpture is seen at its best. The subject and style are intriguing and have a bizarre quality suggesting comparison with some of the hybrid creations of Romanesque sculptors of Western Europe.[42] A fascinating image such as Plate 28 is not unusual in Makonde carving. One finds, for example, a representation of an expectant mother entitled *Woman with Child Thought,* in which an extra pair of arms

27. Anonymous. *Fertility Spirit*, wood. Collection of J. Anthony Stout, Washington, D.C.

28. Anonymous. *Spirit,* wood. Collection of Professor and Mrs. Izaak Wirszup, Chicago.

29. Anonymous. *Spirit Group*, wood. Collection of J. Anthony Stout, Washington, D.C.

growing upwards out of her ears supports an infant.[43] Another strange figure portrays either a sorceress or a female spirit.[44] Here the neck is omitted, leaving a vacant space, and the head is supported by two upraised arms. Highly unusual are the figure's breasts. Carved as balloonlike forms, they are suspended over the shoulders, one in front and one in back. Countless other examples of Makonde predilection for fantastic treatment of the human figure in the representation of spirits and sorcerers could be cited.

An example of a Makonde group composition in the round, a fairly common sculptural type, may be seen in Plate 29, *Spirit Group*. A half dozen or so human figures, some superimposed, dance around what appears to be a human body at the circular base. According to Stout, "The presence among the spirits of elements associated with ancestor ritual (mortar, serpent, unidentified animal, and inverted bodies) suggests that the scene is a resurrectionary apocalypse derived from traditional belief."[45] In contrast to the single figures just discussed, anatomical distortions are not apparent in individual bodies. Distortions do appear, however, in the poses of figures and in their relations with each other. In this composition arms gesticulate wildly, legs are akimbo, heads thrust backward. Figures meet figures at every conceivable angle: head to head, head to stomach. The composition is an intricate tangle of frenetic forms. It shows once more the imaginativeness of Makonde carving.

It might be valuable to consider possible reasons for this originality of subject matter and style. Because of the occasional portrayal of men smoking in the Makonde repertoire Stout asserts that some "carvings strongly suggest that consciousness-altering drugs have been part of the experience of these artists, presumably either in their past traditional life or in their adaptation since migrating northwards."[46] He offers no further documentary evidence of the use of hallucinogens either in the traditional life of the Makonde or by members of the souvenir artist community in and around Dar es Salaam. It is known, however, that hallucinogens have been used in East Africa, Somalia, and Zaïre.[47] Until more fieldwork is done on the possible use of drugs by the Makonde it is highly speculative to assume that drugs are a prime factor in the fantasy apparent in the Makonde souvenir-art style.

A more valid explanation for this creativity probably lies in what has happened in the last several years in Dar es Salaam. The capital and major port of Tanzania, it has recently become a major tourist center in Africa. As a result of the increased influx of foreign visitors the souvenir-art business has flourished. Dealers, and especially the more astute ones, discovered that the highly original Makonde pieces sold more readily and fetched better prices than standardized African souvenir styles, particularly the ubiquitous Wakamba carvings.[48] Consequently it is probable that a few dealers encouraged the Makonde carvers in every possible way to continue in this vein.

Although it is readily apparent from the preceding analysis that the style of Makonde souvenir carvings is quite different from that of the Wakamba, there are certain distinct influences from the earlier, established, more widely known style. In both souvenir arts there is a predilection for slender, elongated figures, which invariably rest on a carved, usually round, base. Enhancing these body proportions are long, delicate arms and legs. In both styles smooth surfaces are highly polished and largely devoid of such features as descriptive details rendered by incised lines or low relief carving.[49]

Today souvenir art is certainly the best known of any of the new African arts. Its astonishing success has been achieved by fulfilling three needs that have, perhaps, only an indirect relationship to art collecting: It often serves a functional purpose (as bookends, salad sets, and chairs or tables); it seemingly satisfies a universal urge of travelers everywhere to acquire remembrances of places visited; and the large export market for this work seems to indicate that even those not fortunate enough to visit Africa desire to own an "authentic" piece of African art.

IV: The Emergence of a New Art: Introduction

T HE GROWTH of a new, major art that is still relatively unknown in the United States is certainly the most promising development to take place in the last fifty years in sub-Saharan Africa. Various older artists have been working in this new art style for some years, and now an increasingly large group of the younger generation are turning to it. Many of these artists have been trained in African, European, or American art schools and are aware of contemporary and historical art trends in other parts of the world. Some of their work may be influenced by traditional African art, but much of their subject matter, forms, and techniques are new to the continent. Their art is clearly a learned and dedicated one, with no relationship to either mission-inspired work or souvenir art.

A few of these artists are self-taught or have served such varied apprenticeships as working in a souvenir art workshop, an advertising agency, an architect's office, or a sultan's palace. But by far the great majority have been trained in African art schools or, usually as recipients of government scholarships, in art schools abroad.[1] African art schools, almost without exception, have been established by Europeans and until recently also staffed largely by expatriates.

It is not at all surprising, therefore, that these artists have often adopted techniques that were unknown or rare in traditional African art. For example, the medium of painting is as important as that of sculpture.[2] Western-derived techniques are conspicuous: in painting, gouache and oils often

AFRICAN
62   ART

appear; and in sculpture, work in cement, plaster, and even fiber glass occurs. Recently mosaic, stained glass, and tapestry have been added to the list. Many of the themes in present-day African art, such as portraits, landscapes, and figure compositions, are similar to those in Western art.

The representation of this new subject matter is varied in style. There are works that are conservatively and academically rendered as well as abstract paintings that are reminiscent of Abstract Expressionist work. Most of this new African art, however, falls between these two stylistic poles, and as a consequence it avoids a close following of either.

The manner in which these works are produced and sold is also comparable to Western practice. For instance, unlike the situation in traditional African societies, where works were usually produced on commission, artists now largely create on their own initiative and sell when the opportunity arises. These new African artists have a much wider choice of patronage: individual collectors, private groups, and business firms, particularly the large European and American companies, who have occasionally commissioned works for their new African offices. With government support, African museums have also begun to collect the new art, and governments themselves have ordered examples of it for their ambitious building projects.

Since the majority of Africans today live as they did traditionally, in rural villages, they are usually unaware of the new art. Those who have moved to the large, rapidly growing cities may become acquainted with this work through exhibitions and newspaper and magazine articles. Although the urban African may at times meet artists and may even appreciate the new art, the average person does not have the money to purchase it.

A few members of the uppermost strata of contemporary African society, often denoted as "the new elite," do occasionally collect these works. Many of them are intellectuals and professional people, often graduates of African or European or American universities. But since the African universities have been largely staffed by expatriates, the outlook of this "elite" is often Western-oriented. Thus the concept of "art for art's sake," which is only occasionally a motivation for traditional African art, is an idea readily understood by this group, who will in fact purchase works whose only function is an aesthetic one. Some of these professionals, moreover, are knowledgeable about world art, having studied art history and visited European and American museums.

It should be stressed, however, that only a small fraction of the African "elite" society collect art. They are much more interested in politics and sports, and many of them regard the development of a new African art as a needless luxury. A small number of these people also feel that for the present Africans can coast along on the reputation made by their ancestral artists. Lack of interest more than anything else explains the lack of support for this art. Price is rarely a factor for upper-strata Africans, as it is for the average wage earner, since prices are usually low by Western standards and African professional people earn salaries often comparable with those in Europe.[3]

Westerners are more important individual patrons of the new African art. They include businessmen, engineers, teachers, architects, diplomats, and their wives, who have come to work in Africa, usually for a short period. They attend exhibitions, meet artists, read and write reviews, and frequently buy works. Although it may be convenient and lucrative at the present time, the dependence on expatriate patrons is undesirable for the future development of the new African art. African artists sometimes adjust and adapt their themes and styles to gain approval from buyers. It is also of considerable significance that with expatriate patronage the works leave Africa permanently with the departure of the buyer. Consequently there is bound to remain in Africa only a portion of the few important works which can guide future artists.

Besides individual patrons there are several important groups in Africa interested in this art. Privately organized and supported, these groups are patrons in the broadest sense, for although they may occasionally buy or commission works, their primary role is to provide encouragement and assistance to artists. They do so mostly by sponsoring exhibitions, through which the artists are introduced to their public. Subsequent newspaper and journal notices and reviews further publicize the art. It is substantially from these exhibitions that most works are sold.

Sometimes these supporting groups eagerly search out the works of artists to exhibit. Since the motivation for the exhibitions is rarely commercial, as with privately operated galleries in Europe or the United States, and there are as yet few African artists, many young painters and sculptors, some freshly graduated from art school, receive comprehensive one-man shows at the beginning of their careers. Whether that is detrimental or not is controversial. Early uncritical acclaim may inhibit a young artist's growth, but encouragement tempered with the proper criticism can aid in his development toward a more mature style.

Private sponsoring groups are located primarily in Nigeria and Ghana, countries where the new art movement is strongest. The oldest organizations are Ghanaian: the Akwapim 6 and the Ghana Society of Artists, both founded in 1955. Until the early 1960s the latter was the larger and more influential of the two. Its former president, the late Kofi Antubam, stated that the Society's aims were threefold: to organize conferences of artists, craftsmen, and art teachers in order to exchange ideas; to arrange annual exhibitions of members' works; and to cooperate with government bodies, such as the Ghana Arts Council and some of the foreign embassies that were interested in Ghanaian art. The Society became inactive shortly before Antubam's death.[4]

The Akwapim 6, although a smaller group, has been continuously active since its founding. The group's title refers to the six founding members living on the Akwapim ridge, an area encompassing seventeen towns north of Accra. Membership has risen beyond the original six, and includes the noted sculptor and founder of the group, Dr. Oku Ampofo. The Akwapim 6 holds regular annual exhibitions, unlike the Ghana Society of Artists.

Among the most important art groups in Africa have been Nigeria's Mbari Clubs.[5] Since the founding of the first club in Ibadan in July 1961 under the impetus of the critic Ulli Beier, Mbari has consistently supported and encouraged the best in the arts.[6] Founding members included many of the leaders in Nigeria's flourishing art movement, such as the playwrights Wole Soyinka and J. P. Clark, and the writers Ezekiel Mphahlele, originally from South Africa, and the Nigerians Amos Tutuola and the late Christopher Okigbo.[7] The response to the Ibadan Mbari was so favorable that a branch was opened in Oshogbo in 1962.[8] Still later branches were begun in Enugu, capital of the former Eastern Region, and in Lagos. In the late 1960s Mbari Clubs were opened at Ife and in Benin City.

For several years the Ibadan Mbari Club had a vital impact on Nigerian intellectual life. The club gave music and dance recitals, as well as plays by leading Nigerian writers. A surprisingly large number of art exhibitions were held almost without interruption. The club's policy was to exhibit the work of young, relatively unknown Nigerian artists and to bring the work of other African and European artists to Nigeria. The opening exhibition, the works of Nigerian painters Demas Nwoko and C. Uche Okeke, began the program on a high level, one continually maintained. It was followed by numerous outstanding shows of works by other Nigerian artists. Non-Nigerian artists have also been represented; for example, a group exhibition of work from Makerere University College in Uganda, and a one-man show of sculpture by the Ghanaian Vincent Kofi. The Ibadan Club also published paperback books illustrating the works of contemporary artists. The drawings of C. Uche Okeke and a book of poetry by Christopher Okigbo illustrated by Demas Nwoko are among them.

The activities of the Ibadan Club declined after the Oshogbo Club opened. The latter group became an important cultural force, arranging exhibitions, producing plays, dance recitals, and folk operas, and publishing monographs on the work of Nigerian artists. Most noteworthy of its accomplishments was the emergence of several highly individual artists from a series of workshop courses given at the club (see below, pp. 147–56).

Subsidies for Mbari Club activities have come from several sources. The Ibadan Club was initially funded by the Congress of Cultural Freedom in Paris, then by the New York-based Farfield Foundation, and still later by the Nigerian government through the University of Ibadan. The Farfield Foundation has been responsible for supporting much of the work done at Oshogbo since its inception.

The active and diversified programs of Nigeria's Mbari Clubs have been emulated in East Africa. Ezekiel Mphahlele established the Chemchemi cultural center in Nairobi, an artists' and writers' club based on Mbari principles. In 1966 Mphahlele came to the United States and Chemchemi's role was adopted by the newly formed Paa ya Paa Art Gallery. Under the aegis of Elimo Njau, a well-known painter, Paa ya Paa has exhibited works of most major East African artists as well as artists from abroad. Like the Mbari Clubs it maintained a workshop to discover and encourage new talent.[9]

Several European and American organizations have also actively encouraged the development of the new African art, among them the influential Societé Africaine de Culture in Paris, which founded centers in Cameroun, Ivory Coast, Senegal, Nigeria, Ghana, Kenya, and Haiti. The society was supported from its inception by such influential intellectuals as Albert Camus, Richard Wright, and Aimé Césaire, as well as by Jean-Paul Sartre and Léopold Sedar Senghor. Its interests are much broader than those of any group previously discussed; it has been concerned with all aspects of contemporary African life—economics, politics, and religion—as well as with the arts.

The Society's most important activity has been the publication several times a year of the excellent journal *Présence Africaine*. Started in 1947 by the Senegalese writer Alioune Diop, this journal was intended to affirm "the presence, or ethos of the black communities of the world and to defend the originality of their way of life and the dignity of their culture."[10] One of the early issues of *Présence Africaine,* nos. 10 and 11 (double volume), was devoted entirely to art, while over the years articles on painting and sculpture have frequently appeared.

Highlighting the Society's activities in the arts were two conferences convened in the late 1950s: the "Congress of Negro Writers and Artists," held at the Sorbonne in September 1956, and its sequel, convened in Rome in March 1959. The prominent African painters and sculptors Ben Enwonwu, Kofi Antubam, and Gerard Sekoto presented papers, which were later printed in special issues of *Présence Africaine* devoted to these conferences.

Two American groups, now inactive, also had as one of their major aims aid and encouragement of the new African art. Founded in 1957, the American Society of African Culture (AMSAC) was associated with the Societé Africaine de Culture, and was, like that organization, concerned with all aspects of present-day African life. (Between 1965 and 1967 AMSAC regularly published a quarterly journal, *African Forum.*) Art exhibitions were held at AMSAC's several conferences, and it gave one-man shows to the late Kofi Antubam and Sam Ntiro in its New York offices. In 1961 AMSAC opened a center in Lagos, where it attempted through conferences and exhibitions to initiate and expand contacts between African and Afro-American artists. It exhibited the works of the painters Jacob Lawrence and Elton Fax, for example, in addition to shows by Nigerian painters. Financial difficulties have forced AMSAC to curtail its activities drastically.

The Harmon Foundation, a New York philanthropic organization now defunct, arranged exhibitions which appeared in New York and elsewhere in the United States. In various ways it also aided African artists studying in the United States, even purchasing some of their works. One of the major contributions of the Harmon Foundation were listings, including some biographical information, of many of today's African artists. The first, a mimeographed publication issued by the Foundation in 1960, was compiled by the late Afro-American sociologist Forrester Washington. It was followed in 1966 by a more ambitious effort written by Evelyn Brown, the foundation's assistant director. Both works have several defects, largely because the research was carried out in the United States. Some of the artists discussed are of minor importance, and because the authors were not able to spend time in Africa they had little contact with original works of art. As a result, both publications lack an evaluation and analysis of the new art.

The most ambitious American encouragement to date of the new African art has been the quarterly journal "African Arts," published by the African Studies Center of the University of California at Los Angeles with aid from the Ford and Kress Foundations. Its first issue appeared in the autumn of 1967, and since then it has consistently shown and discussed a good deal of the new work. Particularly impressive is its generous use of color reproduction, which has served as an excellent introduction to much of this material for American audiences.

As previously mentioned, European and American businesses in Africa are becoming increasingly important as patrons of contemporary African art. Concerns with offices in major African cities have begun, often in conjunction with architects, to incorporate this art into their new buildings. Since many of these modern buildings are severely functional in appearance, art frequently relieves their stark simplicity, often providing a contrast of texture and materials. The use of art, in addition to its aesthetic function, creates a favorable impression among the peoples and governments of the strongly nationalist African states. Although discussed more fully elsewhere in these pages, a few of the outstanding examples of the work commissioned by these business firms should be mentioned briefly here: carved doors by Sam Songo for the Wankie Colliery in Rhodesia, carved doors for the Co-operative Bank in Ibadan by Felix Idubor, and a large pierced concrete relief by Festus Idehen and Paul Mount, commissioned by the Chase Manhattan Bank for what is now a branch of the Standard Bank of Nigeria in Lagos.

The most significant patrons of present-day art, however, are the various African governments. They not only patronize African artists on a much grander scale than do individuals, groups, or businesses but they also aid and encourage art in various ways. They often commission murals, mosaics, and sculpture to decorate both interiors and exteriors of government buildings, and several governments, among them those of Nigeria and Ghana, have organized and subsidized groups such as arts councils, which have arranged exhibitions and conferences to aid artists.

Two additional functions relative to the arts are being performed increasingly by African governments. One is the subsidy of art museums.[11] Although the principal purpose of these museums is to preserve and exhibit traditional art, they often buy, exhibit, and occasionally commission examples of the new work. Many governments also have established and are supporting art schools, often the only such schools in the area.[12]

In numerous instances the extent of government encouragement of the new art movement depends on the attitude towards the arts of the previous (or present) colonial power. For example, the Portuguese government, which still retains its colonies, has done nothing to encourage cultural developments. In contrast, former colonial administrations of France, Belgium, and Great Britain have assisted, in varying degrees, the growth of the new African art. The policies of these three colonial powers have frequently served as a basis for the development of contemporary art by independent African nations. The fact that during colonial times Great Britain offered considerable encouragement to the arts has resulted in the present significant position of art in Nigeria and Ghana; today these nations lead all African governments in art subsidies.

The Belgian colonial administration in the Congo, on the other hand, made only minor efforts to aid the development of art. With the recurrent political upheavals since Independence the Republic of Zaïre has had little opportunity to improve the situation. Among the few important public commissions during the colonial period in that vast territory are the sculptured columns and reliefs for the Salle des Fêtes at the Kinshasa Zoo, executed by that city's Académie des Beaux-Arts, and the large mural by the painters Kabingo and Kabongo for the modern theater in Lubumbashi.

Government-supported museums in Zaïre have been concerned almost exclusively with traditional art. A museum was established in Kinshasa in 1935, and smaller ones were started in the provincial centers of Luluabourg in the Kasai in 1959 and Lubumbashi in Katanga in 1942, but they were devoted to Congolese traditional work. Only the Lubumbashi museum displayed any of the new art—the paintings, sculpture, and ceramics of the Desfossés studio in Lubumbashi, formerly an important art school. None of the works produced by the school after the death of Desfossés in 1954 were exhibited. Unfortunately the museums at both Lubumbashi and Luluabourg were victims of the Congo's political upheavals and both are presumed defunct.

The Belgian colonial administration did not establish any art schools in the Congo. In the 1950s, however, they belatedly supported schools begun by private organizations or individuals: the Académie des Beaux-Arts in Kinshasa and a similarly named institution in Lubumbashi.

In the former French colonial areas in Africa few public commissions were given to new African artists of note. The museums established by the Institut Français d'Afrique Noire (IFAN) in most of the former French colonies are excellent, but they, too, are concerned exclusively with traditional art.[13] The French, however, not only encouraged art schools in their areas but also provided them with adequate facilities. They subsidized the École des Arts and the Poto-Poto School, both in Brazzaville, as well as a painting section in the Lycée Technique in Libreville, Gabon. They also founded an important colonial school, École des Arts du Sénégal, in Dakar in 1957. Since achieving independence, the Ivory Coast government has established with the aid of UNESCO a major school in Abidjan, the Institut Nationale des Arts.

In general, however, the African states that were formerly British colonies have most advanced the development of the new art. An excellent example in former British East and Central Africa is the Rhodesian National Gallery in Salisbury. The gallery owns a number of examples of new African art and has exhibited them in its annual national exhibitions along with other works of African artists. The museum's director Frank McEwen established at the museum an art workshop for Africans, where working space and materials are supplied (see below pp. 119–23).

One of the most important and oldest of African art schools was established in the late 1930s at Makerere University College in Kampala, Uganda.[14] Begun by Margaret Trowell, and later given government support, it has trained a number of talented painters and sculptors. More than any other institution or individual, this school is responsible for the intensive interest and growth of art in East Africa.

A government-sponsored school in the former British colony of the Sudan has assumed great importance in recent years. Now called the School of Fine and Applied Art, the institution had its origin in Khartoum in 1945. It has produced several young painters whose work is among the most interesting in all of Africa.

In Africa below the Sahara, however, government support of art is greatest in the former British West African colonies, Nigeria and Ghana. These two nations not only sponsor several excellent art museums and schools but also commission new works and subsidize groups encouraging the development of a new art. The Ghana Arts Council and the Nigerian Council for the

Advancement of Art have given grants to support artists and have held exhibitions.[15]

The Nigerian Council may be used as an example of the way in which such organizations function. It serves as a parent group to the Society of Nigerian Artists and the Federal Society of Arts and Humanities. The former organization was begun in 1964 to create a forum for artists and to arrange exhibitions, symposia, lectures, and film showings. Its membership is drawn from professional artists within Nigeria. The Federal Society of Arts and Humanities has an altogether different function. Since its formation in 1963 it has been collecting examples of contemporary Nigerian work for a projected art museum.

The Council also operates a shop, the previously mentioned Galerie Labac in Lagos. Although much of its stock is souvenir work it does display and sell works by several young artists, giving them what amounts to a permanent exhibition.

These groups were preceded in both countries by the operations of the British Council, an organization whose chief mission was to promulgate the British way of life. Often it also aided the new African artists. Between 1943 and Independence in 1957, for example, the British Council in Ghana organized fifteen exhibitions of Ghanaian painting and sculpture and provided a scholarship for a local artist.[16]

An unusual form of governmental encouragement of art is seen in the periodical *Nigeria Magazine,* which has performed an important and vital role in the growth of the new Nigerian art. Subsidized for over thirty-five years by the Nigerian government, it is a quarterly of wide international distribution, devoted to all aspects of present-day Nigerian life. Illustrated articles on new developments in art and reviews of most exhibitions appear frequently. Furthermore, the magazine has maintained a large exhibition hall beside its office in Lagos, in which many leading Nigerian artists have received their first one-man shows.

The Ghanaian and Nigerian governments have frequently commissioned art for public buildings and facilities. Among Ghanaian works, Kofi Antubam's carved doors and state chair in Parliament House in Accra and the bronze fountain figures by Vincent Kofi outside that city's State House are most notable. Antubam also decorated dining rooms in the government-owned Black Star Line ships and in the Ambassador Hotel in Accra. Nigerian government buildings are often similarly embellished. The National Parliament in Lagos, for example, has doors carved by Felix Idubor; the Western Region House of Assembly in Ibadan contains the previously mentioned speaker's table and chairs carved by Lamidi Fakeye; and the new Lagos City Hall is decorated with mosaics by Yusuf Grillo and a monumental carved wood partition by Festus Idehen. Ben Enwonwu, art adviser to the government, has executed a number of works for the state, among them a bronze, full-length portrait of Queen Elizabeth, which stands before the National Parliament, and a similar study of Nigeria's former president Dr. Nnamdi Azikiwe, which before the Civil War stood in front of the Eastern Region House of Assembly in Enugu.

Museums in both these West African countries have been unusually active in patronizing the new artists. The national museums in Lagos and Accra have had space permanently devoted to exhibitions of this material. The Accra Museum, furthermore, owns paintings by such Ghanaian artists as Asihene and Antubam, which, together with traditional material, are permanently displayed on the main floor. Both museums have commissioned large sculptured works for their buildings' exteriors. Ben Enwonwu's bronze, *Anyanwu,* is silhouetted against the modern facade of the Lagos Museum, and an over life-size stone figure by Dr. Oku Ampofo stands before the Accra Museum.

In former British West Africa, government subsidies for art departments in universities and teacher-training colleges have been of utmost importance in the growth of the new art. The finest art schools in this area are in Nigeria, at Ahmadu Bello University in Zaria and the Yaba Technical Institute in Lagos. Art is also taught to advanced students at the Teacher-Training College, Freetown, Sierra Leone, the Teacher-Training College, Winneba, Ghana, and the University of Science and Technology, Kumasi, Ghana.

African countries that have remained independent of colonial rule for most if not all of their history show varying degrees of government participation in art activities. In Liberia, for example, there have been no important government programs for aiding art and there are no new artists of note. The Republic of South Africa is a different situation. The government spends a fair amount of money encouraging art by supplying funds to enable museums to form collections and by supporting several art schools. The money, however, is spent almost entirely to further the emergence of a white or European art. Black South African artists, and there are several interesting ones, are forbidden to attend the established art schools, are not encouraged, and in fact are largely ignored by the government. The closest approach to a government-subsidized art school for Africans has been a studio at the Bantu Men's Social Centre in Johannesburg. Here, a group of individuals worked together but without organized courses or instruction.

The attitude of Ethiopia is refreshingly different. The government aided the establishment in 1957 of the Fine Arts School in Addis Ababa, a diploma-granting institution with a full curriculum in the fine arts. The government has also awarded major commissions, the most impressive of which are three monumental stained-glass windows by Afewerk Tekle in Africa Hall, headquarters for the United Nations Economic Commission for Africa.

The growth of the new African art has been, and will continue to be, at least for some time, dependent largely on the patronage herein discussed. Both Western and African support has stemmed from individuals as well as various groups, including business concerns and governments. The new African art certainly could not have developed without these benefactors. They not only encourage the artists' work but they also aid in the publication of reviews which include illustrations of paintings and sculpture. Most important of all, they help to contribute funds necessary to train new artists. They hold exhibitions and conferences and buy works. For the continuance and further development of this art these various sources of support must offer at least the same encouragement, and preferably at a faster tempo.

V: Art Schools in French-Speaking Africa

M AJOR African art schools may be grouped regionally on the basis of the cultures introduced by the colonial powers. There seems to be a correlation between the various European cultures and attitudes towards art instruction. In schools founded in different areas of Africa, methods vary from an almost complete lack of formal instruction to well-organized art programs leading to recognized academic degrees. The first approach was most successfully pioneered in French-speaking areas, those formerly ruled by Belgium and France.

In the Republic of Zaïre, formerly the Belgian Congo, three schools merit attention. The most interesting and perhaps most influential was founded by Pierre Romain-Desfossés in Lubumbashi (formerly Elisabethville) in 1944. On his death ten years later the school was integrated into Lubumbashi's Académie des Beaux-Arts et des Métiers d'Art, a school established in 1951 by Laurent Moonens. Another similarly named Congolese school, Académie des Beaux-Arts, was established in Kinshasa in 1943 by Frère Marc.

The Desfossés school in Lubumbashi was at first simply called "Le Hangar" and later became known as "L' Académie de l'art populaire Congolais."[1] This school is important not only because it was one of the first art schools in French-speaking Africa but also because Desfossés pioneered an attitude toward art instruction that has been widely influential in other African art schools. Desfossés affirmed that his intention was not to suggest themes, provide models, or even give advice as to color, composition, or modeling. He offered a congenial place to work and supplied necessary materials, including paper, canvas, and paints. The sole rule he imposed was that artists did not repeat themselves. Desfossés asserted that in this way an artist was able to create works based entirely on his own experiences. These experiences, he believed, were, in turn, without benefit of any obvious and direct contact with Western art values.

Desfossés felt that the artists in his school produced works that were wholly African. It is true that his students' works, unlike the art of some other schools claiming similar teaching methods, lacked obvious derivations from either European academic or modern painting. The production of his atelier was "wholly African" only in the sense that it was done by Africans in Africa in a style that fits a rather condescending Western stereotype of what African painting should be: above all, decorative, having bright colors, flat forms, and simple compositions.

Desfossés failed to recognize, however, some of the less obvious and subtle European influences to which his students were exposed. He was unaware that it is difficult for an African artist today to visualize a purely traditional African experience. Much of modern African life is, in fact, an amalgam of ancestral traditions and encroaching Western values. Moreover, the materials Desfossés supplied and the ways in which they were used, especially in easel paintings, are in themselves Western-derived. It is certain that these artists, irrespective of their backgrounds, had seen examples of European pictorial representations if only in Bible illustrations and in advertisements. Although he disclaimed giving any formal instruction, Desfossés did indirectly mold his students through praise and disapproval. A discerning student could not fail to note certain "approved" ways and might consequently change his style. Despite Desfossés' attitude toward instruction, the paintings produced by his students did develop a closely recognizable "style."

The Lubumbashi school, interestingly enough, began by accident. One day during his employer's absence, Desfossés' Congolese chauffeur picked up the artist's palette and produced a painting. Desfossés was so intrigued with the work that he gave him more materials and paints. Before long the chauffeur's friends joined him and in time there developed a number of "regulars" who worked steadily day after day in Desfossés' studio. The "school" was at first entirely supported by Desfossés and it was not until several years later that the Belgian colonial administration helped finance its operation. The school's fame soon spread, and several exhibitions were held in Europe and the United States.[2]

While the most accomplished of the school's artists created easel paintings in oil or gouache on cardboard, Desfossés also encouraged experimentation in other techniques. There were several painters who carved wood blocks with which they printed fabrics and book illustrations, a sculptor who carved figures and decorated stools and tables, and a woman potter.[3] One of the first artists to join the Lubumbashi school was the painter Bela. Originally from a family of fishermen near Fort Archambault, Chad, he was hired upon Desfossés' arrival in Zaïre as a servant and remained with him until his employer's death.[4] Bela subsequently moved to Kinshasa, where he occasionally paints for the Alhadeff workshop. There has been no noticeable change or development in his style since Desfossés' death, and he frequently repeats former successful compositions.

Bela's technique, unique in the new art, is easily recognizable. He paints with his finger tips, eschewing brushes because he believes, incorrectly, that they were never used in traditional tribal Africa.[5] His method consists of the pointillist or dot technique. While the dots often give a nervous vibrancy to the form's silhouette, their uniformity in size tends to vitiate this vitality.

Bela's paintings are in many respects similar to those of other Desfossés artists. He frequently utilizes subjects from traditional African life, such as ceremonial dances and animal hunts. Like Pilipili, a fellow student, he has painted a number of underwater views of fish and sea greens, views that might be seen from the window of a bathysphere. Bela's figures are quite flat, despite an embryonic, rather stylized attempt at modeling, and his expression of movement is stiff and awkward. Forms, usually in profile, are silhouetted against a neutral background lacking a horizon; this frieze-like compositional arrangement parallels the picture plane, with only an occasional grouping of figures in depth.

Pilipili Mulongoya, who signs his paintings simply Pilipili, is another noteworthy Desfossés student. Born near Lubumbashi, he, too, comes from a family of fishermen. He worked in that city as a house painter from 1944 until 1947, when he joined the school.[6] He has continued to paint after Desfossés' death, and, like Bela, he has not changed his style significantly.

Pilipili's specialty is paintings of birds, animals, and fish portrayed either at rest or in mortal combat. His birds and animals are placed in simple landscapes of greens and trees, and his fish, perhaps his best-known pictures, are seen as if underwater amidst aquatic plants (Plate 30). Delicate and precisely painted forms are clearly and sharply delineated. Pilipili's work always contains an easily recognizable trait: the filling of the background with small, equal-size spots. This background treatment, together with his delicate and precise treatment of forms, is evidence of the decorative qualities inherent in the work of all students of the Desfossés school. Pilipili's style is certainly the most decorative of all.

Mwenze Kibwanga, commonly called Mwenze, is one of the most creative artists of the Lubumbashi school.[7] He was born in Katanga Province at Mwanza in 1924, a member of the Baluba tribe. He began taking painting lessons in Lubumbashi in 1946 with a European, M. Pletinckx, and started work in the Desfossés school four years later. Since Desfossés' death Mwenze has been very active, teaching as well as painting and exhibiting periodically.[8]

In his painting, Mwenze, like Bela and Pilipili, uses easily recognizable elements. His forms are constructed with heavy, straight brush strokes of contrasting color laid next to each other so that the ends are uneven and produce a jagged silhouette (Plate 31).[9] Backgrounds are composed of parallel brush strokes, often arranged in a free interpretation of a traditional Baluba decorative motive, a motive which consists of the opposition, often at right angles, of small groups of parallel grooves.[10] In Mwenze's work, however, there is more irregularity in the way in which separate groups of lines are juxtaposed.

The paintings of Mwenze are much more vigorous and dramatic than the more decorative works of Bela and Pilipili. These qualities are created only partially by Mwenze's mode of building up forms with heavy parallel lines of contrasting color. Within the forms themselves a very active element consisting of a variation of light and dark tonal values serves to integrate his compositional forms dramatically by the use of highlights. In contrast to Bela and Pilipili, his figures, although still somewhat stiff, are more fluid, interrelate better, and even occasionally intertwine. Moreover, they are usually large, often filling the entire picture area. The dramatic quality of his style is also due to his choice of themes. He prefers scenes of violence, such as life-and-death struggles between animals and between men and animals.

After Desfossés' death his school was integrated into the Académie des Beaux-Arts et des Métiers d'Art in Lubumbashi. The Desfossés group, called Section D of the academy, continued to operate separately according to Desfossés' own methods. Several of his former students, including Pilipili and

30. Pilipili Mulongoya. *Crocodiles and Fish,* gouache on cardboard. Collection unknown.

31. Mwenze Kibwanga. *Devouring of an Antelope,* oil on cardboard. Collection unknown.

Mwenze, became teachers in the Lubumbashi academy. The existence of this section as a separate entity lasted only a short time and was then abolished.

The Lubumbashi Académie des Beaux-Arts et des Métiers d'Art was established in 1951 by Laurent Moonens, a Belgian artist.[11] From its founding, the aims and practices of the academy differed from those of the Desfossés school. It was more nearly a conventional art school in that a definite curriculum was followed. Several courses of study—painting and sculpture as well as architecture and commercial design—were offered. In keeping with this more conventional aspect, instruction was given and the students were examined and then divided into sections based on their ability.

In spite of this obviously more academic procedure Moonens, like Desfossés, allowed considerable freedom and apparently did not wish to impose a ready-made European style. In fact, the paintings produced by the two schools exhibit certain similarities. Above all else they are usually decorative; forms are flat, often silhouetted against plain or ornamental backgrounds in which there is frequently no representation of real space. The subject matter, which includes birds and animals and picturesque customs, in most cases is treated in a decorative manner.

The work of the Lubumbashi Moonens' school does, however, differ in some important respects. Paintings from this school evidence a greater technical proficiency, while the figure construction is more controlled and less awkward and even more fluid than that of the Desfossés group. Moreover, there is greater variation in style among artists of this school. Kamba and Mode, two of its more gifted painters, illustrate perfectly this variation in style.

Jean-Bosco Kamba, a Baluba born in Luluabourg, graduated from the Lubumbashi academy in 1958. His paintings, like most of the works of the academy, are executed in gouache on colored paper or, less commonly, on cardboard. Intertwined birds, animals, and snakes are often placed within quite artificial plant backgrounds, as in his *Serpent and Birds* (Plate 32). He usually ignores the real world, often combining birds and animals that do not appear together in nature. Narrative subjects are almost nonexistent. Like the Desfossés artists, Kamba developed a distinctive style trait. Dots or sometimes parallel or concentric lines appear within his outlined forms. They are so delicate that they give a more decorative, rather than expressive, quality to his work.

Mode, who graduated in 1959, is unique among the artists of the

32. Jean-Bosco Kamba. *Serpent and Birds,* gouache on wood. Collection unknown.

33. Mode. *Figures,* gouache on cardboard. Collection unknown.

Lubumbashi school, for he is primarily interested in the human figure. His figures are given a stick-like interpretation devoid of all facial features, and are often arranged in quite complex compositions. Mode's forms usually have heavy outlines of pure color with the often meager interior volumetric space filled in with contrasting color. A vigorous, active movement characterizes his figurative expression. Flexed and attenuated legs and arms are often joined to an elongated torso and give the figure this expression of activity. Characteristic of his style is the often open outline of the hands and feet. Backgrounds for his figures are either plain or dotted (Plate 33). It is interesting and perhaps important to note that Mode's stick-like figures and their elongation of proportions resemble to a degree some of the early rock paintings of Rhodesia and South Africa.[12] This analogy may perhaps not be fortuitous since it is possible that he had seen examples or illustrations of the rock art. Regardless of this possibility it seems more likely that Mode may have been influenced by one of the popular styles of the Poto-Poto art school in Brazzaville (see below pp. 83–89). Interestingly enough, this latter style, which predates Mode's works, also shows some parallels with the early African rock paintings.

Moonens, director of the Lubumbashi school, returned to Belgium in 1958. Subsequently, Jean De Maegt, the academy's instructor of sculpture, was made director.[13] Under De Maegt's leadership the school was reorganized to conform more closely to the traditional Belgian art school. Consequently a more academic art instruction was emphasized and certain new sections were added, such as ceramics and a cours général (French, geography, and arithmetic). As might be expected, the majority of new instructors in the school were both conservative and academic in training.

The third important art school in Zaïre was founded in Kinshasa. Originally named the École St. Luc, it was founded by the Reverend Frère Marc-Stanislas at Gombé Matadi, west of Kinshasa, in 1943.[14] When the Governor General became aware of its accomplishments, it was moved in 1949 with government assistance to Kinshasa, where it received an annual government subsidy. In 1959, two years after the École St. Luc was renamed the Académie des Beaux-Arts, Frère Marc left the school and was succeeded by Frère Denis, but the direction and policies established by the former were continued.[15]

Although painting, architecture, ceramics, and graphics were offered, the course of study most stressed at the Kinshasa academy was sculpture.[16] It was under the direction of Andre Lufwa, Frère Marc's first student (Benjamin

34. D. Bakala. Effigy cup, wood. Académie des Beaux-Arts, Kinshasa, Republic of Zaïre.

Mensah and Ignace Mankana, also students of Frère Marc's, instructed in the sculpture section, too). The pattern of instruction set up within the school required that within their first three years students carve decorative objects and furniture based on certain basic designs and motives found in traditional Congolese art. In the fourth year they sketched plants and animals. The last three years of the seven-year course of study included the sketching and carving of the human figure and the modeling and casting in plaster of larger than life-size figures.

Typical examples of beginners' work may be seen in Plate 34, illustrating a cup signed D. Bakala, 1960. While its design concept is based on traditional Bakuba effigy cups, it departs from this source in several important respects; for instance, the traditional base has been eliminated, a cowrie shell fillet has been added at the hair line, and a torque with Baluba designs encircles the neck. A more significant difference, however, is the somewhat more realistic treatment of facial features.

In their final four years Kinshasa students apparently ignored their early training in certain traditional African forms and designs. In the works done in these years all traces of traditional Congolese art were, in fact, eliminated and replaced with the dull realism of European academic art. This realism is related to the work of the teachers Benjamin Mensah and Andre Lufwa.[17]

The styles of Mensah and Lufwa reflect the teaching of Frère Marc, who has firmly stated that his students should "be taught in the classic manner"; that is, they should be instructed as if they were academic Belgian art students.[18] Consequently, the Kinshasa students drew from casts of ancient art, sketched nature out-of-doors, and modeled the human figure from life. Such a conventional European art school curriculum was in keeping with the conservative and academic attitude held toward art by the school's administration. During the students' last three years, courses in art history were given at one time by the director of the Kinshasa Museum; the major emphasis has always been on the history of European art.

Two of the three Congolese schools are historically important in this discussion of the new African art. The art schools begun by Frère Marc and Pierre Romain-Desfossés were among the first in sub-Saharan Africa. As early as 1943 and 1944, respectively, they established two different approaches to the teaching of art. Frère Marc intensively indoctrinated his students in a European style and introduced them to Western techniques and past styles of art. Desfossés preferred, on the other hand, a laissez-faire approach, where no instruction was given and no examples of any other art were shown to the students. These two extremes recur constantly in other African areas, and sometimes the actual methods used in these schools have been borrowed and utilized.

Several major art schools have also been established in former French colonies. The most historically important is the Poto-Poto school, founded in 1951 in the similarly named African quarter of Brazzaville, People's Republic of Congo.[19] Another school was established in 1957 in Dakar, the École des Arts du Sénégal, and in 1966 the Institut Nationale des Arts was begun in Abidjan, the Ivory Coast.

The Poto-Poto school, known officially as the Centre d'Art Africaine, was begun by Pierre Lods, a French mathematics teacher and amateur painter.[20] Poto-Poto is widely known and its reputation abroad is based largely on the exhibitions of its work held in South Africa, Germany, France, England, and the United States. Within Africa itself some of the school's paintings are extremely well known.

Lods has said about the school's beginning:

[I]n my studio at Poto-Poto I employed an African boy called Ossali, who showed a very lively interest in my work. One day he suddenly failed to turn up; the day after he was still missing. I noticed that a few tubes of oil paint and some brushes had also disappeared and I decided to go and call on him at his own home. There I found him painting away on an old nautical chart of the Oubangui; the yellowing paper was rapidly being covered with knife-like silhouettes of ultramarine and turquoise birds painted with all the superb purity and simplicity of line that is found in African art. It was a revelation to me—an artist making his bow.

Seeing my pleasure, Ossali, who had at first been apprehensive, opened out. He whistled, burst into song, and finally started to dance around his room waving his brushes. The next day, in vermilion and black, he painted palm trees against a mountain, the whole on a black background. There was no getting away from it; I had to find another boy, for Ossali had turned painter. He painted every day, and with such frenzied enthusiasm that I dared not interrupt him, even to give advice, for the results he produced were so striking despite technical imperfections.

Ossali was rapidly followed by his "little brothers," who came to try their hand. They were followed in turn by cousins, friends, big brothers, little cousins, and little brothers' big cousins until very soon the studio was far too small. Then they spilled over into the grounds and the nearby cabins. They painted all the time, it didn't matter what, and they used any material they could find.

Visitors began coming, and they started to buy; enthusiastic journalists encouraged our pupils, and at this stage friends of mine introduced me to the director of the Division of Social Affairs, who said to me: "Draw up the plan for a studio, and we will build it wherever you want." We moved into this palm-thatched studio in June 1951 with ten or so painters, one of whom was Ossali.[21]

Although the original Poto-Poto studio was burned, a similar one was built on the site, and it is here that the artists work. Lods directed the school until 1961, when, at President Senghor's invitation, he left to teach at the École des Arts in Senegal. Mme. Edith Gandelin succeeded him and continued his policies. She also taught sculpture at the school.

Concerning his method of instruction Lods has also been articulate:

> I left them to work on their own, without schedule or guidance. My part was to provide the material—paper, paints, brushes—but I left them to work out their own techniques, and find it they did. . . .
>
> Once or twice, as an experiment, I tried to guide or influence my pupils in what they painted. Inevitably I found that this led to unsatisfactory results. I therefore limited myself to giving technical advice, especially when they were working in oils, so that their paintings would last longer. I then collected their successful works, where they were sometimes done on mere scraps of paper, and used these to encourage them when they went through a period of downheartedness. Sometimes, too, we read African proverbs that I had collected, or legends and poems written by African authors or by Europeans who corresponded with me on Africa.
>
> I surrounded my student painters with traditional African objects, and in the grounds I grew a large variety of native plants. I also tried to organize festivities and parties. And that has been the extent of the "teaching." It has already shown promising results. The complete success of our experiment will come only when African painting is once again integrated in the whole art of the country—in its music, dance and acting. For Africa is a country where there is no strict frontier between life and art; the same rich emotional intensity permeates both.[22]

Lods obviously adopted the approach pioneered in the French-speaking areas of Africa, but in contrast, he more actively encouraged familiarity with traditional African objects, plants, music, and dance. This encouragement doubtlessly accounts for the reminiscences of traditional African styles frequently found in the works of his school. Lods, like Desfossés, believed that works executed by his students as a result of his method of instruction were purely African in essence, and in his words "were enriched by the innate sense of composition of rhythm and of color harmony so natural to Africans."[23]

Typical Poto-Poto painters such as Zigoma, Thango, and Ondongo illustrate the various styles of the school.[24] These artists favor gouache on watercolor paper, although they occasionally work in oil on canvas. Each artist, it would seem, is adept in several different styles, although most seem to prefer and excel in one of them.

35. Ondongo. *Drummers,* gouache on paper. Collection of Rolf Italiaander.

36. Zigoma. *Figures,* gouache on paper. Collection of the artist.

The most popular of the Poto-Poto styles, and a virtual trademark of the school, is the stick-like rendering of figures seen in a painting by Ondongo (Plate 35). Active figures such as hunters, dancers, and market women are portrayed against a neutral background without reference to a base line. The stick figures are elongated, with small heads and long, thin arms and legs. At times they twist gracefully or lurch in angular, staccato movements. The figures are often interrelated through the versatile and intricate patterns formed by their arms and legs. Such accessories as drums, headdresses, loin cloths, and jewelry are frequently emphasized by vibrant color and rich pattern contrasts.

Imitations of this Poto-Poto style are found throughout sub-Saharan Africa. Paintings simulating in simplified fashion the popular Poto-Poto stick-figure style can be readily purchased in any large city. Quantities of these works are produced by scores of artists who have had no connection with the Poto-Poto school. These imitations are hawked with other souvenir art goods in the airports and European-frequented cafes and hotels. Among them are forgeries supposedly painted and signed by popular Poto-Poto artists.[25] Details from mediocre Poto-Poto paintings have also been adapted to textiles and even lampshades sold within Africa.

The Poto-Poto style, as previously mentioned, closely resembles rock paintings in Rhodesia and South Africa. Figure proportions, movements, and even some of the compositions in the Poto-Poto paintings are strikingly similar to rock art, suggesting an influence. Pierre Lods, however, vigorously denied having shown his students reproductions of rock art, but it is, of course, possible that they had seen examples elsewhere.

Zigoma, another artist of the Poto-Poto school, illustrates a different style of painting (Plate 36). While there is a complete lack of ground line, these figures differ radically from the stick-figure style, since they are large and clearly outlined shapes. Highly abstract torsos are surmounted by stylized masklike heads which have geometric facial features and sharp, angular projections. The colors used in these paintings are rarely descriptive, consisting of intense reds, blues, and greens.

In still another Poto-Poto style, exemplified by the Zigoma painting shown in Plate 37, stylized masks are often crowded into a composition, filling the entire picture area. In these works similarities to traditional mask styles are sometimes apparent. The flowing curves of the form at left recall profile views of typical masks from the Guro tribe of the Ivory Coast as well as re-

37. Zigoma. *Masks,* gouache on paper. Collection of the artist.

38. Thango. *Composition,* gouache on paper. Collection of Leo Alhadeff, Kinshasa, Republic of Zaïre.

liquary heads from the Fang peoples of Gabon. At the right the horns represented on this form are comparable to the masks of the Baoulé and Senufo tribes of the Ivory Coast.[26] Heads from Kuyu tribal sculpture of the Middle Congo are also frequently represented in the paintings of this Poto-Poto style.[27] The masks represented in these paintings have, most commonly, no traditional prototypes but are fantasies, composed of geometric shapes. In the Poto-Poto examples the colors are usually vivid although some are restricted to black, gray, and white.

The last Poto-Poto style discussed here is practiced exclusively by Thango (Plate 38). The highly stylized masks of the previous styles are replaced by richly colored, varied, abstract shapes, although occasionally a mask is still recognizable. Shapes in his paintings are often so tightly compressed as to become severely elongated. Also in many areas Thango's paintings are practically nonobjective, with color contributing to this abstract quality, as highly saturated hues are juxtaposed in quite unconventional color combinations. The artist characterizes his paintings as "marriages of color." Thango's style frequently recalls Cubist paintings of Picasso and Braque in the abstract forms, compositional compression, and occasional simultaneity of vision.[28]

Four styles, then, represent the basic repertoire of Poto-Poto school artists. A number of elements in common link their work with the paintings of the Desfossés and Moonens group. All three schools have basically decorative styles. Bright and vivid colors, rarely used in a descriptive manner, are primarily expressed as flat forms in which little or no interest in space is evident.

The Poto-Poto school, in contrast to those of Desfosséss and Moonens, has a much greater range of more clearly distinguishable styles. This range varies from representations of semi-realistically treated figures, through schematically handled masks, to largely nonobjective compositions. That Lods allowed his students more freedom than Desfossés and Moonens is therefore clearly evident. With few exceptions, unlike painters at the other schools, Poto-Poto's artists are skilled in executing different styles. It therefore appears that Lods also permitted the artists to be influenced by the work of fellow students. Moreover, Poto-Poto work, with elements derived from traditional African tribal art as well as from modern European painting, shows a wider range of influence.

The continuing influence of Pierre Lods on contemporary African art is seen in his work in Senegal. Upon his departure from the Poto-Poto school in 1961, he joined the faculty of the École des Arts in Dakar, where he taught painting. He shared these duties with two Senegalese artists, Ibrahim N'Diaye and Papa Ibra Tall. The painting division of the École was organized in a rather unusual fashion in that it was divided into two sections. One, directed by N'Diaye, followed the practices of European art schools. The other, directed by Tall, in which Lods taught, followed the methods employed by the Poto-Poto school, that is, supplying materials but claiming to offer no formal teaching. These divisions had separate space and equipment and there was, as a result, little contact between them.

N'Diaye left the École in the mid-1960s for Paris, where he worked as an independent artist (see below, pp. 165–67). About the same time, Tall also departed. Lods continued teaching painting at the École, however, and he also maintained an atelier in his home in an African quarter of Dakar.

Under the influence of Lods, Poto-Poto's theories and practices were obviously followed in the École des Arts, and, as might be expected, results were similar. Certain resemblances to traditional styles and modern European painting are consequently apparent. The Senegalese school's works are, however, even more decorative than the Poto-Poto paintings, showing much more interest in color and pattern. This greater decorativeness may perhaps be explained as a consequence of the strong Moslem influence in this area and a subsequent absence of a traditional figurative style.

Papa Ibra Tall left the École des Arts, where he had taught tapestry making as well as painting, in order to found a tapestry school in Thiès, east of Dakar, in 1966. In 1968 four designers and sixteen weavers were working at the school, La Manufacture Nationale de Tapisserie. The course of study lasts from three to five years. Tapestries produced there are expensive; for example, one approximately four by five feet costs about $3,400. Consequently, the Senegalese government has been the major purchaser, buying works for its ministries and embassies abroad.

Most tapestries made at the school are based on designs created by Papa Ibra Tall.[29] A Toucouleur born in 1931 near Dakar, Tall went to Paris to study architecture in 1955. An exhibit there in 1959 of paintings done in his spare time prompted President Senghor to urge him to become a painter. He enrolled briefly at the Académie des Beaux-Arts and in 1960 returned to Dakar to work in the École. A U.S. State Department grant enabled him to tour American museums, and while in New York he painted his impressions of Harlem. His paintings have been exhibited not only in Paris but also in Dakar, Rome, and Moscow, and his work has been bought by President

39. Papa Ibra Tall. *The Stride of the Champion,* oil on masonite. Collection of the artist.

40. Papa Ibra Tall. *Peace Will Come,* tapestry. Collection of La Manufacture Nationale de Tapisserie, Thiès, Senegal.

Senghor and other important government officials. He has illustrated, with elegant and sophisticated drawings, the book *Un Voyage du Sénégal,* in which contemporary Senegalese life is well portrayed.

Two of Tall's works, a painting in oil on hardboard, *The Stride of the Champion* (Plate 39), and a tapestry, *Peace Will Come* (Plate 40), illustrate the artist's style. Although perhaps a bit slick and superficial, they are both technically accomplished figure compositions. Tall's overwhelming interest in design is apparent; the figures contain interior parallel lines which echo the silhouettes, while concentric lines radiate outward, integrating the figures with their environment. The artist, moreover, shows some interest in the traditional decorative arts of Senegal, as is seen in the geometric motives on the figure of the *Champion,* motives derived from traditional weaving and leather work.[30]

The newest of the major art schools in French-speaking Africa is the Institut Nationale des Arts in Abidjan. It was begun in 1966 by Albert Botbol, a Moroccan sent to the Ivory Coast by UNESCO. Music, dance, and drama as well as fine arts are taught.

The fine arts curriculum, modeled on the art schools in France, is the most structured course of art study offered in the former French colonies. At the completion of the five-year program a student is granted a diploma equivalent to those given by French schools. The curriculum includes painting, sculpture, drawing, graphic art, ceramics, textile design, and history of art.

Christian Lattier, instructor of sculpture at the Institut, is the most exciting sculptor to have developed in French-speaking Africa. Born in Grande Lahou, west of Abidjan, in 1926, Lattier spent most of his life in France, returning to his native country in 1961. He studied sculpture at the Académie des Beaux Arts in Paris from 1947 to 1956. He has had one-man exhibitions in Paris, Abidjan, Munich, and Rome, and at the Festival of Negro Art in Dakar in 1966, an exhibition of contemporary works gathered from all over sub-Saharan Africa, Lattier won the grand prize.

The prize was for one of his rope sculptures, a most unusual technique he first experimented with, independent of instruction, in Paris in 1952. In this sculpture, usually of large scale, Lattier covers an iron armature with rope often soaked in sisal oil. The works are sometimes colored by mixing earth with the oil.

41. Christian Lattier. *The Chicken Thief,* rope and iron. Collection of the artist.

Lattier's subject matter is quite varied, including genre themes, animals, and the mother-and-child motive. The last theme occurs often in his work, and may possibly be inspired by the traditional wood sculpture of the Anyi tribe, in which this subject is extremely popular. The Anyi, neighbors of the Godie, Lattier's tribe, are an influential cultural force in the Abidjan area. It was one of Lattier's animal sculptures, his monumental *Panther,* that won the grand prize in Dakar. Perhaps most unusual are his representations of jazz musicians. He shares his interest in jazz with the Senegalese painter Papa Ibra Tall and with Gerard Sekoto, a South African expatriate painter who has lived in Paris for several decades (see below, pp. 167–69). This concern with jazz performers as a valid artistic theme seems to be limited to artists living in French-speaking areas.[31]

Exemplifying Lattier's style is a large work, *The Chicken Thief* (Plate 41). Paradoxically, it combines the three-dimensionality inherent in the sculptural medium itself with a linearity resulting from the materials and technique. As may be seen in frontal and profile views, the composition extends aggresively into its surrounding space. Thus the sculptor established his work in three dimensions; then he proceeds to break this three-dimensionality down by the introduction of large, inner areas of open space. Into these open spaces project essentially linear forms, resulting in intricate patterns of negative space. Furthermore, even the solidity of the individual forms, of the bodies of the man and the rooster, tends to disintegrate since these forms are created by rope stretched across wide spaces with interstices between.

The three major art schools established in former French colonies have continued instructional methods pioneered by Pierre Romain-Desfossés and Frère Marc in Zaïre. The approach used by Pierre Lods in his Brazzaville Poto-Poto school was apparently influenced by Desfossés. Lods continued this manner of teaching in the École des Arts in Dakar. In the Dakar school the Lods method was, for a time, used concurrently with the more conventional European art school approach, comparable to that employed by Frère Marc. The latter approach continues in the newly founded Institut Nationale des Arts in Abidjan.

VI: Art Schools in English-Speaking East and Central Africa

FOUR art schools of importance are found in the large area of English-speaking East and Central Africa.[1] Two of them, the School of Fine Arts at Makerere University College, Uganda, and the School of Fine and Applied Art in Khartoum, Sudan, were established during the British colonial administrations. These two schools, begun in the 1930s and 1940s, were followed in the next decade by the School of Fine Arts in Addis Ababa, Ethiopia, and finally by the newest school in the area, the workshop of the Rhodesian National Gallery, founded in the 1960s.

The most influential of the four is the school at Makerere University College in Kampala, Uganda.[2] It was founded in 1937 by Margaret Trowell, a British teacher and painter. The first art classes at all associated with Makerere took place one afternoon a week on Mrs. Trowell's verandah.[3] After an exhibition of students' works in London in 1939, classes were moved into college buildings and were thereafter limited to college students. During the next two decades the School of Fine Arts established an affiliation with the University of London and developed its programs. In 1957 the first diplomas were awarded for completion of a four-year course of study. This program paired a major and a minor field of work, including painting and drawing, sculpture and pottery, and textile and graphic design. History of world art, including traditional African sculpture, was compulsory for all students.[4] The inclusion of traditional sculpture undoubtedly stemmed from Mrs. Trowell's early and long-standing interest in the subject.

Margaret Trowell claimed she gave no instruction in art to her students.[5] The works of these students, however, form a clearly identifiable "school style" that is obviously European-inspired. Unlike the paintings of the Desfossés, Moonens, and Lods workshops, where similar claims were made, Trowell students' paintings contain such Western elements as deep space within which figures and forms are modeled with light and shade. Picturesque African subjects and Bible themes were done in lifeless, academic fashion.[6] Solidly modeled forms are placed in believable, detailed landscapes in which rocks and various species of plants and trees are accurately rendered. Colors are drab with a taste for ochre tones. Although much of the work of her school was undistinguished, Mrs. Trowell inspired, encouraged, and partially trained three of East Africa's best-known artists: the painters Sam Ntiro and Elimo Njau and the sculptor Gregory Maloba.

Gregory Maloba was Mrs. Trowell's first serious student. Born in 1922 in Munias, Kenya, he joined her classes in 1941 at the instigation of the English sculptor, Henry Moore. During a visit to East Africa Moore had been impressed by some of Maloba's modeling in clay when the latter was a student in secondary school. In 1942 Maloba began to assist Mrs. Trowell in the teaching of painting. Shortly afterward Mrs. Trowell, in her words, "captured" a Wakamba carver whom she brought to her school for a day so that he might demonstrate to the students his sculptural technique.[7] Following this experience Maloba turned seriously to sculpture, and from then until 1966 he was the chief instructor of sculpture at the school. During his tenure at Makerere he executed several commissions, the most ambitious being the colossal cement fondu Independence Monument erected in Kampala's main park in 1962. He has made three trips to England; in 1948–50 he studied art at the Bath Academy of Art, Corsham Court, and in 1957–58 and 1963–64 at the Royal College of Art in London. In 1966 he left Kampala to become head of the new Department of Design at University College, Nairobi.

Maloba's favored subject matter are portrait busts, which he executes with sensitivity and competence. His finest is perhaps that of Ham Mukasa, cast in bronze in 1952 for the Uganda Boy Scout headquarters in Kampala (Plate 42).[8] Mukasa's massive head, with its large, clearly delineated features, is treated broadly without attention to small-scale details. Its rough surface reveals the small clay units used in modeling the preparatory bust.

In the surface treatment and, in some works, in the expressiveness of emaciated features with deep, hollowed eyes, Maloba's portraits strikingly

42. Gregory Maloba. *Ham Mukasa*, bronze. Uganda Boy Scout Headquarters, Kampala, Uganda.

resemble those of the late British sculptor Sir Jacob Epstein. Maloba would probably admit this affinity if questioned, for he has stated that:

> students ought to look at work by artists of every race and generation if possible. Freedom for each individual to develop along his own line (whether or not it be influenced by another individual artist or school of thought), this must be there.[9]

It seems clear, then, that Maloba was certainly directly influenced by Epstein's work, which he learned about during his study in England.

One of the most widely known East African painters, Sam Ntiro, was for many years also an instructor at the Kampala school. He is a Chagga born in 1923 near Mount Kilimanjaro, Tanzania. Ntiro joined Mrs. Trowell's classes shortly after Maloba did, and upon his graduation in 1948 was made a painting instructor at the school. He taught until 1961, when he joined the diplomatic service of the newly independent Tanzania. After serving as that government's High Commissioner in London, he returned to Kampala to teach painting at a teacher-training college there. Several years later he moved to Dar es Salaam to become a commissioner again in the Tanzanian government.

Ntiro, like Maloba, continued his art education during several trips abroad. From 1942 to 1956 he studied at the Slade School and at the Institute of Education of the University of London. In 1960 he received a Carnegie travel grant for ten weeks of art study in the United States; while in New York he was given a one-man show at the Merton Simpson Gallery. At this exhibition the Museum of Modern Art in New York bought one of his works for its permanent collection.

Despite these years abroad, Ntiro, unlike his colleague Maloba, has been little influenced by twentieth-century Western art. His style, formed in his early years at the School of Fine Arts, has remained practically unchanged and is obviously related to that of typical Trowell students. Ntiro's works, however, are not as academically realistic, since his figures and landscapes are less detailed. His paintings have a naiveté resulting largely from his flat, rather awkwardly drawn figures (Plate 43). It is this latter quality which has prompted one observer to relate Ntiro to another modern primitive, Grandma Moses.

Ntiro has said of his themes, "My painting is a memory of what I know best of the life of my people. . . ."[10] Consequently his paintings *Beer Making, Working in the Banana Grove, Making a Hut,* and *The Market Day* are vignettes of Chagga daily life. Such genre subjects are also incorporated into an important mural series executed in 1959 for the University's Northcote Dining Hall. This series includes six twenty-foot-high paintings with main themes such as Drawing Water, Going to School, and Raising Food—all appropriate subjects for the Hall.

Drawing Water (Plate 43) is a typical Ntiro composition. Tiny figures are placed without benefit of linear or atmospheric perspective in a vertical, horizonless landscape. The bare landscape is spotted, in most unrealistic fashion, with different varieties of trees. Figures are aligned schematically in single file, forming a large chevron which fills the entire painting. The figure grouping in the lower half is dramatically but unrealistically highlighted along its length. The flat, repetitious figures are amorphous and unarticulated; they wear simple, brightly colored clothing, contrasting with the somber landscape. The figures are in every instance typically out of scale with their surroundings.

43. Sam Ntiro. *Drawing Water,* tempera. Wall of Northcote Dining Hall, Makerere University College, Kampala, Uganda.

Another major commission of Ntiro's, executed the same year, is an altar mural done in oil mixed with beeswax on plaster for the mission church at Kakindo, Uganda. Unlike most of his works, Ntiro deals here with Christian themes: Preaching the Word, Conversion of St. Paul, Crucifixion, Entry into Jerusalem, and Feeding of the Multitude. These subjects are Africanized; everyone, including Christ, is black, and the environment is also African. The composition, as in his Northcote paintings, is rather schematic. His five scenes are separate and distinct circular groups placed in the foreground; within each group the most important figure is centered and larger than the rest.

A contemporary of Ntiro is Elimo Njau. Like Ntiro, he is a Chagga born near Kilimanjaro. He received his diploma in 1957 and was then appointed art instructor at Makerere's teacher-training school in Kampala. In 1960–61 he studied in London, and shortly after his return left Makerere to work in Nairobi. He became, in succession, assistant director of the now defunct Sorsbie Gallery, head of the visual arts program at the Chemchemi Cultural Centre, and founder and director of the Paa Ya Paa Art Gallery. Njau also established the Kibo Gallery in Moshi, Tanzania. In the early 1970s he began teaching at the University of Dar es Salaam.

Njau's most ambitious works were executed for the Church of the Martyrs in 1956. The church was built in Fort Hall in the Kikuyu country of Kenya as a memorial to victims of the Mau Mau uprising.[11] Njau's paintings, covering an entire nave wall, are the largest mural series in East Africa. They depict five important episodes from the life of Christ, and like Ntiro's Kakindo paintings, the scenes are Africanized. *Nativity* (Plate 44), for example, takes place within a simple Kikuyu hut in the steep, fertile valleys of the surrounding Fort Hall area. *Baptism of Christ* includes typical Kikuyu figures, such as a woman supporting a heavy burden with a head strap, and in *Last Supper,* enacted within a Kikuyu hut, Christ and his disciples sit before a table laden with African food. *Agony in the Garden* is set before nearby, rugged snow-capped Mount Kenya.

As the narrative unfolds there is a radical transformation in style. The fertile, rolling hills of *Nativity* change in the final two scenes to a bleak landscape filled with jagged rocks, stumps, and fallen trees. Color, too, is used to denote change; the warm colors of the early pictures become, in *Agony in the Garden,* cold, gray, and somber. In the final scene, *Crucifixion,* Njau

44. Elimo Njau. *Nativity,* tempera. Nave Mural for Church of the Martyrs, Fort Hall, Kenya.

juxtaposes warm and cold, an intense yellow and blue, to symbolize both hope and despair.

In comparing Elimo Njau's style with that of Sam Ntiro, the latter's influence is apparent in the preference for spacious landscapes spotted with relatively small figures. Njau, however, paints with greater freedom and confidence. His compositions are more complex and convincing, while his figures do not have the awkward stiffness of Ntiro's. Njau's brush strokes are longer and looser and give a certain vitality and freshness to his style.

Changes in curriculum and especially in attitude began at Makerere when Mrs. Trowell left in 1958. Her successor as director of the School of Fine Arts was Cecil Todd, a former professor of art at Rhodes University, South Africa. Under Todd's direction students are now exposed to much more Western art, including a wide range of modern styles. Todd's own modern work and attitudes have been reinforced by the influence of the head of the Department of Painting, Jonathan Kingdon. A talented graphic artist and painter, Kingdon joined the faculty at Todd's invitation. Among other innovations, Todd has expanded the study of history of art to a compulsory four-year course that includes a full year in modern European art. Techniques favored in more advanced European art schools, such as stained glass, mosaics, and metal casting, are now being offered. Courses of study terminating in the Bachelor and Master of Fine Arts degrees were offered initially in 1969–70.

A large, well-designed gallery housing the extensive permanent collection of the school was opened in the fall of 1968. Because most of East Africa's prominent artists have been associated with the school, the collection provides examples documenting the growth of contemporary art in the area. This kind of documentary collection, unusual in Africa, should prove of great significance in the continuing development of East African art.

The effects of Todd's policies are apparent in the work of two former students who are now faculty members. George Kakooza, a student of Maloba's, who succeeded his teacher as head of the Department of Sculpture, received his diploma from Makerere in 1962. He studied in Paris for two years at the École des Beaux-Arts and the Sorbonne. In 1964 he had a one-man exhibition in that city, and since his return to the Makerere department in 1965 he has executed several commissions for public buildings in East Africa.

His most impressive work to date is a monumental free-standing figure group unveiled in 1967 at the University College, Dar es Salaam (Plate 45).[12] Entitled *Thinkers,* the group consists of four standing figures, over three times life-size, holding a book aloft. As with most of his work, the group is made of metal, being composed of brass sheets covering a concrete core. Small pieces of bronze are welded to it to provide textural variation.

Typical, too, of Kakooza's sculpture is the extraordinary elongation of figures with severely attenuated arms and legs, which are then abstracted to geometric shapes. The arrangement of sharply flexed arms is exploited for its design possibilities. Except for his taste for textured surfaces, Kakooza's work bears little stylistic relation to that of his teacher, Gregory Maloba. His inspiration seems to have been derived instead from the style of the modern Swiss sculptor Giacometti.

Teresa Musoke, another former Makerere student, now teaches graphic arts there. Born in 1941, she received her diploma in 1964. From 1965 through 1967 she did postgraduate work in graphic design at the Royal College of Art in London. Solo exhibitions of her works have been held

45. George Kakooza. *Thinkers,* bronze, brass and concrete. University College, Dar es Salaam, Tanzania.

46. Teresa Musoke. *Symbols of Birth and New Life,* oil on hard-
    board. Mary Stuart Dining Hall, Makerere University College,
    Kampala, Uganda. Detail.

in Kenya, Uganda, and Tanzania, and she has also been represented in group
shows in London and New York.

Her work, like Kakooza's, illustrates some of the changes effected under
Todd's leadership. Her most important commission is a large oil painting
entitled *Symbols of Birth and New Life* (Plate 46). Executed in 1964, while
Musoke was still a student, it hangs in the Mary Stuart Dining Hall at the
College. The long rectangular work pictures a complex series of tightly
interrelated forms. The primary interest of the artist appears to be an abstract composition concerned solely with line and color. Upon closer inspection it is apparent that there are representational forms interspersed within,
and at times making up, these shapes. These representational forms are complete or fragmented human figures, animals, birds, trees, and flowers.

The dramatic changes in the work of students since Todd's arrival are
evident. Their paintings and sculpture have much more individuality, vigor,
and, above all, originality than previously. Subject matter and even styles, are
now associated with modern Western or even Near Eastern prototypes, although in a few cases inspiration is derived from traditional African styles.
Todd, therefore, has infused new strength and spirit into the Makerere
School.

Thus, the School of Fine Arts at Makerere University College has played a crucial role in the development of art in English-speaking East and Central Africa. It has not only been the leading art school in this area but it has also been the training ground for the major artists of this region, who have now returned to Makerere to teach the younger generation.

The Sudan supports an art school that has produced artists of exceptionally high caliber. The School of Fine and Applied Art in Khartoum began in 1946, when the School of Design of Gordon Memorial College was reorganized to become the Department of Arts and Crafts of Khartoum Technical Institute. In 1958 a broader and more intensive curriculum was introduced and the name of the department was changed to its present form. It is hoped that the School of Fine and Applied Art will soon become an autonomous institution, awarding its own diploma; the government plans to expedite this development by building a separate college and incorporating several new faculties.

The present course of study leading to a diploma is a four-year program. The first or "foundation" year is devoted to work in drawing, design, modeling, history of art, and general studies. From the second year a student may specialize in one of six fields: painting, sculpture, calligraphy, graphic design, ceramics, or textile design. Future plans include adding interior and industrial design, bookbinding, weaving, and studies in folk art to the curriculum. According to school officials it is expected that in all subjects there will be attempts to utilize the best of traditional Sudanese arts and crafts.

An exponent of this attitude is the instructor of graphic design, Ahmed Mohamed Shibrain. Born in 1932, he was trained at the Khartoum School, graduating in 1955, and was appointed to the faculty the following year. From 1957 to 1960 he studied in London at the Central School of Art. He has had one-man exhibitions in London, Ibadan, Beirut, and Khartoum, and has shown his work in several dozen group exhibitions both in Africa and abroad, including New York. Moreover, he was a winner of a UNESCO art competition held in 1964.

Shibrain has been more profoundly influenced by his religious background than has any other contemporary African artist. He is a devout Muslim, a descendant of al Mahdi, the much revered spiritual and temporal nineteenth-century ruler of the Sudan who gained fame as the opponent of General Gordon. Shibrain fervently believes in reinstituting strict adherence to the orthodox tenets of his religion in modern Sudanese society.

It is not surprising, therefore, that he should turn to Arabic calligraphy as the basis of his artistic expression. Calligraphy has held a place of importance in Muslim life that is sometimes difficult for Westerners to comprehend. As a way of preserving and revering the scripture, verses from the Koran have long been displayed in Muslim homes. Furthermore, the calligraphy in which these verses were inscribed took on aesthetic significance because the taboo against figurative representation, or more precisely, against anything that casts a shadow, prevented other artistic expressions. It became, in fact, the only traditional pictorial art in the Sudan, where even today most homes use metal plaques or drawings of Koranic verses as decoration. The role of Arabic calligraphy has been well stated by Denis Williams, who says it "exalt[s] the language as a sacred vehicle; [its] beauty is to the Arab equally as important if not more so than the conveying of the bare, verbal message."[13]

The relation of Shibrain's style to traditional Arab calligraphy may be seen in his *Calligraphic Abstraction* (Plate 47). Using pen and black ink, the artist arranges Arabic-like characters on a neutral ground. Like all letters, these forms are flat and unshaded. The aesthetic effect, flat black forms against a stark white background, is similar to that encountered in the script of other cultures, for example, in medieval Latin manuscripts or Japanese scrolls.

In Shibrain's work, however, traditional Arabic calligraphy becomes something different. Individual characters are barely, if at all, decipherable; they are shortened or elongated, compressed or expanded. The width of the lines constituting the characters is constantly varied so that within one work the range is from the line made by the finest pen to a solid black form which may measure several inches in width. Furthermore, the Arabic-like characters lose their individual identity, and are combined in such a way as to make a single, aesthetically pleasing, overall composition. The composition shows great unity, within which the artist manages to create sharp contrast between curvilinear and rectilinear lines and shapes as well as between areas of heavy, dark, static forms and light, free-flowing lines. This taste for varied and often dramatic juxtapositions makes the work an extremely exciting one and in this respect it bears some relationship to European Baroque art.

Although Shibrain's favorite technique has been pen and ink, he turned to oil painting in 1968 for the first time since his student days. In *Message 40* (Plate 48) his concern with calligraphy is still evident in the right side of the canvas. In addition he has included traditional Islamic motives: a rosette, a crescent, and diamonds. Perhaps presaging a change in his style and a break

AFRICAN
106 ART

48. Ahmed Mohamed Shibrain. *Message 40,* oil on canvas. Collection of the artist.

47. Ahmed Mohamed Shibrain. *Calligraphic Abstraction,* pen and ink. Collection of Ulli Beier, Ife, Nigeria.

from the strict adherence to nonfigurative representation is the appearance in this work of the prominent pitcherlike form in the foreground and the off-center, paired concentric rings strongly suggestive of staring animal eyes. The subtle pastel colors of the painting reflect essentially the colors encountered in the Sudanese landscape. The blue and bluish green are the colors of the Blue Nile, the yellows and light reds those of the desert, earth, and traditional mud architecture.

Ibrahim el Salahi, head of the painting and drawing department at the Khartoum school, is another fine Sudanese artist. Born in Omdurman in 1930, he was trained at the school and began teaching there in 1952, while still a student. From 1954 to 1957 he studied at the Slade School of Art in London. He has made trips to the United States and South America on fellowships from UNESCO and the Rockefeller Foundation, and his work has been shown in Europe and the United States. A number of his paintings are in American collections, including that of the Museum of Modern Art.

In his paintings and drawings, Salahi, like Shibrain, usually employs traditional Islamic motives and calligraphy, for example, the Arabic-like characters and crescent-shaped form in the painting *Allah and the Wall of Confrontation* (Plate 49). His dependence on Islamic sources is readily under-standable, for Salahi's father is a teacher of Muslim theology who formerly conducted Koranic classes for children. The painter's early exposure to Koranic script was reinforced through study of Islamic manuscripts in the British Museum while a student at the Slade. Upon his return to the Sudan, Salahi became passionately interested in the traditional arts and crafts of his country, such as weaving and basketry, and patterns and painted decorations on house walls in the northern Sudan. Even the Arab regiment flags from the last century displayed in the Museum of the Mahdi in Khartoum are inspiration for his ideas.

Salahi, unlike Shibrain, however, makes considerable use of non-Islamic motives. He combines human figures, animals, and natural elements with forms of Islamic derivation. Salahi does not feel that this inclusion of representational elements is inimical to his Muslim faith. When questioned about this seeming conflict he responded:

> There are many Islamic scholars who have been asked this question and they say there is nothing at all to restrict you from reproducing the human image as you want. In a way it's a kind of a prayer, too, because

AFRICAN
108 ART

49. Ibrahim el Salahi. *Allah and the Wall of Confrontation,* oil on hardboard. Collection of Transcription Center, London.

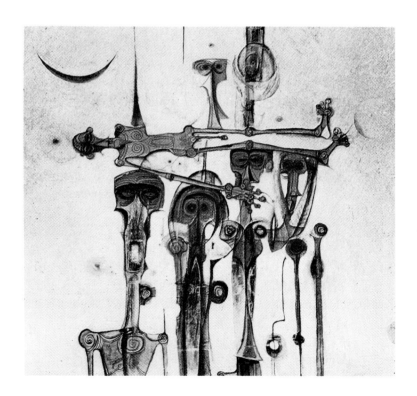

50. Ibrahim el Salahi. *Funeral and Crescent,* oil on hardboard. Collection unknown.

you are appreciating God's creations and trying to think about them and meditate on his creativity.[14]

So, to the Islamic motives in *Allah and the Wall of Confrontation* a human face is added.

The painting *Funeral and Crescent* (Plate 50) is concerned solely with the representation of human figures. Under a crescent moon a procession of mourners carries the deceased aloft. Salahi's figures tend to be tremendously elongated and frightfully emaciated. There is a stress on the extremities; hands and feet are greatly enlarged. Points of articulation—knees, elbows, and places where arms and legs join the body—are emphasized and delineated with spirals, an aesthetic convention found elsewhere, for example, in the figure sculpture of the Maori of New Zealand. In contrast to the negation of flesh in his skeletonlike bodies, the fleshy male sexual organ is exaggerated. It is curious that some stylizations—figure elongation and exaggerated sexual organs—are also seen in much African tribal sculpture. This affinity is evident, too, in his treatment of the face. Within his skeletal heads are geometrically stylized facial features, a handling of form common in traditional African masks. Like the traditional sculptor, Salahi feels free to exaggerate, suppress, or eliminate individual facial features. Although these formal relationships with traditional art exist, it would be a distortion to maintain that the painter's highly original figures and faces were directly influenced by specific tribal styles. It seems instead that Salahi and traditional artists have understood and been motivated by similar basic aesthetic concepts.

More important than the formal considerations concerning the rendering of human body parts and their composition is the extraordinarily expressive effect of Salahi's figures and faces. His elongated emaciated figures cannot be anything but expressive! And the faces, with their staring, often deeply set eyes and open mouths, sometimes with teeth bared, contribute immensely to the emotional impact of Salahi's work. In this expressiveness another affinity with African tribal sculpture, particularly with work from Zaïre (whose borders adjoin the Sudan), is apparent, albeit perhaps unintentional.

Most of these figure stylizations and the intensity of expression are also evident in Salahi's drawing *Poor Women Carry Empty Baskets* (Plate 51). Here he is concerned with contemporary Sudanese life. A woman in traditional costume carries on her head a basket patterned with geometric designs. The work transcends a portrayal of picturesque native life and becomes a haunting image of hunger and poverty. In such a work Salahi exhibits a social consciousness rare among contemporary African artists. This awareness is not restricted to mere recordings on paper and canvas in the artist's studio, for Salahi is involved in the public affairs of his country. He has conducted a weekly program on government-operated television, a program that has been by no means limited to art, and has treated such controversial issues as the severe problems of unemployment and inflation in the Sudan.

In a completely different vein is Salahi's painting *The Embryo* (Plate 52). Although there are veiled references to naturalistic forms, the painting is essentially an abstract composition of juxtaposed organlike and geometric shapes. Flat color areas contrast with sections broken up by geometric designs and colors that blend one into the other. The colors are those overwhelmingly favored in Salahi's palette, varying shades of brown. Dark-brown and blue forms are silhouetted against a light-brown background, the latter strongly suggesting the desert landscape of Khartoum. Also apparent in large areas of this work is the impasto painting technique, a device much used by the artist. It not only provides textural variation but also projects important forms into low relief. This relief effect is particularly dramatic in those paintings in which humans with large, staring eyes are portrayed.

Ibrahim el Salahi is one of the truly great contemporary African artists. A synthesizer, as one must be in the Sudan, where the Arab culture of the North meets the Negro cultures from the South, Salahi combines many of the essentials and fundamentals of the arts of these disparate groups. In the process he creates new images and has developed a style uniquely his own.

Ethiopia has an art school organized much like those in Kampala and Khartoum.[15] Called the Fine Arts School, it was founded in Addis Ababa in 1958. A five-year program offers painting, sculpture, graphic and commercial art, industrial design, lettering, history of art, and teacher-training courses. History of world art is stressed in the curriculum; four years are devoted to the painting, sculpture, and architecture of Europe and one year to non-European art.

Skunder Boghossian, one of the most talented artists in Africa, teaches painting at the Fine Arts School. Born in Addis Ababa in 1937, he received only informal art training there before leaving for Europe on a government scholarship in 1955. After several frustrating years in London, where he decided in rapid succession that St. Martin's School, the Central School, and the Slade were not to his liking, he moved to Paris. He found the Parisian

52. Ibrahim el Salahi. *The Embryo,* oil on hardboard (?). Collection of the Hamilton Gallery,
London.

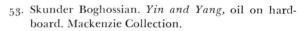
51. Ibrahim el Salahi. *Poor Women Carry Empty
Baskets,* pen and ink. Collection unknown.

53. Skunder Boghossian. *Yin and Yang,* oil on hardboard. Mackenzie Collection.

atmosphere more stimulating and so remained there, studying at the Académie de la Grande Chaumière until his return to Ethiopia in 1966. Skunder's[16] first one-man show was given at the Merton Simpson Gallery in New York in 1962 and was followed by a second exhibition there in 1965. He has also participated in shows in major European cities as well as in Ibadan, Nigeria. He was the first contemporary African painter to be represented in the collection of the Musée d'Art Moderne in Paris, and the Museum of Modern Art in New York also owns one of his paintings. He has been the recipient of Ethiopia's most prestigious art award, the Haile Selassie I Prize for Fine Arts.

Skunder's paintings mirror his interest in the arts and culture of Ethiopia, Europe, and West Africa. Influences from his native country and West Africa are juxtaposed in a recent work, *Yin and Yang* (Plate 53), a title inspired by the painting's phallic and oval and circular forms. The picture area is filled with the representation of an icon, or more precisely a diptych, obviously inspired by the traditional icons used in Ethiopia's Coptic religion. Topping the icon's frame is a series of semicircular forms recalling the numerous cupolas of a Coptic church. Furthermore, the rich reds and deep browns of this work, as well as of his more recent productions, suggest similar colors used in traditional manuscripts and church wall paintings.

Not only does Skunder show his affinity with this art form but in addition he demonstrates a knowledge of fundamental stylistic elements in other traditional Ethiopian arts. His concern with Ethiopian traditional art has been apparent at different periods in his career. His first significant works, exhibited in his initial New York showing, were representational scenes of Ethiopian life such as the marketplace and traditionally garbed figures. Following these early works this native influence was rejected, only to reappear in a different form in his more recent production. In the last few years Skunder has traveled considerably within his country, studying its traditional art and archeology. A visit to the rock-hewn temples of Lalibela left him so impressed he was "unable to paint for weeks."[17]

Influences from other parts of the continent may also be traced in *Yin and Yang*. Superimposed on the icon's picture area are faithful depictions of West and Central African hair combs. Skunder employs stylizations found in the original African works in the heads decorating the combs; for example, one comb closely resembles those carved in the Ashanti kingdom of Ghana. The eyebrow, a continuous line, extends the full width of the flat, round face, and the eyes are elongated ovals. Especially characteristic of Ashanti art is the long, ringed neck. Despite this painting's relationship with traditional African art and Skunder's professed fascination with the subject, formal influences from West African sculpture are rare in his work. Skunder's interest in the subject is nevertheless quite real, for during several of the years he lived in Paris the painter studied and sketched African tribal art every day in the Musée de l'Homme. At this time Skunder carved a number of masks closely approximating in style their West African prototypes.

Skunder's best-known works are those created from the early to the middle 1960s. These paintings, like his *Yin and Yang,* bear titles dealing with basic and elemental themes in human life and the universe, for example, *Primordial Effort, Song of Eclipse,* and *Inside the World Egg.* A series called *The Nourishers,* which broke with his earlier figurative style, initiated the period and includes *Explosion of the World Egg* (Plate 54), dated 1963. Another painting produced at this time and in the same style is *Cosmological Explosion* (Plate 55).[18]

In the works of these years Skunder clearly demonstrates his contact in Paris with significant paintings of twentieth-century European art. There are clearly discernible influences of fantasies and dream images from the Surrealist movement. Skunder has credited several artists as having had a major effect on his style, among them Paul Klee, Roberto Matta, and Wilfredo Lam. The impact of Matta and Lam has been recounted:

> In passing I just happened to look in a small gallery. I saw drawings in the window that actually gave me a bodily shock. So impressed by the dramatic play of forces and the supernatural quality of that work, I really couldn't move. I don't know how long I stood there. That was Lam. When I finally went inside I was startled again by Matta. In his paintings there was a cosmic coordination in space and time and his metallic rhythm vibrated in such a way that the canvases seemed to move. The effect of all this was confusion about my work, but eventually that confusion became a suggestion.[19]

The compositions of *Explosion of the World Egg* and *Cosmological Explosion* are typical of this period. A circular, often brightly colored, shape, sometimes resembling an egg, is placed near the center of the canvas. From

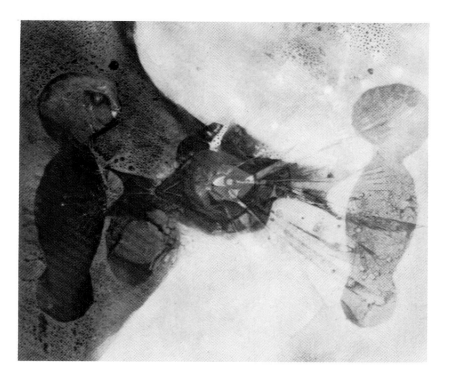

54. Skunder Boghossian. *Explosion of the World Egg,* oil on hardboard. Collection unknown.

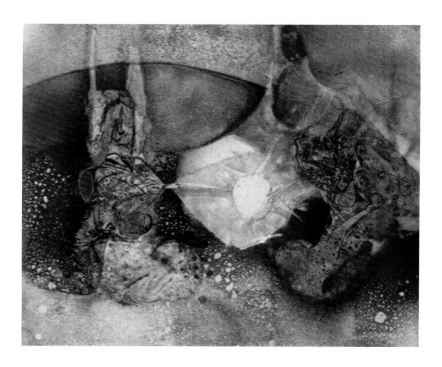

55. Skunder Boghossian. *Cosmological
Explosion,* oil on hardboard. Collection of Dr. G. Liersch, Munich.

this nucleus thin lines and forms radiate, silhouetted against a neutral background. These lines contrast with the solid masses of the forms, which in turn, are broken up with linear, often decorative, details that in some cases shape organic elements. Because of the use of light this breaking up of form and shape creates a feeling of space and texture.

Skunder Boghossian is one of the most talented contemporary African painters. Like Salahi, he successfully blends influences from several disparate cultures in a highly original and imaginative fashion.

Gebre Kristos Desta is also a teacher of painting at the Fine Arts School in Addis Ababa. Son of a calligrapher and manuscript illustrator, he was born in Harar in 1932. His first paintings were done while he was still a science student at University College in the capital. In 1957 he won a government scholarship to study at the Academy of Art in Cologne, Germany. After three years at the Academy and another year of work and travel in Europe he held his first one-man show at the Galerie Kuppers in Cologne. Since his return to Ethiopia he has exhibited in Europe, South America, and Asia, as well as at home.

Like Skunder, Gebre Kristos has won the Haile Selassie I Prize. It was awarded to him in 1965 for being "largely responsible for introducing non-figurative art into Ethiopia." The citation might have been even more meaningful had it credited Gebre Kristos as being one of the earliest exponents and now the foremost practitioner of abstract art in sub-Saharan Africa.[20] Impetus for this style came from his stay in Cologne, where he met painters of this persuasion and became acquainted with works of the Russian pioneer abstractionist, Wassily Kandinsky. Since his return to Ethiopia the artist has frequently been sharply criticized for adopting this mode and neglecting traditional Ethiopian art. Gebre Kristos has replied:

> It's really funny that some people who know nothing about the history of art attach such exaggerated importance to the art of their own country. They don't realize how international art really is. Picasso would hardly have created his cubism had he not seen African art. Matisse was influenced by Islamic traditions. Gauguin went as far as Tahiti to find new inspiration. We create ultramodern houses in our developing countries. We build superhighways on which we drive the latest model cars from all over the world. We use all sorts of up-to-date international styles in technology, science, education, medicine and what have you. Why in the world should art be any different?[21]

The painter, continuing, explains that traditional Ethiopian church art itself, supposedly an indigenous style, was actually imported from the Byzantine Empire.[22]

Exemplifying Gebre Kristos' style is *Green Abstract* (Plate 56), dated 1966. He illustrates his penchant for combining expressive, not-quite-straight lines with irregularly shaped circles of differing size. Circles, a leitmotif in his work, have a dual role. According to the artist, "They are symbols of universal things: mouth, earth and sun, etc., and more important they also make interesting patterns."[23] The linearity of *Green Abstract* breaks down in *Red Abstract,* done two years later. Although his interest in lines and circles continues, these forms are now executed in a painterly fashion. Lines and circle contours are less defined, and colors that blend one into the other replace clearly defined color areas.

Gebre Kristos also shows a concern with texture and materials. *Green Abstract* and *Tin Cans* (Plate 57) employ an impasto technique, and in addition, a cluster of round cans of various sizes are affixed to the oil-on-hardboard background of the latter painting. Rope has been added to other paintings.

Gebre Kristos' dedication to abstract art is a courageous act in the artistic climate of contemporary Africa. Frequently African artists are asked by their governments to execute commissions fulfilling a social function. The role of these works is essentially an educational one: to glorify accomplishments of the state and its leaders and to revive interest in traditional values, thereby developing national self-confidence. This social role of art has particular relevance in present-day Africa, where in many areas 90% of the populace is illiterate. But Gebre Kristos has had another obstacle to overcome, one which is specific to Ethiopia—the vital and continuing importance of traditional art. Illuminated manuscripts and highly decorative silver and brass crosses are still being produced for use by the powerful Coptic church. There is strong allegiance to the church, not only among peasants but also among the aristocracy and intelligentsia. Gebre Kristos' life as an artist in Addis Ababa might have been much easier if he had retained some of the techniques and forms of this art and had not made such a sharp break with Ethiopia's past.

In the early 1960s a workshop school was established at the National Gallery of Rhodesia in Salisbury by the gallery director, Frank McEwen. McEwen's interest was originally aroused by paintings produced by an untrained museum guard, Thomas Mukarobgwa. He provided this man and other interested experimenters with materials and encouragement. Gradually

56. Gebre Kristos Desta. *Green Abstract,* oil on canvas. Collection of the artist.

57. Gebre Kristos Desta. *Tin Cans,* oil and metal on hardboard. Collection of the artist.

the circle grew until in several years a dozen or so artists were coming regularly to a workshop school held in the museum storerooms. Other artists worked in their homes, bringing their paintings and sculpture to McEwen for criticism and discussion. In addition, several soapstone carvers living in the mountain region of Inyanga, 150 miles from Salisbury, also relied on him for advice, although obviously less frequently.

McEwen left Rhodesia in 1973, and since then he has lived in Europe and the United States. He tried to maintain the workshop artists by selling their works abroad, but was hindered by the sanctions on the export of Rhodesian art.

Because of the efforts of McEwen and the critic Ulli Beier, the work of these new Rhodesian artists is widely known in Europe and particularly in the United States. Both men have written ardently about its importance and originality. There have been two exhibitions in London, including "New Art from Rhodesia," a show accompanied by a handsome, profusely illustrated catalogue, held at the Commonwealth Institute in 1963. The Museum of Modern Art in New York purchased workshop paintings and encouraged McEwen in other ways, including circulating an exhibition of Rhodesian art throughout the United States. In the fall of 1971 there was an exhibition of workshop sculpture at the Musée Rodin in Paris.

Frank McEwen's attitude towards teaching art is entirely different from that found at Makerere, Khartoum, and Addis Ababa. There has been no formal instruction at the workshop school, and McEwen asserts that his role has been limited to providing materials and space, encouragement, and occasional criticism. He feels African artists should remain free from the "corrupting" influence of Western art schools and express instead their innate African qualities.[24] The flaws inherent in this argument have been discussed in earlier pages. Moreover, McEwen's approach, unlike that of similar schools mentioned previously, is compromised by the museum environment in which the artists work or at least receive criticism. Painting and sculpture from major periods in the history of Western art and European-influenced, white Rhodesian work are displayed prominently on gallery walls. It would be a rare artist who could remain untouched when faced with this wealth of unfamiliar styles and techniques.

The teaching methods espoused by McEwen are not new to Central Africa. In the 1940s Reverend Edward Paterson claimed to have used the same approach in his art teaching at the Cyrene Mission near Bulaywayo,

Rhodesia, although his results indicate there was more influence than he realized. Schools using this kind of instruction to develop new styles, as pointed out earlier, have been more common in the French-speaking areas of Africa. It is tempting to speculate on the reasons for McEwen's sympathy with this outlook. There is, of course, the example of Reverend Paterson's earlier Rhodesian school. Perhaps of pertinence, too, is McEwen's French orientation. He lived in Paris for thirty years, where he served as a liaison for art activities with the British Council and, as a consequence, developed friendships with Picasso, Braque, and Brancusi. Probably even more important has been his friendship with the Austrian-born Ulli Beier, who established several somewhat similarly oriented workshops in Nigeria during the 1960s.

The best-known and most talented painter produced in the workshop remains its initial participant, Thomas Mukarobgwa. His oil on hardboard, *View You See in the Middle of a Tree* (Plate 58), owned by the Museum of Modern Art, is characteristic of his style. He shows a predilection for subjects from nature, particularly landscapes such as this one from which man has been excluded. The scene bears little relation to objective reality. It is, instead, an exercise in the juxtaposition of highly saturated, contrasting colors which appear to have been applied with great verve and spontaneity. Contributing to the total pictorial effect is the use of impasto. These qualities added together serve to make this work highly expressive and akin in some ways to the paintings of the German Expressionists and the post-Impressionist painter Vincent Van Gogh. An interesting, albeit fortuitous, relationship to Van Gogh is the fact that both painters sign their works prominently and with only their first names. By so doing the artists enhance their emotional impact and establish closer rapport with the spectator.

There is more sculpture than painting at the workshop school. Carvings are made by a number of sculptors working in and around Salisbury and in the enclave at Inyanga, including such men as Bernard Manyandure, Boira and Richard Mteki, Lemon Moses, Joram Mariga, Denson Dube, and Nicholas Mukomberanwa. They utilize varied stones, ranging from soft soapstone to granite. Their preferred themes are the human figure and head, although occasionally an animal is represented.

Strong Man (Plate 59), a self-portrait by Bernard Manyandure, is typical of this work. There is extraordinary stress on volume and mass, which is reinforced by a conscious compositional compactness. Arms remain wedded to

58. Thomas Mukarobgwa. *View You See in the Middle of a Tree,* oil on hardboard. Collection of Museum of Modern Art, New York.

59. Bernard Manyandure. *Strong Man,* stone. Collection of National Gallery of Rhodesia, Salisbury.

60. Boira Mteki. *Granite Head,* granite. Collection of National Gallery of Rhodesia, Salisbury.

the body. The large head rests firmly on the shoulders. These qualities as well as an intensity of facial expression observed in other workshop carvings frequently call to mind Romanesque sculpture.

This relationship to Romanesque art is not as farfetched as it may appear. A probable prototype for the workshop style, by virtue of proximity in time and space, is the Romanesque-style sculpture carved by Reverend Paterson and some of his former students at the Cyrene Mission. It is only necessary to compare this Manyandure work or numerous other workshop examples with a sculpture discussed earlier in these pages, *Mother and Child* by the Cyrene graduate Lazarus Kumalo (Plate 13). Produced in 1959, it is one of many works by Kumalo done in the same style, and it is, in turn, similar to the work of other Cyrene-trained sculptors.

The most powerful of the Salisbury carvers, Boira Mteki, eschews the soapstone favored by many of his colleagues, preferring to carve in granite. This choice probably is the result of his youthful training as a cutter of semiprecious stones. Mteki's repertoire is rather limited; he carves heads almost exclusively, for example, *Granite Head* (Plate 60). The power in his work springs from a certain primitiveness, a quality which may in part stem from the medium. Because granite is so hard, Mteki's forms are large and devoid of fussy detail and his surfaces remain rough, giving the work strength and vitality. Surprisingly, there is a close stylistic relationship between this and other Mteki works and canoe prow ornaments called musumusu made by the Solomon Islanders of Melanesia. Strikingly similar is the highly individual treatment of the face: the exaggerated prognathism, the long, narrow nose and its diagonal placement, and the extremely narrow forehead. His *Great Phallic Head,* in the collection of Mrs. R. Burrell, a less successful example of the same style, is very close indeed to the well-known, frequently reproduced Solomon Islands canoe prow in the collection of the Museum für Völkerkunde in Basle.[25]

VII : Art Schools in English-Speaking West Africa

IN ENGLISH-SPEAKING West Africa art schools are concentrated in Ghana and Nigeria.[1] The oldest is the art department of the University of Science and Technology in Kumasi, Ghana, a school whose origin dates to the 1930s. It was not until the 1950s that two schools were established in Nigeria: the art department of Ahmadu Bello University at Zaria and Yaba Technical Institute at Lagos. Most recently, in the 1960s, a workshop school was begun at Oshogbo, Nigeria.

The art department of the University of Science and Technology in Kumasi has had a long and complex history. The department began at Achimota College, just outside of Accra in 1936.[2] At that time, H. V. Meyerowitz, a sculptor and designer, was the department's director. He established a three-year arts and crafts course that included mural painting, modeling and traditional wood carving, basketry, pottery, weaving, lettering, and wood engraving. Since both Europeans and Africans staffed this department some African as well as European styles were taught.

The late Kofi Antubam, a graduate of the Achimota art department, was for decades Ghana's best-known artist. Born in Opon Valley in southwestern Ghana in 1922, Antubam was the son of an Akan paramount chief. Two years after graduation from the college in 1946 he was awarded a two-year scholarship to study at Goldsmith's College of Art in London. When he returned to Ghana in 1950 he began his directorship of the art department of Achimota School, Ghana's finest secondary school, a position he held until his death in April 1964. In addition to his teaching Antubam gave many public lectures and wrote extensively on both traditional and contemporary Ghanaian art.[3] One of his most important contributions, however, was his aid in the founding and support of the Ghana Society of Artists. He was also active in other Ghanaian and British art societies.

In addition to numerous local exhibitions in Ghana, Antubam held one-man shows in London, Paris, Rome, Düsseldorf, and New York. An accomplished artist in various media, he painted portraits of prominent Ghanaians and large murals in oil on plaster for the Cocoa Farmer's Cooperative Headquarters and the Ambassador Hotel, both in Accra, as well as murals in two United Nations buildings in Geneva. His work in mosaic is well illustrated in the Accra Community Center. He decorated the interiors of two ships of the Black Star Line, Ghana's national shipping company, and designed several postage stamps issued soon after Independence. Among Antubam's most important sculptures are the wood reliefs he carved for Accra's Central Library and the main Assembly Hall in the Ghana Parliament building. He also carved in the round the Ghanaian State Regalia, which included a chair, a sword of state, and a mace.

Certainly among his most ambitious commissions are two thirty-foot murals painted in 1956 for Accra's luxurious Ambassador Hotel. They portray traditional Ghanaian activities, such as a paramount chief with his spokesman or linguist, men playing the game called oware, and collecting cocoa pods.[4] These murals evidence a mastery of many European-derived compositional devices, which seem obviously a consequence of his earlier studies at Goldsmith's College together with his knowledge of Western European art.[5] Separate scenes are united by a single continuous landscape, and a patterned undulating ground line leads the eye from scene to scene. Figures are arranged in each of these vignettes as a spatial circle, a device reminiscent of some fifteenth-century Italian painters. The feeling of depth is enhanced by sharply foreshortened objects such as overturned stools placed in the foreground. As in many of Antubam's works colors are bright with a pronounced emphasis on blue and orange.

The style of Antubam's small canvases is typified by the oil painting *Paramount Chief* (Plate 61). His often-used technique of outlining parts of figures and objects with dark lines is quite apparent here. Despite the flattening effect this method produces, his forms retain mass and solidity. When included, descriptive details are handled broadly and simply. A characteristic

61. Kofi Antubam. *Paramount Chief and Attendant,* oil on canvas. Collection unknown.

element in his style should be noted in the caplike treatment of hair given to the fourth figure from the left.

The conventional, often realistic, style seen in Antubam's paintings was continued in many of the artist's carved wood reliefs, such as that in the Accra Central Library, executed in 1961. It represents a mother distributing books to her children. She is surrounded by traditional Ghanaian objects and symbols: an Ashanti linguist staff, an akua-ba figure, stools, bowls, and utensils. Placed at the relief's apex is a design commonly identified by the Ashanti as a symbol of wisdom: four symmetrically arranged lobes, each with a circular core attached to its outline.

Despite his oft-stated distaste for traditional African art, Antubam worked effectively in a sculptural style in which he refined, elaborated, and even stylized Ashanti symbols and designs.[6] Objects carved in this style are primarily functional, such as lecterns, chairs, and doors. Many of these objects are Western-derived, although Antubam has embellished them with old African motives, as, for example, in the large wooden double doors for the Assembly Hall, Parliament House, Accra (Plate 62).

Completed in 1960, these doors contain six highly polished reliefs plus elaborately scrolled wooden handles. Unlike traditional African doors, the reliefs were carved separately and then inserted into the framework. Ashanti symbols, however, appear on the reliefs. The center left relief illustrates a state sword with its double wrought-iron blade and its gold-leafed wooden handle. The two attached door handles are carved with symbols denoting welcome and wisdom. The bottom section of the handle, signifying welcome, consists of two vertical addorsed spirals above two horizontal spirals at either end of an S.

In 1946, the year Antubam received his diploma from Achimota College, Meyerowitz died. J. M. Mackendrick, a Scottish painter, was made department head a year later. The school expanded and moved north to Kumasi in 1951, forming a major department in what is now called the University of Science and Technology. That same year a new teacher-training course was established within the department to train primary and secondary school art teachers. Ten years later the original three-year art training course was expanded to four years. Mackendrick resigned in 1962 and was replaced by S. V. Asihene, formerly instructor of painting in the school.[7] The department, renamed the School of Fine Arts, has offered the following sections: painting, sculpture, ceramics, commercial and graphic design, research and extramural

62. Kofi Antubam. Carved door for the Assembly Hall, wood. Parliament House, Accra, Ghana.

63. Vincent Kofi. *Drummer,* wood. Collection of the artist.

studies, textiles, jewelry, and art education. In addition, a course in European art history has been compulsory. The largest enrollment in the school is in the painting section, where the instruction has followed essentially the theories and procedures of the typical English academic art school. Still lifes, portraits, and nudes have often been done in a lifeless, realistic style with little originality.

The sculptor Vincent Akwete Kofi is the most noteworthy artist to have graduated from the art department after it moved to Kumasi. He was born at Odumasi in the Krobo district in 1923. His father, a minister, was a part-time sculptor who had won several prizes, and his twin sister (Akwete means twin in Akan) is a potter and textile designer. After his graduation from Kumasi College of Technology, Kofi attended the Royal College of Art in London from 1952 to 1955. In 1959-60 he studied traditional African and Oceanic art with Paul Wingert at Columbia University and various techniques at the Sculpture Center and the Sculptors and Ceramic Workshop, all in New York. It was here he learned the cire perdue casting method, a technique traditional among the Ashanti. That year proved an extremely influential one in the development of Kofi's style.

Returning to Ghana, he headed briefly the art department of Prempeh College, a secondary school in Kumasi, before becoming head of the art department at the teacher-training college in Winneba, a position he held from 1961 through 1969.[8] He has returned to Kumasi, where he now teaches at the University.

Kofi has exhibited not only in his own country but in Ibadan (Nigeria), London, and New York as well. Unlike Antubam, he has executed only one important commission for the Ghanaian government, two fountains for the State House in Accra.

He has carved several larger than life-size figures in a dense, heavy wood, using the traditional African adze. His themes are at times African, such as the extraordinarily powerful figure, *Drummer,* or Okyerema (Plate 63).[9] In this work the simplified compact body, whose legs and feet are treated as amorphous shapes, is given interest by the delineation and contrast of arms and hands. The raised and bent right arm, holding a drumstick, expresses energy and tension. Most impressive, however, is the strong, powerfully carved, upturned face. The sharp-lined definition of the jaws, ears, and mouth contrast with the other massive, rounded facial features. Supplementing the force and vigor of the forms is Kofi's characteristic treatment of the surface as pattern, with chiseled grooves reinforcing the basic shapes.[10] This patterning, with its close similarity to that found in most stilt-step figures of the Marquesan Islands in the South Pacific, is but one of the figure's relationships with primitive art. In addition, there are reminiscences of traditional African art: the eyes recall those found on masks used by the Ibibio tribe of southeastern Nigeria; the placement and enlargement of the figure's left hand bring to mind Bayaka and Basonge fetish figures of the Congo; and the large, upward-tilted head evokes Lower Congo commemorative figures.

In Kofi's *Pregnant Mother and Child* (Plate 64) the compact body is again left relatively undefined, in this case to stress the close relation of mother and child. A tremendously large slab-like hand (the hands and feet in Kofi's works are commonly elephantine) supports the baby. Mother and child each face sidewards in opposing directions, establishing an interesting contrapuntal design. Perhaps because of the tender theme, forms are more rounded and surfaces smoother than in *Drummer*. Relations to traditional African art are also evident in this figure. The baby's flattened head and its slanted placement on the body are style traits suggestive of Ashanti Akua-ba figures. Recalling these figures also is the concentration of facial features in the lower part of the face: eyebrows which are continued by the nose, and a long narrow mouth. It might be noted in this work that the child's upraised arms without hands are reminiscent of another style, some of the Dogon figures from Mali. But the Ashanti akua-ba figures also have arms which are without hands.

While Kofi was studying in New York he became interested in the sculptural techniques of cire perdue casting and metal welding. An example of the former is seen in the reclining young girl entitled *Awakening Africa* (Plate 65). Because of the material's greater strength, Kofi's metal figures are less compact, and body parts are thinner and lighter than in his wood sculpture. This work, however, like his wooden figure *Pregnant Mother and Child,* has style traits drawn from traditional Ashanti akua-ba figures. In *Awakening Africa* certain parallels are seen with these figures in the cylindrical treatment of the body, the deeply grooved neck, and the geometric handling of specific facial features.

Vincent Kofi is one of the most gifted new African sculptors. Unlike the work of many of his confreres, specific features as well as a simplicity, power, and monumentality relate his style to much traditional African art. Yet, at

64. Vincent Kofi. *Pregnant Mother and Child*, detail, wood. Collection of the artist.

65. Vincent Kofi. *Awakening Africa*, bronze. Collection of the artist.

the same time, there is a modern aspect that ties much of his work to European twentieth-century sculpture. Both styles are often successfully synthesized in Kofi's works.

Vincent Akwete Kofi and Kofi Antubam are the outstanding graduates of the art department which is now part of the University of Science and Technology in Kumasi. It is unfortunate, however, that more artists of note have not been trained during the long history of the department.

The second art school to be established in English-speaking West Africa was the department of the Nigerian College of Arts, Science and Technology, renamed Ahmadu Bello University, at Zaria in northern Nigeria. Founded in 1953 in Ibadan, the department was transferred two years later to its present site. The University at Zaria has given a four-year art course, which, as in all other British-established art schools in Africa, may be supplemented by a one-year education course. Three major fields are taught: painting, sculpture, and commercial design, the last including graphic and textile work. The student begins with a two-year general course in which he samples the major art fields, and in his final two years he specializes in one subject. Art history is scheduled to be taught in each of the four years, but qualified instructors, as well as slides and photographs, have not always been available. There is, however, an adequate art library, and conversations with graduates indicate that they had made good use of books and illustrations available to them.

The Department of Fine Arts at Zaria has become Nigeria's leading conventional art school, drawing students from the entire country. Despite its location in the Northern Region, there are few students from the North. This can be traced to two causes: the general backwardness of the North, with its lack of sufficiently qualified students, and the traditional Islamic prohibition against representational art.

Commercial design and painting have been the most popular fields taught in the school. Under the direction of instructors such as Eric Taylor, the design students have produced highly competent and original posters.[11] Skilled commercial design is sorely needed throughout Africa. Increased demands for informational and display materials are accompanying the growing importation of European manufactured goods and expansion of government services by independent African states. Mediocre Western artists who have had little knowledge of traditional African art styles, customs, or prejudices have, until recently, largely filled these needs. It is hoped, therefore, that Zaria commercial design graduates will fulfill an important function.

The painting section has trained a number of talented, highly creative artists, such as Grillo, Akolo, Simon Okeke, Onobrakpeya, C. Uche Okeke, and Nwoko. Graduated in the early sixties, these young men are now the art establishment of Nigeria. In the exhibition celebrating Independence held in Lagos in October 1960, their works were shown publicly for the first time. Since then many of these artists have exhibited all over the world. They have received numerous public commissions and have also sold many works.

Yusuf Adebayo Grillo, a painter who is the most conservative of the Zaria group, is presently head of the art department at Yaba Technical Institute in Lagos. Of the various commissions he has received, monumental mosaics executed for the new Lagos City Council Building in 1968 are perhaps the most important. Although adept in the mosaic medium, his style can be seen best in his oil paintings, for example, *Yoruba Woman* (Plate 66), a favorite subject of the artist. Because Grillo, a Yoruba, was born in the large cosmopolitan city of Lagos, he has not had as much contact with his traditional tribal life as certain other Zaria graduates. In spite of that, usual forms of Yoruba dress as well as the dignified and impressive stateliness characteristic of these women are well rendered. Design is all-important; the simplified figure, without descriptive detail, is flattened and exaggeratedly elongated. Basic shapes within this figure are simplified and also repeated in the background. Color plays an important role in unifying the design. Discarding the customary blue of Yoruba dress, Grillo has replaced it with white and lavender.[12]

Especially in their interest in design and color, Grillo's paintings reflect influences from twentieth-century Western painting. When questioned about these influences the artist responded,

> The contemporary Nigerian artist must accept those influences which are vital to him. It does not matter whether these are drawn from Yoruba sculpture or Picasso paintings, both of which, incidentally, I find exciting. The artist should not worry about the results of these borrowings because the work, if sincere, cannot help but be a Nigerian work since it is created by a Nigerian.[13]

Jimo Akolo, who is another highly competent Zaria graduate, paints intricately constructed pictures. Born in 1937 near Ilorin, the northern boun-

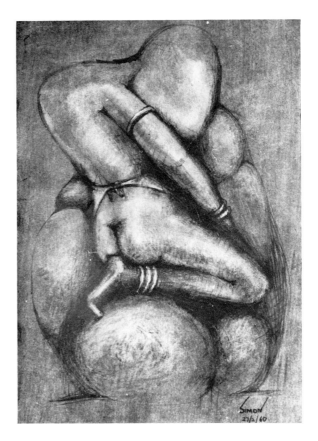

66. Yusuf Grillo. *Yoruba Woman,* oil on hardboard. Collection of Peter Whitehouse and Edward Moore, Lagos, Nigeria.

67. Simon Okeke. *Girl Who Was Turned into a Calabash,* watercolor. Collection of the artist.

dary of Yoruba country, he graduated from Zaria in 1961. Shortly afterwards he was awarded an honorary mention in the Biennale at São Paolo, Brazil.[14] He was commissioned to paint a large mural series for the Northern House of Assembly in Kaduna, the capital of the Northern Region of Nigeria. During the year 1964-65 Akolo studied in the United States at the Audio-Visual Department of Indiana University. He now teaches in the Department of Education at Ahmadu Bello University.

Akolo is interested above all in design and color, and he might be considered the colorist of the group. Unlike some other Zaria artists, his figures express no action or emotion; they are, instead, dignified mannikins in a tightly balanced and often exciting aesthetic composition.

Of the Zaria graduates, Simon Okeke's painting is the most unusual. An Ibo born in Onitsha Province in 1937, he graduated from the Zaria school in 1960. Shortly thereafter he was employed by the National Museum in Lagos to aid in the restoration of traditional Nigerian art objects and in the preparation of exhibits. He studied new techniques in these fields at the British Museum and in museums in the United States during leaves of absence from the Lagos Museum. With the outbreak of hostilities between the Federal Government of Nigeria and secessionist Biafra in 1967, he left the Lagos Museum.

Simon, as he signs his works to avoid confusion with his friend C. Uche Okeke, is a watercolorist with a wholly individual approach. Starting with white paper he builds up his dark, richly colored forms so that they have a density and mass uncommon in watercolor technique. The roundness of the forms is achieved not only by the use of light and shade but also by the scratching away of the paint in the highlights. Many of these forms are then silhouetted against a dark, densely pigmented, plain background.[15]

Simon's subjects are drawn mostly from Ibo life and folklore, as in the *Girl Who Was Turned into a Calabash* (Plate 67). His preference for simple, compact figures in which heads, legs, and arms are drawn tightly to the bodies, is apparent. In other group compositions the figures are so densely crowded that it is visually difficult to disentangle them. Furthermore, Simon frequently distorts figures and objects to enhance the compactness of his designs. His figures are composed of simple, rounded shapes free of most descriptive detail. His heads are typically massive and featureless ovoid shapes. Sometimes intertwined with his figures are simple, spherical objects such as calabashes and bowls.

Bruce Onobrakpeya is a fourth talented Zaria alumnus. Graduated in 1960, he is a member of the Urhobo tribe and lived in Benin City for many years. In 1963 he began teaching art at St. Gregory's College, Lagos. Among his commissions are a series of paintings depicting stations of the cross in St. Paul's Church, Ebute Metta, Lagos, and a concrete mural at Lagos University. He has also illustrated novels and books of legends and folktales.

Onobrakpeya excels as a graphic artist even though he has also produced paintings and sculpture. He has executed scores of extremely interesting black and white and color prints within the techniques of lino-cut, etching, silk screen, and woodcut.[16] The artist is often drawn to subjects from Benin legends and myths he learned as a boy, for example, *Quarrel between Ahwaire the Tortoise and Erhako the Dog* (Plate 68). Ahwaire's activities interest the artist deeply, for they appear in many of his works. The contestants in this print are enfolded within a stylized, upward-spiraling rock formation subservient to the large design pattern produced by the rocks. His particular concern with pattern is evident in the way he has cleverly alternated solid black-and-white shapes with simple lines and patterned areas.

Since 1965 Onobrakpeya has been experimenting with bronzed reliefs, a unique technique that evolved from his preoccupation with graphic arts. He sprays carved lino-cut blocks with bronze paint and then inks in the interstices so as to simulate patinated bronze low-relief sculpture. One of these reliefs, *Three Spirits* (Plate 69), combines two other major thematic concerns of the artist: nature and the spirit world. The highly stylized spirits suggest cross and longitudinal sections of tree trunks. *Three Spirits* differs radically in style from the earlier *Quarrel between Ahwaire the Tortoise and Erhako the Dog*. In the bronzed relief there is interest in fantasy and a lessened concern with composition and design. Forms have become much more amorphous and expressive. These new qualities probably stem from the artist's participation in three summer workshops at the Ibadan and Oshogbo Mbari Clubs. He is the only Zaria-trained artist discussed in these pages to have taken part in these programs.

Onobrakpeya's paintings, are not, unfortunately, as effective as his prints and reliefs. His themes are literary, his forms are frequently descriptive, and his compositions often lack the organization evident in other media.

The most exciting and creative of the Zaria graduates are two Ibos, C. Uche Okeke and Demas Nwoko. Close friends, their careers, in the years immediately following graduation, were linked; their first major exhibitions

69. Bruce Onobrakpeya. *Three Spirits,* bronzed relief. Collection of the artist.

68. Bruce Onobrakpeya. *Quarrel between Ahwaire the Tortoise and Erhako the Dog,* lino-cut. Collection of the artist.

were joint ones held in Lagos and Ibadan in 1961, and a year later they exhibited in the Galerie Lambert in Paris. The reactions of critics and public alike were so favorable that several commissions and grants were tendered.

C. Uche Okeke was born in Nimo in the Awka Division of Eastern Nigeria in 1933. His parents were artistically oriented; his father at one time carved wood reliefs traditional among the Ibos of the Awka region, and his mother, a midwife, also taught dress designing. Okeke was encouraged early in his career by one of the first Nigerian painters, Akinola Lasekan, and by the British art critic Dennis Duerden.[17] The latter introduced him to illustrations of modern European art and helped him secure his first one-man exhibitions in Jos and Kaduna in 1956. One year later Okeke entered Zaria. Since his graduation he has held numerous exhibitions, won prizes, and had a book of drawings published by Mbari. He spent 1962 and 1963 in Germany studying mosaic techniques.

Okeke has been deeply involved in problems inherent in the development of contemporary African culture. To discuss theories and practices, he established an Art Society at Zaria that frequently came into sharp conflict with the art department's faculty at the University. More significantly, he began a Cultural Center in his hometown of Kafanchan in central Northern Nigeria, where he had been taken as a child by his parents. He installed a rather large library in Kafanchan in order to encourage the townspeople to read, especially the works of Nigerian writers. His center also included a collection of over five hundred paintings, works of sculpture, and prints. Later, until the outbreak of hostilities in 1967, he directed a similar center in Enugu, capital of the former Eastern Region. Recently he has written and directed plays.

Okeke, unlike most of his Zaria colleagues, is concerned in his painting with varied categories of subject matter. Ibo religious myths, even though he is a devout Catholic, combine with Christian themes. He also paints scenes from everyday life, landscapes, and abstract murals such as those decorating the walls of the former Ibadan Mbari center.

Okeke is drawn to his tribal traditions and, with the aid of village elders, has collected several hundred folktales. His *Fabled Brute* (Plate 70) is, in fact, a character from these tales. It is a fanciful, toadlike animal, whose "ferocity" is suggested by sharp, white teeth and protruding, bulbous eyes. It is among the best examples of his creative work.

Many drawings by Okeke also show preoccupation with Ibo folklore and tribal life. In his *Maiden's Cry* (Plate 71), for example, not only the tradi-

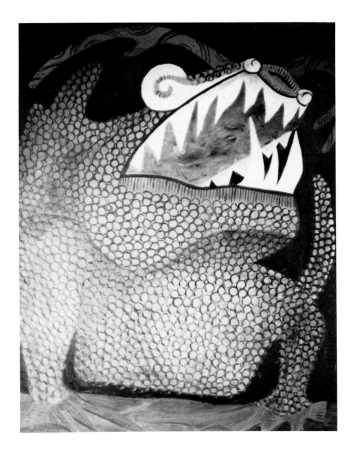

70. C. Uche Okeke. *Fabled Brute,* oil on hardboard. Collection of the artist.

71. C. Uche Okeke. *Maiden's Cry,* pen and ink. Collection of the artist.

tionally attired and coiffured maiden but also the distorted rendering of the figure recall the clay-modeled fertility goddess Ala, who occupies a central position in Ibo Mbari shrines. Features shared by these two figures are the cylindrical body, the elongated neck, the heart-shaped face, and the high placement of breasts. In contrast with the traditional treatment of Ala in Mbari sculptures, the *Maiden* is represented as shedding copious tears while her hands are raised in a gesture of anguish.

Okeke is one of the most accomplished of the new Nigerian artists. His drawings have a freedom and expressiveness of line in addition to a marked interest in pattern. Using themes from many different sources, he creates works that are always exciting and original, and that show an interesting range in style.

Demas Nwoko, born in a small Ibo village, Idumuje-Ugboko, in the Asaba Division of Eastern Nigeria in 1935, graduated from Zaria in 1961. Since the previously mentioned joint exhibitions with Okeke he has studied stage design and fresco painting at the Académie des Beaux-Arts in Paris and has examined stage design techniques around the world on a Rockefeller Foundation grant. More recently he has been employed as a scenic designer in the Department of Theatre Arts at the University of Ibadan. He has also painted a large mural in Tedder Hall for the University, and has illustrated a book of poems entitled *Heavensgate* by the late Christopher Okigbo. In recent years Nwoko has experimented with sculpture and even architecture, designing and building a studio that is both functional and imaginative in Ibadan in 1968.

A great deal of Nwoko's work is pervaded by an intense expressiveness. This quality is apparent in such diverse subjects as a Yoruba Ogboni secret society chief, a mother and child, and even a stand of twisted bamboo trees. Perhaps the most representative examples of this expressive quality appear in *Nigeria in 1959* (Plate 72) and *Beggars* (Plate 73). The former, a scene observed during a Moslem festival at Zaria, shows a group awaiting the appearance of the Emir.[18] Three English officers sit before a line of erect African soldiers. The sharp contrast between the lounging poses and apathetic facial expressions of the Europeans and the power and virility of the Africans creates a nervous, tense atmosphere. The painter reinforces this contrast by the use of color: the English are dressed in pale gray and khaki while the Africans wear deep, richly colored uniforms. Not only are forms and colors expressive but the painting is obviously a commentary on current events, an

72. Demas Nwoko. *Nigeria in 1959,* oil on hardboard. Collection of the artist.

73. Demas Nwoko. *Beggars,* oil on hardboard. Collection of the Ford Foundation.

approach unusual in contemporary African art. The picture, aptly titled *Nigeria in 1959,* suggests something of the social climate in the colony one year before Independence.

Nwoko's social commentary appears very strongly in another example of his work, *Beggars.* The three men are grotesquely and even hideously expressive, typical of many beggars seen today in large Nigerian cities. Although most people attempt to avoid them, Nwoko brings us face to face with these unfortunates. Their distorted grotesqueness seems to relate to "Die Neue Sachlichkeit," the paintings and drawings produced in post-World War I Germany.[19]

Nwoko also paints in a totally different manner. For example, *The Leopard* (Plate 74) displays what can certainly be called a light and whimsical approach and a decorative quality often found in Nweko's work. His portrayal of a reclining, lethargic leopard, with often stiff, body-length whiskers, being inspected by bright-eyed, chattering jungle birds and a monkey represents a completely fanciful and most appealing mood. Facial features, painted entirely in red, are joined in a continuous line; leaf ribs are composed in a regular, geometric, star pattern; while the leopard's tail neatly encircles the perimeter of a leaf.

Demas Nwoko is without doubt one of the most creative of the Zaria graduates. He is a highly original artist who combines a superb decorative sense with expressiveness and a feeling for social comment. He has become one of Africa's outstanding artists.

Although the art department of Ahmadu Bello University at Zaria has become the country's most serious and advanced art school, another school, also subsidized by the Nigerian government, the Yaba Technical Institute in Lagos, has produced commendable work. Founded in 1955, the Yaba art department has a curriculum, requirements, and aims which differ considerably from those of the somewhat older Zaria school. Students are accepted at Yaba largely on the basis of artistic ability. Some students, for example, even lack a secondary school diploma. The curriculum, furthermore, concentrates on subjects useful in business, and some courses are even tailored to meet the specific needs of local business concerns. In contrast to Zaria, Yaba students are not required to take any academic subject except history of art. The two-year art curriculum of the school includes pottery, sculpture, commercial design, graphic art, and painting. In the first year students take a general course, touching upon all the arts; in the second they specialize in

74. Demas Nwoko. *The Leopard,* oil on hardboard. Collection of the artist.

75. Festus Idehen. *Seated Man,* wood. Collection of the artist.

either commercial design and graphic art or sculpture.[20] Recently an additional two-year course of study, designed to train students to continue at other schools, such as Zaria or abroad, has been instituted.

The most gifted graduates of Yaba are the sculptors Festus Idehen and Osagie Osifo, both of whom were trained individually by Paul Mount, a British painter and sculptor who headed the art department until 1961. Idehen, born in Benin City in 1928, came from an artistic background. His grandfather Ebomwoyi carved many of the architectural beams and supports for the Oba's palace in Benin City. His mother, a priestess in the Olokun cult, modeled the life-size, clay figures found in the cult's shrines, a technique she taught her son. In the mid-1950s Idehen entered Yaba, beginning the long association with Mount that lasted until the latter's departure from Nigeria. He has had several one-man exhibitions in Lagos and executed a number of commissions, among them a monumental pierced wood screen for the Lagos City Hall in 1968 and concrete murals for public buildings and private residences, including the new Presidential Palace in Monrovia, Liberia.

Idehen has also executed many wood and concrete figures several feet high, such as his carved wood *Seated Man* (Plate 75). Forms are boldly simplified and surfaces are rough, indicating tool marks. Even more significant, however, are resemblances between this work and traditional African sculpture. The figure is bilaterally symmetrical and rigid in pose, features often found in traditional work, and specific stylizations are adopted and combined in a larger synthesis. Large, projecting tubular eyes, reminiscent of several traditional African mask styles, are placed within a configuration whose forehead, nose, and depressed facial planes closely resemble some of the masks of the Lega tribe of eastern Zaïre. The traditional motives Idehen uses are conscious adaptations of styles originating in various regions of Africa. In this selective adaptation of motives, Idehen resembles the Ghanaian sculptor Vincent Kofi as well as modern European artists such as Picasso and Modigliani. The sculptor was encouraged to work in this style by Paul Mount, who felt that African artists should use traditional African art forms and motives.

One of Idehen's most significant works is the floor-to-ceiling pierced-concrete relief embellishing the interior of the Lagos branch of the Standard Bank of West Africa (Plate 76), which was executed jointly with Mount in 1961 when the office was a branch of the Chase Manhattan Bank.[21] The relief was originally modeled in clay, then cast in concrete which contained a pul-

76. Festus Idehen and Paul Mount. Relief for Standard Bank of
West Africa, Lagos, Nigeria, concrete.

verized pink quartz. Details were then carved on the completed cast.[22] For an important aesthetic effect of the design (as well as to reduce the excessive weight of the relief) large areas of negative space were opened up between the figures. Furthermore, to express the seemingly structural function of support, the major lines within the composition are dominantly horizontal or vertical. Within these design considerations Mount and Idehen enhanced the interest throughout the relief by varying the sizes and poses of the figures. Heads and bodies are reduced to geometric, cubic shapes. The subject is derived from a Benin folktale and certain traditional Benin motives are evident: the ceremonial regalia of the Oba, while stylized, is nevertheless strongly suggested, and certain specific Benin style elements, for example, the double outlining of the eye, are used.

The Standard Bank relief is interesting not only for technical and stylistic reasons but especially because it is the only important commission executed jointly by a modern European and an African artist. Moreover, it is a significant example of contemporary African art because of its size as well as its quality, and because it is one of the most outstanding examples of work commissioned by a Western business firm with offices in Africa.

Osagie Osifo, like Idehen, is a sculptor trained at Yaba Technical Institute. He was born in 1939 in Idumu-Omwana, a village thirty miles from Benin City. He also derives from an artistic environment: the name of his village means "craftsmen of the king." Apparently those who specialized in carving resided there and Osifo has said that consequently he began his career early. He moved to Lagos in 1953, where his elder half-brother, the well-known Nigerian sculptor Felix Idubor, further trained him (see below, pp. 179–81). Four years later Osifo entered the Yaba school, where he began a close association with Paul Mount, who had a major influence on his style. Upon his graduation from Yaba he opened a studio and salesroom in Lagos.

Osifo has exhibited frequently in Nigeria. Among his most important commissions are a large Yoruba-style pillar for Queens College, Lagos, several carvings with Christian themes for St. Paul's Church in Ebute Metta, and some figures which are now in Southwell Minster, Notts, England.

Osifo, with Mount's encouragement, also became interested in African traditional sculpture. Unlike Idehen, he frequently copied such works (largely from illustrations and in some cases from actual objects) as Fang reliquary heads, Yoruba ibeji, and Benin bronze plaques (the last curiously cast in fiber glass). Most of Osifo's works are, however, original conceptions, and although they recall traditional African sculpture, it is almost impossible to pinpoint the specific sources of their forms and motives.

An entirely different kind of instruction from that offered in the art departments of Zaria and Yaba was introduced into Nigeria by the privately supported Mbari cultural centers. It had its origin in a summer workshop held at the Mbari Club in Ibadan in 1961. Ulli Beier, Mbari's guiding spirit, invited a young South African architect, Julian Beinart, to lead the workshop. He had run a similar program the previous year with Amancio Guedes in Lourenço Marques, Mozambique (see below, pp. 160–61). Beinart taught a condensed basic design course which concentrated on the importance of line, texture, perspective, composition, and paint mixing. His students, mostly primary and secondary school art teachers and Zaria graduate Bruce Onabrakpeya, attempted abstract sculpture and collage using such previously unused familiar materials as wire, mud, and bits of paper and glass. Beinart returned the following year to conduct a similar course, and was assisted by a painter from British Guiana, Denis Williams.

Although Beinart's summer courses were too short to have had a traceable effect on contemporary Nigerian art, they did encourage Beier to initiate a somewhat similar venture at the newly established Mbari Mbayo center in Oshogbo, the town in which the critic lived.[23] Beier asked Williams to teach a summer course there at the conclusion of his work with Beinart and to repeat it in 1963. The social and cultural milieu of Oshogbo was quite different from that of Ibadan. In the latter, a city with almost one million inhabitants, site of a major university, and a center of Nigeria's intellectual life, Williams' educated, middle-class students clearly had had preconceived aesthetic concepts. In contrast, Oshogbo, a town of 140,000 people, lacked Ibadan's cosmopolitan character and instead was an important center of Yoruba traditional life. Williams' students here were mostly jobless primary-school dropouts with few preconceived Western notions about art. Williams was much less theoretical and abstract in his teaching than Beinart, and imparted only a minimum of technical knowledge. He concentrated instead on stimulating his students to evoke from the depths of their consciousness sincere and highly individual images. He then helped his students to select images that he considered genuine and pure, and to reject those he considered false and derivative.[24]

The first of the Oshogbo artists, painter and printmaker Jacob Afolabi, who was an actor with Mbari's resident theater company, was discovered during the summer program in 1962. The following year, painter Rufus Ogundele, also an actor, showed talent. Beier relates the success of these two with their continuing presence at the center, and most important, their economic security as members of the theater company.[25]

With Beier's marriage to the painter Georgina Betts, the Oshogbo school acquired a knowledgeable, talented artist-in-residence. With the help of Afolabi and Ogundele, she conducted a third summer school in 1964, during which a number of talented newcomers were discovered: Twins Seven-Seven, Muraina Oyelami, Adebisi Fabunmi, and Jimoh Buraimoh. At the end of the summer Georgina Beier established in her home a permanent workshop where artists could come for materials, advice, and encouragement. For the next three years, until the Beiers' departure from Nigeria in 1967, these four artists plus Afolabi and Ogundele worked there occasionally.[26] Georgina Beier's methods of instruction were apparently similar to Williams', and because she was available all year round, her results were more impressive.

Certainly the most interesting of the Oshogbo workshop artists is actor, author, and playwright Twins Seven-Seven.[27] Beier describes his first appearance in Oshogbo as a spectacular one:

> Seven-Seven appeared one night at a dance held at the Mbari Mbayo Club. His appearance fascinated us at once: a blouse of rather bright Nigerian cloth which had "Seven-Seven" embroidered across the back, narrow trousers with pink buttons sewn along the seams, zig-zag edges cut into sleeves and trousers, pointed Cuban-heel shoes and an embroidered, tasseled cap. Even in a colourful town like Oshogbo he caused a minor sensation. But his dancing was even more exciting than his appearance: his imaginative variations on accepted highlife dancing proved so spectacular that the large crowd cleared the floor for him— a rare happening in a community where nearly everyone is a born dancer. I felt attracted by the young man's personality and was somehow reluctant to let him drift away again.[28]

For several weeks Seven-Seven entertained visitors to the Mbari Mbayo Club but with the advent of the third summer school he began painting and his talent was immediately apparent.[29]

Twins Seven-Seven creates pen and ink drawings colored with gouache on paper or hardboard. After Beier's departure the painter started coloring with oil paints. Essential to his technique is a final varnish coat which gives a much-needed luminosity. His themes are richly varied: Yoruba deities and myths, everyday events, and most frequent, his fantasies, which often incorporate elements from the other two realms.

Among these fantasies is *Inspiration of Mr. Kelly and Twins Seven-Seven and the Ghost of the Voice of America* (Plate 77). Painted in 1968, it was purchased by Mr. C. Kelly of the Lagos headquarters of the Voice of America. As is evident in his other fantasies, the painter's visions here are personal and private and therefore difficult to interpret. Seven-Seven is able to explain many of his visions but unfortunately for the critic his explanations vary with the artist's mood. In this work two seated figures in the foreground probably represent the artist and Mr. Kelly. A rectangular shape with knob-like projections, the third largest unit in the painting, resembles a radio and may possibly represent the ghost of the Voice of America. Enlivening Seven-Seven's work is a delightful sense of humor. The artist's face is replaced by a bovine head,[30] and the radio is animated by four humanlike feet extending from its base.

Seven-Seven's interest in decorative pattern is everywhere apparent. Heads are surrounded by dentate forms. Figures are dressed in dramatic red and white striped clothing. Seven-Seven's self-portrait juxtaposes striped pants and a polka-dot shirt, and Mr. Kelly's chair rests on a red-and-white checkered floor. Furthermore, every bit of open space is filled with pattern: stars, circles, and wavy lines (towards the picture's center these lines form the letters U.S.). This pattern resembles nothing so much as a painter's doodling with line. Seven-Seven's compulsion to fill all space is a contemporary Nigerian version of the horror vacui seen in early arts such as Egyptian tomb painting or geometric and archaic Greek vase painting.

Jimoh Buraimoh, a painter and mosaicist who has also been an electrician for the Mbari Mbayo theater company, is the most recent Oshogbo artist to come to prominence. Although he commenced his artistic activity in Georgina Beier's 1964 summer course, it was not until after the Beiers left that the artist began to attract attention and to receive important commissions. The first of these commissions was a mosaic for India Loom House, Lagos, in 1967, followed the next year by mosaics for the Ikoyi Hotel in Lagos and the Conference Hall, University of Ibadan. Partly as a result of these commissions he is among the best known of the Oshogbo artists.

Among this group Buraimoh's techniques are the most unusual and varied. Beginning as a painter, he soon began adding strings of beads to his

77. Twins Seven-Seven. *Inspiration of Mr. Kelly and Twins Seven-Seven and the Ghost of the Voice of America*, crayon and oil on plywood. Collection of C. Kelly, Lagos, Nigeria.

painted surfaces. Early in his career he also worked in mosaic, inlaying numerous coffee tables with glass tessarae. Later, in his Lagos and Ibadan commissions, he experimented by utilizing additional African materials: cowrie shells, beads, pebbles, and potsherds. Buraimoh's repertoire also includes lino-cut prints.

Obatala and the Devil and *Flute Player* (Plates 78 and 79), beaded paintings, illustrate subjects, forms, and colors favored by Buraimoh. His themes, like many of Twins Seven-Seven's, are derived from Yoruba daily life and mythology or from personal, highly individual fantasies. Obatala is the Yoruba creator god. The Yoruba character of *Flute Player* is obvious not only in the flute and agbada but especially in the depiction of a tall beaded cap. The verisimilitude of the cap is enhanced by the addition of real beads. Beads are also affixed to other large areas of the work, their bright colors blending well with the primary colors of the artist's palette. Human figures in Buraimoh's style are amorphous and rubbery in appearance, but are given strength and stability by the introduction of straight lines and well-defined decorative units at critical intervals in the figures. The most significant details are the eyes and nose. The not-quite-straight nose is tremendously elongated and the irregularly shaped eyes made up of concentric circles are much enlarged. This distortion as well as large areas of white give the eyes their very expressive character.

The Oshogbo artists developed individual styles of great imagination and creativity. Unlike the work of other similarly organized workshops in other parts of Africa, there is no readily identifiable "school style," nor are there clearly traceable stylistic derivations from European or traditional African art. This achievement must be largely credited to the intelligence, taste, and efforts of Georgina Beier and her husband. Ulli Beier's role as catalyst, guide, and proselytizer for both the literary and artistic production of Nigeria during his years in residence there cannot be overestimated.

After the Beiers' departure, Suzanne Wenger, an Austrian-born painter and sculptor, took on some of the duties of workshop director. As Beier's first wife she had lived in Nigeria for many years and had become deeply immersed in Yoruba traditional religion and art. Her orientation, therefore, was somewhat different from Williams' and Georgina Beier's. Her interest lay primarily in finding modern expression for the ancient traditional culture. At a summer workshop she led in 1967 several other artists developed

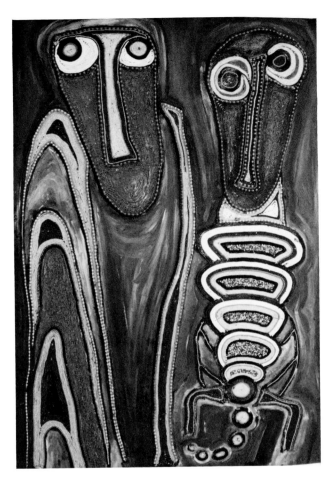

78. Jimoh Buraimoh. *Obatala and the Devil*, oil and glass beads on hardboard. Collection of W. Grutzmann.

79. Jimoh Buraimoh. *Flute Player*, oil and glass beads on hardboard. Collection of Peter Whitehouse and Edward Moore, Lagos, Nigeria.

whose efforts were in large part directed towards the building and decorating of religious shrines.

Suzanne Wenger also helped and encouraged two other important artists, Asiru Olatunde and Adebisi Akanji, who began working in Oshogbo before the formation of the Mbari Mbayo summer schools and remained independent of them. They must, however, be considered here because they were both discovered by Ulli Beier and because they know well the artists and works of the Oshogbo workshop.

The better known of the two is Asiru Olatunde, a sculptor in metal. He was born into a blacksmith's family in Oshogbo about 1922 but was forced by poor health to abandon the trade of his father. He remained unemployed for many years until Beier and Suzanne Wenger encouraged him in 1961 to produce jewelry and sculpture in the more malleable metals.

Lion-shaped copper earrings, his first works, were inspired by the modeled cement lions decorating Brazilian-style houses popular in Western Nigeria during the 1930s and 1940s. His patrons then urged him to create larger, more impressive, free-standing sheet-metal animals and later, metal reliefs to be hung on walls or used as doors. It is these reliefs that have brought him his present popularity. His early works were in copper and sometimes brass, but he soon turned to sheet aluminum because of its resemblance to silver and its lower cost. The personal fantasy evident in paintings by Twins Seven-Seven and Jimoh Buraimoh is almost wholly lacking in Asiru's work. He is, above all, a documenter of Yoruba religious and genre activities, although recently he has undertaken Christian themes for church doors in Oshogbo and Ilesha.

Perhaps his most effective work occurs in his representations of birds and animals. *Elephant* (Plate 80), an early free-standing sculpture, is cut from sheet copper with details—eyes and toes—hammered out in low relief. Within the elephant's body are a raised snake, crocodile, and chameleon. Surrounding these smaller animals the background is punched from the front to provide textural variation that contrasts with the smooth surfaces of the reptiles and the elephant's head and legs. The gentle charm of this artist is immediately apparent. Asiru's elephant is delightful, with a naiveté that results perhaps from the artist's never having seen an elephant, since these animals disappeared from this part of Nigeria long ago.

Pigs Cavorting Around a Tree (Plate 81) is characteristic of Asiru's work.

80. Asiru Olatunde. *Elephant,* sheet copper. Collection unknown.

81. Asiru Olatunde. *Pigs Cavorting around a Tree,* aluminum. Collection unknown.

Numerous elements recall traditional bronze plaques from the kingdom of Benin. The proportions are similar, and Asiru's range of thematic material corresponds to that favored by Benin bronze casters. But most significant are the stylistic relationships; Asiru's forms are clearly silhouetted against a patterned background in the fashion of traditional plaques. This decorative patterning, unusual in relief art, interferes with the optical representation of atmosphere and depth. The lack of depth is further reinforced by forms that are flattened and often arranged above one another rather than receding into space. Individual forms are usually depicted in their broadest possible aspect, that is, profile animals and frontal humans. This relationship to Benin relief art is perhaps not coincidental since most artists either own or have easy access to books on traditional African art. Moreover, Oshogbo is relatively close to important collections of Benin art in government-operated museums in Benin City and Lagos.

Adebisi Akanji, a sculptor in cement, began his career in much the same way as Asiru did. In 1962, when Adebisi was a bricklayer, Ulli Beier commissioned him to model in cement animals and figures for a one-man exhibition in Oshogbo. Beier's request for cement sculpture from a bricklayer was not without historical precedent in Western Nigeria, for it was artisans of the same craft who had created the heraldic lions for the Brazilian-style houses. This earlier sculpture, essentially folk art, disappeared with the advent of the dull, modern-style cinder block houses favored today. Beier, then, was attempting to revive an art form that had disappeared and chose for this task someone who had shown artistic talent in this medium. The exhibition proved successful, and Adebisi next created large openwork cement screens with registers of forms strengthened by a wire armature.

Adebisi's most celebrated screens enclose three sides of an Esso service station in Oshogbo (Plate 82). Each screen is divided into three wide registers of figures, animals, and other motives. As in Asiru's work there is a strong relationship with traditional African sculpture, in this case to the Yoruba doors commonly gracing entrances to palaces of the Obas, or kings. Yoruba doors, unlike other carved West African doors with a single, overall design, are divided into registers. Adebisi's range of subject matter also relates to the older art, for he combines subjects from many realms: Yoruba deities stand beside palm-wine tappers, ancient mythical events are juxtaposed with very contemporary ones, birds and animals consort with humans. Stylized animals—a leopard, a snake, and lions are found together with Ulli Beier driving a Volkswagen.

Adebisi's style, however, differs from that of Yoruba sculpture. Forms are more stylized than those of the relatively naturalistic traditional art. Adebisi's stylizations, moreover, exhibit an unusual combination that contributes to the interest and expressiveness of his work. He combines fluid, curvilinear forms with shapes whose outlines are interrupted by angles. These free-flowing forms derive naturally from the technique of modeling in soft, wet cement. Inspiration for his angular forms, however, must have another source. They are similar to forms found in the starch-resist dyed fabrics, the paintings, and particularly the carved wood screens of Suzanne Wenger. These stylistic affinities with Wenger's work are partially explained by Adebisi's close relationship with her, for they have collaborated in the reconstruction and embellishment of important religious shrines in Oshogbo.

Asiru Olatunde and Adebisi Akanji have a distinctly different artistic approach from Oshogbo workshop artists such as Twins Seven-Seven and Jimoh Buraimoh. The sculpture of these two men is much closer to traditional Nigerian art styles. The older art is the basis for their choice of media, subject matter, composition, and often, the style of the forms themselves. Although this dependence must be recognized, Asiru and Adebisi have created fresh and original interpretations that are wholly successful. It is not necessary to be aware of affinities to the older art to enjoy and appreciate their sculpture.

Ulli Beier realized that in order to survive, the Oshogbo artists must have regular outlets for their work. Concerning this need he wrote:

> The Oshogbo art school was not an aesthetic experiment: it was designed to create a living for these artists and to build up a new function and a new social status for them. All the artists mentioned here can now live off their work. Moreover, their work is not geared to the European collector alone. . . . More than any other workshop group in Africa, they have become integrated in the local community.[31]

During the author's visit to Oshogbo after the Beiers' departure in 1967 there was evidence that Beier may have been overly optimistic. The artists had for a while turned to other patrons—Mr. and Mrs. Richard F. Wolford, an American couple in Lagos who had energetically promoted and sold Oshogbo works until they, too, left Nigeria. Only a very few public com-

82. Adebisi Akanji. Screen for Esso Service Station, Oshogbo, Nigeria, cement.

missions have been given these artists and little interest in buying their work has been evidenced by Nigerians. They were, therefore, like workshop groups in the Congo, Zaïre, and Rhodesia, almost wholly dependent for their livelihood on sales to Westerners. Today in Oshogbo there are fewer non-Africans and therefore fewer potential customers than there were several years ago.

In June 1969 another Mbari-type center, Ori Olokun, opened at Ife, a city not far from Oshogbo, and the site of a relatively new university. Here Oshogbo artists painted murals on club and courtyard walls and found new outlets for their work. The Ife center functioned for several years under the aegis of Michael Crowder, who was director of the University's Institute of African Studies. Crowder is a writer and scholar who, as editor of *Nigeria Magazine* in the early 1960s, was responsible for a number of excellent exhibitions of contemporary Nigerian art in the magazine's Exhibition Centre in Lagos. In mid-1971 Ulli Beier returned to Nigeria and took up a post at the University of Ife. It will be interesting to follow developments at Ori Olokun since his arrival.

The "nonteaching" approach to training artists resulting in original and largely non-Western styles (such as the work of the Mbari Mbayo artists and, to a lesser extent, painting from the workshop of the Rhodesian National Gallery in Salisbury) is a new development in English-speaking Africa.[32] The artists encouraged in these studios were largely uneducated men who could not usually qualify for admission to conventional art schools. With a minimum of instruction the Oshogbo workshop was able to achieve highly original results.

Conventional art schools, in contrast, have had a long history in English-speaking Africa. They are not only more numerous but were established earlier than those in French-speaking areas. The art departments of the University of Science and Technology in Kumasi and Makerere University College, both founded in the 1930s, are the oldest art schools in Africa. The facilities of conventional schools in the English-speaking areas are usually excellent and their equipment and materials more than adequate. Course offerings are large and varied, and usually provide students with a choice of work in the fine or applied arts.

Several criticisms, however, may be leveled at some of these art schools, criticisms that are not easily applicable to most schools in the French-speaking areas. For example, their geographic location sometimes seems undesirable. The art department at Kumasi University is far from Ghana's capital at Accra, the site of the National Museum as well as the center of the country's cultural activities. Similarly, Ahmadu Bello University's art department at Zaria, located in vast and undeveloped Northern Nigeria, is far from the center of that country's contemporary cultural activities. This part of Nigeria is, moreover, dominated by Islam, a religion traditionally hostile to the figurative arts. The school's campus is located so far from town that art students find it difficult to witness traditional activities that might serve as subject matter.[33] Some critics feel the University was placed at Zaria simply because British officials in Nigeria favored the climate and environment of that area.

In the past rapid faculty turnover has been another disadvantage of some English-area schools. Those that were staffed largely by British instructors, such as the schools at Kumasi, Zaria, Yaba, and Makerere, were especially susceptible. Often there was a complete change of staff every few years; for example, in the early 1960s Zaria changed department chairmen three times in four years. Temporary faculty can hardly be expected to institute major changes and conceive long-term developmental projects. With the increasing Africanization of art-school faculties in the last few years this disadvantage has almost disappeared.

Perhaps the most serious criticism of English-area art schools has been the specifically British orientation of their programs. Most of the African schools were, for example, affiliated with English art schools which required them to meet English standards. Compliance with these standards was, moreover, insured by periodically sending examiners from English schools to Africa to test students and observe the courses. Departures from established British practices were consequently frowned on and attempts to relate programs more closely to African life and realities were rarely made. This disadvantage is now, however, being overcome, since many African schools have severed formal ties with their British counterparts.

VIII : Artists Independent of African Art Schools

AMONG twentieth-century African artists there are some who have had little or no connection with African art schools. A few are self-trained, while others have studied overseas. Some of these artists have full-time jobs in such varied fields as medicine, advertising, and government service and can devote only part of their time to art. A very few, however, such as Felix Idubor and Gerard Sekoto, support themselves solely from sales of their works. While the majority of these artists are from English-speaking areas, several come from other regions of Africa.

Valente Goenha Malangatana of Lourenço Marques, Mozambique, is the only important contemporary artist in Portugal's large African colonies (Mozambique, Guinea, and Angola). That there are no other artists of importance is undoubtedly a consequence of Portugal's complete lack of interest in stimulating the growth of any African art.

Malangatana was born in 1936. He received only a rudimentary primary school education and has had little formal art training. He has, however, devoted much spare time to drawing, to the dismay of friends and relatives who said he was always "playing." In the early 1960s he was discovered and encouraged by Amancio Guedes, a brilliant, imaginative, Portuguese architect, who has designed several excellent buildings in Lourenço Marques.[1] Guedes became his patron to the extent of supplying materials and furnishing a studio, as well as buying works and arranging exhibitions.[2] The first important exhibition of Malangatana's work was held in Cape Town, South

Africa, in the early 1960s, and was followed by his first one-man show, at the Ibadan Mbari in 1962. Since then he has exhibited jointly with Ibrahim el Salahi in Paris and London. In the early 1970s he studied print making in Lisbon.[3]

Malangatana, unlike most new African artists, paints in a highly charged and emotional fashion both aberrant and elemental aspects of life: madness, suicide, sex, and divorce. The emotionalism seen in *Rape* (Plate 83) results not only from the violent action but also from the painter's distinctive treatment of heads and facial features. The woman has long, flowing hair, an obsession with Malangatana, who has stated that "woman's hair shall be the blanket . . . woman's breasts shall be my pillow."[4] Her terror-stricken eyes are long, white ovals with large, dark irises. Both the woman and her attacker have stylized, aggressive mouths filled with long, sharp teeth, reminiscent of many traditional Congolese masks. Despite a striking compositional arrangement often missing in his works, *Rape* contains several awkward, anatomically impossible positions. Malangatana obviously lacks technical mastery but this lack is more than compensated for by his extraordinary power of expressiveness.

Malangatana has occasionally painted Christian themes, such as *Last Judgment* (Plate 84). The scene takes place in a bizarre, almost surreal, world of nude and clothed men and women, parts of figures, and symbols. Forms float in space, are crowded and inconsistent in scale and nightmarish in their emotionalism. Violence and its results appear everywhere, a characteristic of much of his painting which would almost allow Malangatana to be considered an African Hieronymous Bosch.

Malangatana deals with unusual themes in a direct and vigorous way. Most of his paintings are raw and uninhibited, often shocking and repellent, and yet despite his occasional technical crudities, he is a highly original painter and deserves close watching.

The first independent painter to emerge in French-speaking Africa began working shortly after World War I. He is Ibrayima Njoya, born perhaps as early as 1880. A member of the Bamoun tribe in Cameroun, he worked steadily in the tribal capital at Foumban except for a few short trips within the country. He enjoyed a long and close friendship with his similarly named cousin, the late Sultan Njoya, the progressive and intellectual head of the Bamoun tribe in the early decades of this century. In 1908 the Sultan named the artist principal of his newly founded school in Foumban, at which arith-

83. Valente Malangatana. *Rape,* oil on hardboard. Collection of
    the artist.

84. Valente Malangatana. *Last Judg-
    ment,* oil on hardboard. Collection
    of the artist.

metic, reading, and other elementary subjects were taught. Ten years later the Sultan placed him in charge of construction of the monumental pseudo-German Romanesque palace in Foumban.[5]

About this time, c. 1920, the Sultan, whose interest in the arts was evident in his establishment of a museum of traditional Bamoun art in Foumban, requested Njoya and Ibrayima Titabohou to create an original Bamoun painting style. As a result, these two men are among the earliest of the new African artists. Njoya produced approximately thirty-five paintings, while the less creative Titabohou produced only a few works before returning to farming. Njoya rarely exhibited, although he remembered with pride an exhibition in 1927 in which he won first prize. Several of his paintings are permanently displayed in the museums at Foumban and Douala, the largest city in Cameroun, and the remaining works are in European and American private collections.[6]

Njoya's paintings, on heavy watercolor paper, combine unusually the media of watercolor, India ink, and pencil. Bamoun customs, geneology, and folklore make up his subject matter, which favors especially the exploits of past Bamoun kings and sultans. During his long career Njoya passed through several style phases. His earliest works were often eclectic in a naive sense, but in the 1940s and 1950s he began to paint fairly naturalistic, deep landscapes crowded with small figures. In his late years he frequently reverted to his earlier style.

An intriguing example of his early painting is the scene shown in Plate 85, a detail from a larger work containing many episodes representing the history of Bamoun kings. An inscription in the Bamoun alphabet at the top of the scene may be translated as "Sultan Njoya Teaches the First Letters of His Alphabet to His Nobles" (another innovation of the Sultan's).[7] Below this inscription, which is depicted in the painting as if on a long strip of bark cloth, appear two rows of seated figures copying Bamoun characters on wooden tablets.[8] Several primitive aspects appear in this work.[9] There is, for example, a hierarchical scaling, with the Sultan as the largest figure and the size of the middle-ground figures drastically reduced. In this earlier style the artist represents his figures as flat and linear.

In Njoya's painting *The Battle* (Plate 86) the composition becomes much more complex and the forms are more interestingly arranged. Relatively flat figures are crowded together in a vertical landscape in which proper scale relationships are disregarded.

85. Ibrayima Njoya. *Sultan Njoya Teaches the First Letters of His Alphabet to His Nobles,* pen, ink, and watercolor on paper. Musée National, Douala, Cameroun.

86. Ibrayima Njoya. *The Battle,* pen, ink, and watercolor on paper. Collection unknown.

Many of these stylistic traits also appear in Persian miniature painting, an art well known throughout the Islamic world. The similarity is more than a probable coincidence, since Islam is, and has been for some time, an extremely popular religion among the Bamoun. The present Sultan has made several pilgrimages to Mecca, and in the 1920s Sultan Njoya wrote a small religious treatise combining ideas from the Bible and the Koran.[10] It is entirely possible that along with religious influences, examples or illustrations of Persian miniatures were brought to Foumban and may have been seen by the painter Njoya.

Another aspect of Njoya's style is his interest in decorative pattern. Richly varied, complex geometric designs typically frame his painted scene in *The Battle*. Njoya added a wooden frame carved with similar patterns. The decorative designs are based on either traditional Bamoun or Islamic decorative motives, although in some cases they are original.[11]

Njoya has painted extremely interesting and successful works recounting the history and customs of the Bamoun tribe, but he is essentially a naive painter. This naiveté shows clearly his position among contemporary African artists.

At the other end of the stylistic spectrum is Ibrahim N'Diaye, a painter born in Senegal in 1928. N'Diaye studied and worked in Paris from 1948 to 1960. After several years' sojourn in Senegal, where he taught painting at the École des Arts, he returned to Paris to study stage design. He has recently returned again to Senegal. During his first stay in Paris he worked with the sculptors Zadkine and Coutin and the painter Brayer at the Académie de la Grande Chaumière. For a time he vacillated between sculpture and painting as a career, finally choosing the latter. For the two years preceding his return to Dakar, N'Diaye was associated with the Groupe de la Ruche, a gathering of young painters in Paris who rebelled against abstract art.[12]

N'Diaye has exhibited in Dakar, Paris, and at the Biennale in São Paulo, Brazil, where he won honorable mention, and has sold works to prominent persons in Senegal and France. He was commissioned to paint two murals for the Daniel Sorano National Theater in Dakar and to execute a large mosaic for the new airport terminal.

While in Dakar N'Diaye painted mostly genre scenes of that city, one of Africa's most cosmopolitan centers. Although a Wollof tribesman, tribal customs and folklore rarely interest him. A work typical of N'Diaye's style is *Market* (Plate 87). Each of his oil paintings shows a wide range in texture,

87. Ibrahim N'Diaye. *Market,* oil on canvas. Collection of the artist.

from bare canvas, through thin, transparent washes, to impasto applications. This textural variation, rare in new African painting but common in modern French work, gives vitality to his style.

N'Diaye's figures, often fragmented and occupying much of the picture area, seem close to the spectator, but they are also blurred as if seen from a great distance. This contradiction of optical reality is a basic quality in his style. Most interesting of all is the painter's superb use of color. The dominant colors in *Market* are subdued and constantly changing shades of brown and blue-green. For accent he has spotted small patches of bright red throughout the work, for example, the fruit held by the foreground figure.

The artist enjoys painting still lifes for relaxation. He casually arranges studio objects on tables and chairs. Although many of them have been done in Dakar, they could just as easily have been painted in Paris. N'Diaye's style is one of the most European-oriented in the new African art movement, no doubt because his relation with European culture is stronger than that of most other African painters. He has said:

> j'ai besoin d'y retourner [to Paris] souvent. Ne serait-ce que pour prendre un bain de theâtre, de cinemas; pour me replonger dans un climat. Au point de vue technique, l'École de Paris est très importante; elle offre a l'artiste une confrontation avec des peintres de tous les coins du monde. Si je restais ici, je risquerais me m'endormir. Mais, pour l'inspiration, j'ai besoin de l'Afrique.[13]

Gerard Sekoto, one of the earliest of the independent English-speaking artists to attain a reputation in Europe and the United States, is a Basuto from a small farm in the South African Transvaal. He was born in 1913 and in 1939 settled outside Johannesburg, in Sophiatown, an African shanty-town "location."[14] Here Sekoto met Brother Robert Castle of the Anglican Mission, who gave informal drawing lessons to young Africans. It was Castle who introduced Sekoto to the European South African artists Alex Preller and Judith Gluckman. Preller acquainted him with oil technique, and Gluckman, considering the political climate in South Africa, courageously gave him lessons in her apartment. The first shows of Sekoto's works were arranged by Castle in several Johannesburg galleries.

Sekoto went to Paris in 1947, where he has remained since except for a year's stay in Senegal following his participation in the Dakar Festival in 1966. When he arrived initially in France he had no means of support. He sang African folksongs in nightclubs while studying and painting during the day. As a consequence of this strenuous existence, in 1949 Sekoto suffered an emotional breakdown which incapacitated him for a year. It was during this period, however, that his international reputation was established. In an exhibition of contemporary South African art held at the Tate Gallery in London, Sekoto was the only African artist represented. His paintings at this exhibition attracted considerable attention, including a widely publicized notice from the late Queen Mary.[15] The Tate show later traveled to Amsterdam, Brussels, and finally to the National Gallery in Washington, D.C. Everywhere Sekoto received favorable critical comment. Since then he has often exhibited in Europe, the United States, and South Africa, and has sold many of his works to museums, galleries, and collectors.

Although Sekoto has said he would like to return to South Africa should the political situation change, he has stated:

> Today I can express myself in Paris in a style purely African, but I am ready to come back to my native land to stimulate my artistic origins in a country so rich in subjects so fertile for the inspiration of the artist.[16]

He has no desire to stay in South Africa permanently, however, for Paris has become his home.

Although Sekoto has been an expatriate during most of his career, he has painted his

> native location street scenes, e.g., the backyards with women digging holes . . . to bury their unlawful intoxicating drinks. I very often would have an inspiration after a police raid was performed in these back-yards by a storm of the men in the black helmets, sparkling buttons and each a gun by the side. . . . For my subject matter I would include scenes of little children dressed in ragged clothes some plainly naked playing with old rusted tins. The interiors of houses where quite often families share one room. The fruit seller and the location shops. I would also paint the Sunday parties particularly exciting which were generally composed of several styles of dancing, loud and gay shouts almost drowning the sing-song part of the show. . . .[17]

It is clear that Sekoto, although raised in a rural environment, favors as subject matter the daily activities of the detribalized, urban South African.[18] His painting is often concerned with the meeting of European and African cultures and their impact on each other. In his choice of thematic material he is uniquely unlike many European South African artists. In other words he was not interested solely in the picturesque, exotic, and orderly "native life" often seen in the tribal reserves.

Sekoto's *Mother and Child* (Plate 88) represents a "location" scene in which a tall woman carrying a large burden on her head and a child on her back walks quickly past houses typical of these "towns." This work is completely characteristic of Sekoto's style; his palette knife impasto technique is especially evident in the elegant, wide-flowing skirt of the woman. All figures and objects are blurred, and descriptive details such as facial features are eliminated. Sekoto's colors are bright and vivid; in this painting, for example, he has combined light and dark blues with large areas of brilliant orange.

Sekoto has painted several Parisian street scenes, and his most interesting paintings are his studies of jazz musicians, such as *Negro Clarinetist* (Plate 89). These studies are often executed in deep blues accented by touches of yellow and orange. Dark blue combined with an impasto technique and dramatic contrasts of light and dark results in strong and forceful pictures. Some elements suggest a relationship to traditional African sculpture; for example, the bulging, heavy-lidded eyes can be related to various African styles, and the fleshy noses with clearly demarcated nostrils are similar to those found in Yoruba and Benin work.

Unlike Sekoto, Afewerk Tekle, Ethiopia's first modern artist of note, has been highly successful in his own country. Born in 1932, Afewerk came to prominence in the middle 1950s. After going to England in 1947 to become a mining engineer, he soon decided he would rather paint and so entered the Central School of Art and later the Slade. His first one-man exhibition was held in Addis Ababa in 1954, and he has shown since then in Europe, the U.S.S.R., and the United States. He was the first recipient, in 1964, of the prestigious Haile Selassie I Prize for the Fine Arts.

The award citation emphasized Afewerk's outstanding attribute, his versatility. His prolific output shows competence in a variety of media. He has produced pen and charcoal sketches, lithographs, gouache and oil paintings, murals, mosaics, sculpture, and stained glass windows. Moreover, he has designed stamps, book covers, playing cards, and even a national costume.

This versatility is also evident in his wide range of subject matter. Afewerk has painted Ethiopian landscapes as well as religious murals for the Church of St. George in Addis Ababa. He has depicted heroes and events from the legendary and historical past, for example, a bronze equestrian monument in Harar of Ras Makonnen, father of the present emperor. Included in his recording of more recent historical events is a painting of the coronation of Haile Selassie I. He has executed numerous portraits, including, in 1963, a well-publicized oil painting of the late Kwame Nkrumah, leader of Ghana. Finally, among his best-known works are allegories in different media.

Afewerk defends this variety of subject and media as a requirement of the

88. Gerard Sekoto. *Mother and Child,*
oil on canvas. Collection of John
Akar.

89. Gerard Sekoto. *Negro Clarinetist,* oil
on canvas. Collection of the artist.

contemporary African artist in contrast to the modern Western artist, who is able to specialize. This attitude, not necessarily valid for other African artists, indicates the particular situation in which Afewerk works. His representational style, unlike the surrealist and abstract paintings of the other two important Ethiopian painters, Skunder and Gebre Kristos, is easily comprehended. He has, therefore, been the logical choice for the many commissions required by the church, the government, and the emperor.

Executing monumental stained glass windows for Africa Hall, headquarters of the United Nations Economic Commission for Africa, in Addis Ababa, is the most important commission to have been awarded an artist below the Sahara. It is difficult to convey in illustrations the overwhelming effect these windows have on the spectator. Set in the Entrance Hall, they depict allegories of Africa's past, present, and future. The left window portrays ignorance and brutality during the colonial period. Slavery is given prominence by a disunited family in the foreground and an abandoned child in the center. In the right window the struggle against colonialism is depicted in the foreground by an African killing a dragon. The large central window (Plate 90) portrays the present and future of Africa. Two large foreground figures garbed in traditional Ethopian costume symbolize knowledge and awakening.[19]

The style of the Africa Hall windows is the one in which Afewerk seems most comfortable. Although as with media and subject matter he also shows versatility in style, ranging from competent academic work to near abstractions, most of his work lies between these two poles. It is representational, yet there are stylizations which tend to reduce natural forms to their geometric substructures and to eliminate surface details and individual peculiarities. In his windows, as in his later oil paintings, he juxtaposes large areas of highly saturated blues, greens, yellows, and reds.

The Africa Hall windows have had an important effect upon Afewerk's painting style. Since their completion he has superimposed crisscrossing black lines over his portraits, landscapes, and figure studies, and he has shown an interest in color luminosity. These two new elements have created oil paintings that strongly suggest stained glass.

It is interesting to note the many parallels in the careers and works of Afewerk Tekle and the late Kofi Antubam of Ghana. Both men show surprising versatility in media, subject matter, and style, and both settle for a modernized, representational style. Their positions in their respective

90. Afewerk Tekle. Middle window, Africa Hall, Addis Ababa, Ethiopia. Stained glass.

countries are also similar. They have enjoyed the privilege of being "court" artists to powerful rulers—to the Emperor of Ethiopia and to Kwame Nkrumah of Ghana. Because of that, almost all government commissions in their respective countries were given to these two men. Doubtless the demands made by these commissions necessitated that the artists be adaptable.

Oku Ampofo, a Ghanaian sculptor born a chief's son in 1908, now lives in a tastefully furnished ultramodern house in his birthplace, Mampong, about thirty miles north of Accra. He attended Achimota College and in 1932 received a government scholarship to study medicine in Edinburgh. Between 1932 and his return to Ghana in 1940, Ampofo studied sculpture and visited European museums in the time he could spare from his study of medicine. In the museums he discovered traditional African art.

> I found in these ancient masterpieces the emotional appeal and satisfaction which Western education had failed to cultivate in me. It was as though an African had to go all the way to Europe to discover himself! This is virtually true of most of us. Very little, if any, of what is real in our own culture is taught in our schools and colleges.[20]

Since that time Ampofo has acquired a knowledge and a genuine appreciation of this art.

After Ampofo's return to Ghana he became a highly respected and successful physician. He has, nevertheless, continued to create sculpture and has discovered and encouraged talented young artists. In 1945 he organized with these young artists a group exhibition entitled "Neo-African Art."[21] It was Ghana's first important exhibition of this new art, and it proved so successful that it was brought to New York several years later. It was one of the first exhibitions of contemporary African art held in the United States.[22] Still later Ampofo founded the Akwapim 6, an active, privately organized and financed Ghanaian art group. He has exhibited frequently with this group, although he has also shown independently elsewhere in Ghana and in England and Germany. In 1965 a major exhibition of his sculpture was held at the Union Carbide Building in New York. Several of his works have been purchased by the Ghanaian government, including the larger than life-size figures that stand before the Ambassador Hotel, the National Museum, and the Ghana Broadcasting House in Accra.

Ampofo works in both woodcarving and modeling in cement fondu.[23] His smooth, highly polished wood sculpture is executed in heavy, close-grained dark woods. Occasionally he seemingly copies traditional African sculptural styles such as the two large Ashanti-inspired akua-ba figures attached to the facade of the Ghana Drama Studio in Accra. More frequently, however, he merely uses traditional African art styles as inspiration to create new forms. An example is *Puberty,* a large standing female figure who holds her breasts as a sign of modesty, according to Twi tribal custom (Plate 91). The head is at least partially derived from the Baoulé style of the Ivory Coast, a style Ampofo finds especially appealing and of which he owns several examples. Baoulé relationships are apparent in the treatment of the facial features, including three scarification marks at the bridge of the nose. The preciseness and absolute symmetry with which these features are carved, however, and their resultant frozen, lifeless quality are characteristics found primarily in Baoulé sculpture of recent origin. Moreover, the elongation of the head, the zig-zag design of the hair, and the large, elegantly shaped ears are his own inventions.

Ampofo is more original in his cement sculpture.[24] Using red, black, or natural gray cement mixed with marble chips he has executed approximately a dozen, larger than life-size standing figures representing Ghanaians performing traditional activities. Completed in 1955, *To the Sky God* (Plate 92) is one of his more successful works. The severely elongated torso, common in these cement figures, is here compressed into a tight geometric cylinder related to Ashanti akua-ba figures. The face and arms, turned imploringly upward, also show relationships with other traditional African art styles. The upstretched arms, for example, although sharply flexed and with heavy, formalized hands, are nevertheless somewhat reminiscent of Dogon figures from Mali. Moreover, the face strongly suggests kifwebe masks of the Basonge tribe of Zaïre in the squared-off jutting chin, the protruding, rectangular mouth, the placement of the eyes at the widest point of the head, and the rounded, bulging forehead. The nose and eyes of Ampofo's figure, however, are more realistically handled than those of kifwebe masks.

Dr. Oku Ampofo has been influential in the new African art movement. His works are renowned throughout Ghana. Moreover, through the use of traditional African art style elements in many of his sculptures, he has fostered an appreciation of this older art. He has, furthermore, experimented in materials new to African art. Perhaps, however, his most important contribution has been his discovery and encouragement of younger artists and his organization of the influential Ghanaian art group, the Akwampim 6.

91. Oku Ampofo. *Puberty,* ebony.
Collection of the artist.

92. Oku Ampofo. *To the Sky God,* cement and ter-
razzo. Collection of the artist.

Like Ampofo and Sekoto, Ben Enwonwu, a Nigerian painter and sculptor, is one of the few long-established figures in contemporary African art. A member of the Ibo tribe, he was born in 1921 at Onitsha, the largest city in the former Eastern Region of Nigeria. In secondary school, at Ibadan Government College, he studied with Kenneth Murray,[25] an important figure in African art, who arranged exhibitions for the young artist in London and Glasgow in 1938. Enwonwu was one of the first African artists to have his works shown in Europe. From 1938 to 1943 he taught art in Nigerian secondary schools. His first one-man exhibition in Nigeria was held in Lagos in 1943 and resulted in a scholarship to the Slade School of Art in London. Since then he has spent much time working, exhibiting, and traveling in Europe. During one of his European trips he was "discovered" by Sir Jacob Epstein, who bought a large work from him.

Enwonwu served as Federal Art Adviser to the Nigerian Government from the early 1950s until 1966. Although salaried, he had no specific duties. His position ensured him an adequate income and enabled him to work without economic worries; in addition, he was paid for all government commissions he completed. Enwonwu's position, then, was comparable to that of England's poet laureate, a position unique in Africa.[26] Enwonwu has often been considered a spokesman for the new African art. As such he has presented papers at *Présence Africaine* and American Society for African Culture conferences. A recurrent theme in these talks is Enwonwu's assertion that Europeans are unable to understand or fully appreciate African art.[27]

Enwonwu has executed numerous important sculpture commissions in Nigeria. They include competent and realistic full-length portraits of Dr. Azikiwe, which formerly stood before the Eastern House of Assembly in Enugu, and of Queen Elizabeth II, which stands before the House of Representatives in Lagos. Much more impressive, however, are the four Evangelists in the Onitsha Cathedral, the Risen Christ in the Protestant Chapel at the University of Ibadan, and the bronze figure of Anyanwu, or *The Awakening,* attached to the facade of the Lagos Museum. A copy of the last work has been presented by the artist to the United Nations headquarters in New York.

Enwonwu, moreover, is the only African artist to have received an important sculptural commission in Europe. This commission was granted by the *London Daily Mirror* for six wood figures. Unveiled in August 1961, they now stand in front of the newspaper's main office on High Holborn.

Although he considers himself primarily a sculptor, Enwonwu has completed numerous paintings and drawings, some of which are now in private collections in Africa, Europe, and the United States. Perhaps his most ambitious painting is a large mural which he executed for the Nigerian Broadcasting House in Lagos. He has, in addition, done book illustrations such as those in *The Brave African Huntress* by Amos Tutuola, a noted Nigerian novelist.

Perhaps Enwonwu's most creative work, and certainly one of his finest, is the life-size carved wood *Risen Christ* at the Protestant Chapel, University of Ibadan (Plate 93). This figure group, in contrast to his dull, academic-style portrait sculpture, reveals an extraordinary expressiveness and elegance. The striding Christ with long, flowing draperies, the anguished Mary Magdalen, and the complex, convoluted foliage are charged with emotion. The severe elongation and flattening of figures and draperies are surprisingly reminiscent of French Romanesque sculpture. Enwonwu's elaborate working of the surface both reinforces the major compositional lines contributing to the work's expressive power and creates richly varied textural contrasts.

The contrast of style apparent in his sculpture is also revealed in Enwonwu's paintings. He has portrayed, in realistic, academic fashion, traditional Nigerian personages such as the Oba of Benin, Hausa traders, and Moslem teachers. Another style, however, may be seen in his extensive series depicting African dances, for example, *Ibo Dancers* (Plate 94). The elegance observed in *Risen Christ* recurs in the gracefully elongated young women. The curvilinear lines of their bodies are rhythmically repeated throughout the composition, capturing something of the rhythm and verve of African dancing. Related to the surface texturing of *Risen Christ* are the beautiful and complex geometric body designs of the dancers.

Ibo Dancers shows possible influences from traditional African art as well as from several European painting styles. The nude figure in the foreground of this painting has many similarities with mud figures found in Ibo Mbari shrines, with which Enwonwu, as an Ibo, is surely familiar. The elongated cylindrical torso with small, geometric-shaped breasts, the small head, and the shaping of the features of the face are characteristics both styles share. The painting also bears some resemblance to a well-known European engraving, *Battle of the Ten Naked Men* by the fifteenth-century Italian artist Antonio del Pollaiuolo. Both works evidence an interest in the nude figure in differing poses and movements. Unlike Pollaiuolo's work,

93. Ben Enwonwu. *Risen Christ,* wood. Protestant Chapel, University of Ibadan, Ibadan, Nigeria.

94. Ben Enwonwu. *Ibo Dancers,* oil on canvas. Collection unknown.

however, *Ibo Dancers* shows a marked ambiguous spatial relationship between foreground and middle-ground figures, which is a characteristic of Mannerist painting. These resemblances to European styles may be explained by Enwonwu's familiarity with the history of Western art.

Ulli Beier has attempted to explain the reasons for the extreme style contrast found in Enwonwu's painting and sculpture:

> As somebody put it: 'He cannot make up his mind whether he wants to be an African or a European artist. He wants to be an individual expressing nothing but himself, and at the same time he wants to be a social success.' In an interview with Peter Fraenkel reported in *Ibadan,* February, 1958 Ben Enwonwu brushed such criticisms lightly aside. 'He could switch from one style to the other, just as other artists might do one work in stone and another in bronze.' Yet this variety of styles means to be more than that. It represents a real conflict and a genuine expression of the ambiguous position of the modern Nigerian artist between two worlds.[28]

Beier then proceeds to identify without supporting analyses the academic portrait style as European-derived and the more imaginative, expressive style as African. Although Beier is correct about the source of the former, there is a question whether the latter style is completely African, since it usually bears some relationship to European art.

Ben Enwonwu has been a major figure in the development of the new African art. He has labored steadily for over thirty years, producing a large body of work, some of high caliber. He has been active, furthermore, within African cultural organizations and the Nigerian government, promoting interest in art.

The sculptor Felix Idubor is another well-known independent Nigerian artist. He was born in 1928 in Benin City, where at the age of twelve he was already earning his living by woodcarving. Subsequently he became a member of the Benin Carvers Association, a group of souvenir-producing craftsmen in Lagos. In 1945 he established an independent workshop in that city to produce ebony heads for tourists. Idubor was discovered by Enwonwu in 1951, and with the latter's encouragement gave up souvenir-style carving for more creative work. Two years later the British Council in Lagos gave him his first one-man show, and from then on he exhibited frequently in Nigeria. Scholarships enabled him to travel in Europe in 1957, to study the following year at the Royal College of Art in London, and to study in Germany in 1962.

Idubor has executed numerous commissions in Nigeria for the government, for European business firms, and for individuals. Of major importance are the doors for the Parliament or National Hall in Lagos. He has also carved doors for the Oba's palace in the same city, and, a typical modern African contrast, for the skyscraper headquarters of the Co-operative Bank in Ibadan. He has often been commissioned by the government to produce state gifts for visiting dignitaries, such as the casket given to Queen Elizabeth II. Many of his sculptures have been purchased by collectors from Europe and the United States.

Although Idubor has cast works in concrete and bronze, he is primarily a woodcarver. He uses the traditional African carver's adzes and knives, which, in traditional fashion, he makes himself. He also uses European-made chisels. Employing no preliminary sketches, he works deftly and quickly, producing more than a hundred works a year.

Among Westerners, Idubor's best-known works are his carved heads, idealized portraits of Nigerian peoples. They closely resemble souvenir-style ebony busts and represent, in fact, a continuance of Idubor's early training and career. Idubor's carvings of this kind, however, have more strength and vitality than the busts usually made for the tourist market, since they are not as detailed in treatment and their surfaces are vigorously animated with tool marks.

Idubor constantly experiments with new styles. He has carved several extraordinarily elongated wood figures which were inspired by photographs shown to him by Americans of works of the late Swiss sculptor Giacometti.[29] More interesting are several highly stylized pierced figures whose most obvious stylizations are overall flatness, substitution of a smooth, shallow depression for the facial features, and above all, the piercing of the upper torso and ears. These particular stylizations, although frequent in modern European sculpture, particularly in the work of Archipenko, Zadkine, and Moore, are unique in African art.

Idubor's more successful works certainly are his carved wood doors, the most interesting of which are a series of eighteen executed for the National Hall (Parliament Assembly Hall) in Lagos in 1960. Each of three wide entrances to the debating chamber has three sets of double doors, each door carved with a long rectangular moderately high relief. The entire series begins at the left side with representations on two doors of fantastic Nigerian tree spirits, revealing the sculptor's creativity in handling imaginary subjects (Plate 95a). This kind of creativity with fantastic subjects is often found in traditional African sculpture. The main subject matter of these reliefs, however, are the past and present activities of people from all over Nigeria. Various native industries, such as cloth dyeing and flour making, as well as aspects of ceremonial life of the major tribal groups are represented.

Fifteen of the National Hall doors illustrate three scenes each. In the two doors shown in Plate 95b, from top to bottom, the scenes represented are: left, loading cocoa bags, carrying palm nut kernels, and tapping a rubber tree; right, a ritual bathing scene, education in a Moslem school, and a wood sculptor at work.[30] These doors are characteristic of Idubor's relief style. All figures and objects with few exceptions are seen either in frontal or profile view; proper scale relationships are disregarded; there is a marked predilection for decorative pattern both in compositional interpretation and in details of design.

The sculptor's representation of an African carver, shown on the right bottom panel of Plate 95b, is noteworthy for it reveals a sculptor wearing a European undershirt and working with a European chisel on a European-style figure placed on a table. Idubor, himself, however, works in a more traditional African fashion, that is, seated on the ground with the carving held between his legs.

The last doors in the National Hall series portray, respectively, the arrival of the British in Nigeria and the celebration of Independence, *October First, 1960*. The latter is the more effective of the two. Joyously dancing figures carry aloft the letters and numerals of the date, which are arranged to fill the entire panel and to form a unified effect that is lacking in most of the other doors. Moreover, the liveliness and informality of the poses in this relief contrast with the relatively static quality of many of the figures in some of the other panels.

Felix Idubor has achieved a wide reputation and must, after Ben Enwonwu, be considered the best known of Nigeria's new artists. He has executed a number of important commissions while working in several differing styles, the most successful being his relief style. In the best of these reliefs he shows imagination and inventiveness allied with a sureness of technique and composition.

The youngest of the independent Nigerian artists is the painter and

Tree Spirits

95. Felix Idubor. Two sets of carved doors for the
National Hall, Lagos, Nigeria. Wood.

Peoples of Nigeria

sculptor Erhabor Emokpae. A chief's son, he was born in Benin City in 1934. Except for some carving instruction received in secondary school, he had no formal art training before beginning his career in Lagos in 1959, as a graphic designer for a large advertising agency.[31] He has had several one-man shows in Nigeria and has exhibited in Germany and Brazil. He has executed several important commissions in Lagos, including a concrete and mosaic mural for the Institute of International Affairs (1964–65) and a mosaic for the Standard Bank (1967).

Mother and Child is a theme often found in his work (Plate 96). The artist's interest in textural variation is immediately apparent; the thinly painted, semitransparent background objects contrast with the impasto technique used in the foreground figure and ground. The outline of the figure and the grasses are made of pigment squeezed directly from the tube onto the canvas. Emokpae's overriding interest in design, surely a reflection of his career in advertising, is also apparent. Mother and child are highly stylized forms composed of lines and triangles; facial features and clothing patterns are similarly reduced to geometric shapes. The background consists of a well-ordered, allover composition of calabashes, ladles, and bottles, objects used daily by African mothers. Yet despite the relevance of African culture objects seen in association with the mother and child, the abstract shaping and interpretation of the forms strongly suggest a knowledge of twentieth-century European art.

Emokpae has also carved several wood masks and figures, some of which were inspired by traditional African sculpture. *The Seeker,* a life-size kneeling figure holding a bowl, represents a subject matter frequently found among the Yoruba tribe (Plate 97). The elongated and extraordinarily fluid body treatment is, however, reminiscent of a traditional figure style seen at times in Cameroun sculpture. The dramatic and angular treatment of facial forms and planes is also suggestive of the dynamic and aggressive Cameroun style. In spite of these relations with traditional sculpture, *The Seeker* is a highly original work. It has an expressiveness that is often missing in Emokpae's design-conscious painting. In the sculpture, the dramatic contrasts of lines and forms which sharply change direction reach a climax in the backward thrust of the head and the hysterical expression of its huge gaping mouth.

Independent artists in English-speaking areas thus represent two distinct generations: (1) Sekoto, Ampofo, and Enwonwu began their art careers in

96. Erhabor Emokpae. *Mother and Child,* oil on hardboard. Collection of Bruce Telfer, England.

97. Erhabor Emokpae. *The Seeker,* wood. Collection of J. Newton Hill, New York.

the 1940s and have worked and exhibited steadily since then, producing a large body of work and establishing international reputations. Their works are at times relatively conservative in style. (2) Idubor, Emokpae, and Afewerk, younger-generation artists, first attracted attention in the 1950s. Although Afewerk and Idubor have had difficulty at times in breaking away from their early styles, academic and souvenir, respectively, they have attempted in several works to create in an advanced modern style. Emokpae's paintings, too, with their geometrically stylized figures, interest in design, and extreme textural variations, are essentially modern in conception.

These independent artists, together with the artists intimately connected with African art schools either as students or instructors, have contributed greatly to the new African art. Although they are distinctly in the minority, the independent artists are for several reasons significant in any discussion of this new work. The earliest known is the Cameroun painter Ibrayima Njoya, while other artists, such as Sekoto and Enwonwu, are well known outside Africa. Moreover, the younger generation of independent artists, like Malangatana, N'Diaye, and Emokpae have developed styles which indicate clearly the strength of their creativity and originality.

IX : Summary

FOUR distinct types of art have been produced in Africa in recent decades —art in traditional styles, mission-inspired art, souvenir work, and the new painting and sculpture—and they differ consistently in their aesthetic quality and importance. Traditional African art, now disappearing with the concepts that guaranteed its existence, is continuing in only a few areas with any degree of its former excellence. Souvenir work, the most commercially successful of recent African arts, has developed in response to demands having nothing to do with traditional cultures, and, in fact, the low aesthetic quality of this work reflects the lack of any incentive save a commercial one. Mission-inspired art, often strongly motivated by Christian beliefs, is at times more aesthetically successful than the souvenir work. Its possibilities, however, have not been fully realized.

The new African painting and sculpture has been inspired by the desire of Africans to become part of the larger, modern world. This new art, beginning only decades ago, is the most aesthetically interesting of all the work discussed here. The earliest of these artists, Njoya, was painting in the early 1920s and, in fact, may have created a few works even earlier. This new art, however, had its real beginnings in the 1930s, when independent artists such as Sekoto, Enwonwu, and Ampofo started working and exhibiting. The earliest art schools were also established during this decade—the Trowell workshop, which became the School of Fine Arts at Makerere University College in Uganda; and on the West Coast, the art department of Achimota

College in Ghana. The first graduates of these schools came to prominence during the 1940s: Ntiro and Maloba in Uganda, for example, and Antubam in Ghana. It was this period, too, that saw the establishment of what is now the School of Fine and Applied Art in Khartoum and of the first art schools in a French-speaking area of Africa—the Desfossés school in Lubumbashi and the Académie des Beaux-Arts in Kinshasa, both in the Republic of Zaïre.

During the next decade, 1950-1960, African art developed at an accelerated pace. Several new schools were founded: the Poto-Poto School in Brazzaville, People's Republic of Congo; the Nigerian art departments now at Ahmadu Bello University, Zaria, and Yaba Technical Institute, Lagos; the Académie des Beaux-Arts in Lubumbashi; the Fine Arts School, Addis Ababa; and the École Nationale in Dakar, Senegal. Graduates of schools founded in the 1930s and 1940s—such as Salahi, Shibrain, Kofi, Bela, Pilipili, Mwenze, and Mensah—began teaching a new group of students who were often only a few years younger than their teachers. These years also saw the emergence to prominence of Felix Idubor and Afewerk Tekle, artists working independently in Nigeria and Ethiopia, respectively.

In the 1960s there has been a burgeoning of excellent new artists in Africa. Many of them have real talent and often a considerable artistic sophistication, and even the youngest among them show great potential. They include those who graduated in the early 1960s from Ahmadu Bello University and Yaba Technical Institute as well as recent graduates from Makerere's School of Fine Arts. Three fine artists trained in Europe and now teaching in African art schools have also come to prominence during this period— Lattier, Skunder, and Gebre Kristos—as have the independent artists Malangatana and Emokpae. In addition several new schools were founded in this decade: the Institut National in Abidjan, the tapestry school in Senegal, and the workshops in Oshogbo and Salisbury.

This chronology of the new African art reveals two groups of older artists who were historically of considerable importance in this evolution. The first group are the "untrained" artists. They include those associated with African schools where teaching methods allegedly precluded any conventional art instruction. Among this group, largely found in the French-speaking areas of Africa, should be mentioned in particular the Desfossés students Bela, Pilipili, and Mwenze, the Moonens-trained painters Kamba and Mode, and Poto-Poto students Thango, Zigoma, and Ondongo. Of these the works of the Desfossés group and the Poto-Poto School painters are perhaps the best known. All of these painters, it is true, were introduced to and employed new media, for instance, gouache on cardboard or colored paper. Their works usually depict similar subject matter, such as ceremonial or genre activities in traditional Africa or the flora and fauna of the continent. There is, however, a wide variety in their styles, ranging from often naive paintings produced in the Desfossés school through some sophisticated Poto-Poto compositions reminiscent of Cubist works. Despite this seeming variation, all of the works created by this "untrained" group display a highly decorative quality. Forms are flat with an emphasis on line and geometric pattern, space is negated, and bright colors are used. This decorativeness of style, frequently very marked, certainly owes something to the possibilities of the new media with their range of colors.

There appears to be less future potential, regardless of their early successes, for the early "untrained" men than for any other group of present-day African artists. Although the majority of them have either stopped completely or paint only rarely, a few, such as Mwenze, Zigoma, and Ondongo, have continued to paint steadily. But they usually repeat their earlier successful efforts and do not seem to be developing further.

The second group of older contemporary African artists are those trained in the more conventional art schools of Africa or Europe. They usually received a traditional Western-style art education, which often included the study of art history. Among them are Ntiro and Maloba, graduates of the Makerere School of Fine Arts, and Antubam, a graduate of the art department now at Kumasi College of Science and Technology. Several independent artists, such as Sekoto, Enwonwu, and Ampofo, received most of their training in English or French art schools, and consequently they, too, have a comparable background. These art-school trained men, who are now in their late forties or fifties, included some of the best-known African painters and sculptors. They have been working and exhibiting for many years, and in most cases their work has been shown in Europe and the United States as well as in Africa.

This group includes both painters and sculptors. They use both traditional African and Western materials and techniques in their new art. Although murals, a form of painting occasionally found in traditional African art, are produced, the pictorial works are predominantly Western-derived easel paintings executed in watercolor, gouache, or oil. Their sculpture, on the other hand, usually employs materials and techniques common to traditional African art, such as woodcarving, bronze and brass casting, and clay modeling. Cement fondu, a medium unknown in earlier African sculpture, is on occasion used by Ampofo.

Most interesting, however, is the new importance of painting as a technique. Contrary to traditional art, where sculpture was of paramount importance, these contemporary artists consist of painters and sculptors in equal proportion, and two in this group, Enwonwu and Antubam, are equally adept in both media.

The subject matter used by these artists varies widely. Sometimes it is wholly Western-derived; for example, Sekoto has painted Paris street scenes and jazz musicians, Enwonwu has produced landscapes, and both he and Ntiro have occasionally utilized Christian subject matter. But all the men of this group, like the "untrained" artists, are interested primarily in the ceremonial and genre activities of traditional African life. One painter, Sekoto, has even painted a number of scenes describing urbanized African life in the "locations" ringing South African cities.

Like their subject matter, the styles of these artists are also heterogeneous, a result certainly of variations in the amount and type of art instruction they received. Most Western-oriented in style are artists like Ntiro and Maloba, who did not have a strong tribal artistic tradition and who received quite a bit of their art training abroad. Both of them spent several years studying art in England. Maloba's portrait busts closely approximate those of Sir Jacob Epstein, while Ntiro's paintings display a naiveté reminiscent of European and American folk art.

The majority of these historically important art-school trained artists are, however, eclectic in style, combining both African and Western traits. Enwonwu, Sekoto, and Ampofo, for example, frequently use the characteristic figure proportions and treatment of facial features found in specific African traditional art styles. Antubam also incorporated into his work Ashanti kingdom symbols. The composition of figures and their relationship in space are but a few of the stylistic similarities to Western art in the paintings of Enwonwu, Sekoto, and Antubam; and the sculpture of Ampofo displays a greater realism in the handling of figure parts than is seen in traditional sculpture.

In the 1960s a group of younger African artists were prominent. Some of them were trained in conventional art schools in Africa, where curricula have included the study of African as well as Western art history. In most cases they have supplemented their education by work in Europe or the United States. Most important among them are Salahi, Shibrain, Njau, Vincent Kofi, and in Nigeria, Idehen and the so-called Zaria group. Several noteworthy artists developed in the workshops of Oshogbo and Salisbury, among them Twins Seven-Seven and Thomas Mukarobgwa. A few—N'Diaye, Tall, Lattier, Skunder, and Gebre Kristos—studied exclusively in European art schools. And two important artists, Emokpae and Malangatana, were self-trained.

The media and techniques employed by these younger artists are similar to those pioneered in Africa by the older generation. There are some exceptions, such as the first important appearance of print making in Africa, a technique employed by the painters Onobrakpeya and Musoke. In sculpture, advanced Western methods of welding figures and casting reliefs in fiber glass are seen in the works of Kofi, Kakooza, and Osifo. Thus, as with the previous generation of contemporary African artists, these younger men are Western-oriented in their use of media and techniques. More than three-quarters of them are painters, an even greater departure from the overwhelming predominance of sculptors in traditional art.

Although subject matter in this painting and sculpture is largely the same as that found in earlier works, there are two important exceptions. For the first time in African art, painters, for example, Nwoko and Salahi, represent and, most importantly, comment on social events occurring in the "new" Africa. Malangatana deals with raw and basic themes of emotion in his works, while Salahi, Skunder, Twins Seven-Seven, and Buraimoh are often occupied with fantasy and dream subjects, all innovations in contemporary African art. Most recently, pure abstractions, such as the work of Gebre Kristos, have also appeared.

Some of the younger artists, resembling the older painters and sculptors, are eclectic in style. C. Uche Okeke, Idehen, Malangatana, Kofi, Salahi, Shibrain, and Idubor often draw for inspiration on the arts of both Africa and the West. Most of these new artists—Akolo, Grillo, Nwoko, Simon Okeke, Onobrakpeya, Gebre Kristos, Skunder, N'Diaye, Tall, and Emokpae—have, however, developed styles related in a general way to Western twentieth-century art. Like their counterparts in modern Europe and America, they are interested in abstraction of form, design, and composition and the use of color in a nondescriptive manner. Sometimes reminiscences in style from specific Western art movements and artists are seen; for example, *Beggars* by Nwoko conjures up some of the paintings of the "Die Neue Sachlichkeit." As yet, most of these younger painters and sculptors have not been as original or daring in their use of advanced ideas as the *avant-garde* artists of the Western world. However, both those with eclectic styles and those whose work is largely Western-oriented, are the most original, imaginative, and creative of the painters and sculptors studied.

In the past the major sources of support for the new African art were the colonial governments; now the independent African states are supporting it. They have bought works, organized and subsidized art groups, and founded and financed museums that collect the new painting and sculpture. And most significant, these governments have also established and supported art schools. It is these schools that are training most of the important African artists. At present the most impressive schools are found in Uganda, the Sudan, Ghana, and Nigeria. All of them have good facilities, are adequately staffed, and have graduated some important and interesting contemporary artists.

In contrast to nations in the English-speaking areas of Africa, other countries on the continent have been less successful in their art-training programs. There have been only a few important schools in areas formerly ruled by the French. The Poto-Poto School in Brazzaville never received much government support, and furthermore, although historically important, it suffered a decline with the departure of its director, Pierre Lods. The Institut National in Abidjan is at present the only major government-supported art school in former French Africa, but since it was only recently established it is still too early to draw conclusions about its work. The former Belgian Congo also has only two art schools: the Académie des Beaux-Arts in Kinshasa, which has trained no artists of great interest, and the similarly named school in Lubumbashi, which developed some interesting artists in the late 1950s, but has produced no significant work since then. Finally, neither the Portuguese colonial administration in Africa nor the independent nation of Liberia has established any art schools of distinction.

The new art is one more manifestation of Africa's emergence into the modern world. In its resemblance to Western art it evidences both a break with traditional ideas and a new awareness of concepts familiar to other cultures. The art itself, in its choice of media, subject matter, and style, often bears many relationships to Western art. Furthermore, the motivation for the new art is the same as the raison d'être of most modern Western art—

creation for creation's sake. Consequently, although some of it is produced on commission as in older African society, most present-day African art is created on the artist's own initiative and sold whenever possible.

The future of African painting and sculpture appears bright. The new art is still not well known outside the continent, but the situation is beginning to change. Every year more and more African work is exhibited in Europe and the United States, and examples are beginning to be brought back from Africa by private collectors. In recent years, too, European and American museums have begun buying contemporary African art.

Within Africa itself there is no reason why the new art should not continue to grow. Although now the African "elite" only infrequently patronize their artists, it is likely that their patronage will increase. Perhaps the greatest individual support comes from Westerners now living and working in Africa, but it is quite unlikely that this support will continue to be dominant in future years. Private groups in Africa have already given every indication of continuing support. As this art becomes better known in other parts of the world, it is probable that additional groups in Europe and America will evince interest. Western business firms in Africa have commissioned works for their buildings, and the success of these ventures portend more support. African governments have also found that their public art commissions have helped to foster national pride. It is likely, too, that burgeoning government construction programs will require more, rather than fewer, commissions in the future.

This study, therefore, is largely a pioneer examination of the beginning and growth of a new art. It has already come a long way in just a few decades. Given the proper support, there is no reason why the talent and ideas evidenced by many of Africa's young artists should not continue to develop freely using elements from their own and other arts to describe the exciting and unique experience of life in modern Africa.

APPENDIX

AUTOBIOGRAPHIES OF TWO AFRICAN ARTISTS

1. LAMIDI FAKEYE

I AM a native of Illa. My great grandfather was a famous woodcarver. His name was Obogunjoko. He was living in Omido, north of Illa, on the way to Esie. When war came, he went to Illa. The Oba asked all the carvers to carve something for Oro festival, when all the worshippers bring out their images. When the Oba, who was called Orangun Illa, and whose personal name was Aniyeloye, saw Obogunjoko's work he gave his daughter to be his wife.

My grandfather, son of Obogunjoko, did not like carving, because it was too poor at that time. His son was Fakeye, that is my own father. My grandfather did not want him to carve but to be a farmer like himself, because there is no money in carving. But my father Fakeye began to learn the work by himself, and at the age of 25 went to carve at Oke-odo, which is a quarter in Illa. That carver was called Taiyewe. My father, Fakeye, was under him as an apprentice for more than three years.

All Fakeye's sons began to learn carving at about the age of nine or ten. The first born was Adewuyi, who died in 1957. There is also a David Adeosun who is still a carver. I went to school and did Standard VI. I did not like to be a carver because I thought it was useless work. However, I was carving petty things like trays, *ibeji* (twin figures), spoons and so on from 1942 to 1947. Then I went to Oro, near Ijero in Ekiti, and was carving such things as motors, trains, and bowls in the form of a cock (called Olumeye) which the women like in that district. At that time I thought I was the best carver, until I went to the Oba's palace at Oro, and saw some carved pillars. One of the pillars was a woman nursing a child, according as Yoruba women are nursing their children, and another was a horse-rider with many small figures around him. I heard that a carver called Aerogun [*sic*] from Osi-Ilorin did them. These two pillars are now in the museum in Lagos.

I heard that the Rev. Mr. Jones, of Ifaki Training School wanted a carver. He asked me to teach the students to carve. I worked there for some months.

Father K. Carroll came to Oro one day with Bandele, the son of Areogun, and I introduced myself as a carver. He asked me to come to Oye Ekiti to do some work for testing. When I got there, and I saw the work of Bandele, I was a bit ashamed. Father Carroll asked me to become an apprentice under Bandele. I worked under Bandele for three years and suffered much.

In the evening times I was working on my own work, and began to become a good carver. The first big work Father Carroll gave me to do by myself was to carve big pillars and doors for the Idena gate house of the Oni of Ife. I brought Fayo, another woodcarver, to help me in the work. These carvings can now be seen in the Idena Gate of the Oni's palace. That work was done in 1953. In 1954 the Father brought me to Lagos, where I carved the panels for the door of the Catholic chapel in the University with Christian subjects.

[Move to Ondo] In 1955 I carved panels for the seats and tables of the House of Assembly and House of Chiefs at Ibadan. One big one is the throne for the President of the House of Chiefs, who is Oni. Since 1954 I have been working with Father O'Mahony at Ondo. He understands the work very well. Last year I made carvings for the Office of the Premier of the Western Region.

The Fathers have been advising me to get my own apprentices so that I can increase my work. I have now my young brothers and cousins. What makes me glad is that my two cousins who have finished Modern II in Illa have now come to work for me. They prefer this to any other work like teaching or clerk [*sic*]. Altogether I now have seven apprentices. Akin and Alawode are very good carvers. They can finish the work perfectly when I have done the rough work.

ULLI BEIER,
West African Review,
XXXI, no. 391, p. 31.

2. VALENTE GOENHA MALANGATANA

This autobiography may, in some respects, be similar to the lives of other artists we have discussed.

I was born in Marracuene, in the Regedoria Magaia, under Chief Biqua Magaia on the 6th of June, 1936, on Sunday morning. According to what my mother says, I was always with her and always did with her the work she used to do, that is: going with her to the field, carrying water, going to the bush to cut wood for the cooking, picking mushrooms for lunch or dinner.

For these reasons I was almost like a girl. . . . It was only when I started school and got used to my companions that I improved, but I was a cry-baby and very soft and did not know how to fight, and I was even nicknamed Malenga, or girl. . . .

My mother came from another part of the country to marry my father. In her homeland, according to her and confirmed by me, because I remember having gone there with her when I was already able to see and remember what I saw, the girls were very keen on art work; even after they married they continued to do ornamental work, which is usually done with beads on calabashes, belts for women and men, wide necklaces for women and babies, and also bracelets made of beads for witchdoctors. My mother not only knew how to do this but also how to sharpen teeth.

Beside this she did tattooing on stomachs and faces. She used to make sewing thread from pineapples and sisal leaves.

I went to school in 1942 because my mother wished it, while my father was in South Africa working in the mines. At this school in the Swiss Mission I had a very good teacher. This teacher loved teaching and he also had a great gift for drawing, basket-making and other handwork. Here in this school I first saw pictures in books, but I did not believe they were drawings, and also saw some drawings done by the teacher's brother who had already finished studying at the school and was in the town. After I had passed from the first grade to the second and from the second to the third, this school was closed, unfortunately for us all because the teacher left.

Two years later, that is in 1947, I went to a Catholic school which I did not like so much as the other. I had no ability, but in spite of that I did not stop drawing on my own, chiefly on the sandy paths for want of paper. During this time at school, being together with several boys, I learnt to play some football and other games.

A bad period for me. My mother went completely mad while my father was on his way back from South Africa, arriving a few months later. It grieved me very much when she became like that. It happened one night when I and the children of another wife of my father's had been as usual to play some distance from the house where we lived far from everybody.

When we returned that evening as I came into the house where I slept with my mother, I heard a voice calling me. It was the voice of my half-brother, and my mother was also shouting: "My son, come to me for I am dying, your brother was killed because he was the cleverest in this house and was envied by this woman who used to call him 'white man',", pointing as she spoke to another wife of my father's. My aunt found a witchdoctor who took my mother in, and she stayed there having treatment for a long time. I was staying with my aunt and was attending the Catholic school. On religious holidays I used to decorate the house according to what I saw in the Church and she used to get very annoyed when I lit candles inside the house because she was afraid the house would burn down. So I made a shack outside where I could do everything I liked, where I hung holy pictures and other photographs which I cut out of magazines and also some drawings I made of various religious images which I copied out of books and catechisms . . . at this time my mother returned to where she was married, and my father went away again without leaving anything for me. However, when he got to South Africa he sent me two pairs of trousers—they were the same but were labelled, one for me and one for my half-brother. I then came to the city. When I arrived here, I worked as a children's servant alternating with going back home to teach in the Catholic school, where I earned only 40 escudos (ten shillings) per month, which to me was a lot. I helped my mother with the little I had, while she fed me.

Returning to the city, I gave up teaching and went to work at a Coloured household where fortunately I was well treated but, where, unfortunately, I had not time to go to school, although it was very near.

In June 1953, I went to work at the Lourenço Marques Club, after a short rest at home, during which time I decided to go with the girl who would not leave my heart, Cicilia Matias Machina.

In the Lourenço Marques Club I started by working as a bell-boy and cook for the servants, and I began learning English. During this time I used to draw a lot when I saw many drawings done to decorate the rooms for dances. And I studied. I went to a good night school with a good teacher, so that my drawing improved and my pleasure in drawing increased. . . . I was drawing in charcoal and painting in oils, and everyone who saw my work and ideas admired them and encouraged me. I painted furiously, rather forgetting to visit my parents and my wife.

A few months later, in October 1959, I was discovered painting at night by the architect Miranda Guedes. He admired my pictures and exchanged words with me. At this time too, this architect used to buy paintings from me to help me.

Before the end of 1960 the architect told me that he would like to help and arranged for me to leave the Club and give up my contract at the end of January 1960, so I could work all the time. He offered me a studio and monthly allowance, for which I and my family thank him from the bottom of our hearts.

In the studio I started receiving visits from students. Now and then I wrote poems, as I had already been doing before, and these, and this autobiography, I wrote in Portuguese—they have been translated by Mrs. Dorothy Guedes and Mrs. Philippa Rumsey.

I was always different from those who saw me wasting night after night drawing with a pencil trying to tell stories by sketching on the paper.

When I come to the town there were always people who attacked me for painting and drawing because in the view of many it was just playing about—indeed it was playing, but seriously, was always my reply to those who attacked me. Since I do paint for pleasure not as a profession but because I love art and poetry, apart from this poetry is art written on white paper without color and in repeated letters, but poetry in a picture has life, swell and movement also . . . and I will even say that wherever I am, I shall be painting.

GLOSSARY OF NAMES

NAME	ROLE
Afewerk Tekle	Ethiopian painter and sculptor.
Alhadeff, Leo	Businessman and patron of the arts, Kinshasa, Republic of Zaïre. Has subsidized painting and sculpture workshops.
Akanji, Adebisi	Nigerian cement sculptor working in Oshogbo.
Akeredolu, Justus	Originator of souvenir-style thorn carving, Nigeria.
Akolo, Jimo	Nigerian painter trained at Ahmadu Bello University, Zaria.
Ampofo, Dr. Oku	Ghanaian sculptor.
Antubam, Kofi	Ghanaian painter and sculptor.
Areogun	Traditional Yoruba woodcarver, Nigeria.
Asihene, S.V.	Ghanaian painter. Director, Art Department, Kumasi University of Science and Technology, Ghana.
Bamgboye	Traditional Yoruba woodcarver, Nigeria.
Bandele	Traditional Yoruba woodcarver, Nigeria.
Barranger, Marie	Sponsor of mission-inspired art, Dahomey.
Beier, Georgina Betts	Painter and director of summer school and workshop, Oshogbo, Nigeria.
Beier, Ulli	Critic, editor, and teacher at the University of Ife, Nigeria. Founder and patron of Oshogbo workshop.

NAME	ROLE
BEINART, JULIAN	South African architect and director of summer school, Ibadan Mbari, Nigeria.
BELA	Zaïrian painter trained by Desfossés, Lubumbashi.
BISIRI, YEMI	Traditional Yoruba brass caster, Nigeria.
BONSU, OSEI, SR.	Traditional Ashanti woodcarver, Ghana.
BURAIMOH, JIMOH	Nigerian painter and mosaicist from Oshogbo workshop.
CARROLL, FATHER KEVIN	Priest and writer. Director of Catholic mission workshops in Nigeria.
CROWDER, MICHAEL	Writer and scholar. Former editor of *Nigeria Magazine*. Former director of Institute of African Studies, University of Ife, Nigeria.
DESFOSSÉS, PIERRE ROMAIN-	French painter and art instructor. Founder of school in Lubumbashi, Republic of Zaïre.
DONVIDÉ, AQUEMINON	Souvenir carver and originator of Donvidé style, Dahomey.
DUERDEN, DENNIS	British critic and former teacher in Nigeria.
EMOKPAE, ERHABOR	Nigerian painter and sculptor.
ENWONWU, BEN	Nigerian sculptor and painter.
FAKEYE, LAMIDI	Traditional Yoruba woodcarver, trained at Catholic Mission Workshops, Nigeria.
GEBRE KRISTOS DESTA	Ethiopian painter. Teacher at the Fine Arts School, Addis Ababa.
GRILLO, YUSUF	Nigerian painter, trained at Ahmadu Bello University, Zaria. Head, art department, Yaba Technical Institute, Lagos.
HONUTONDJI, ÉTIENNE	Traditional Fon brass caster and creator of mission-inspired art, Dahomey.
IDEHEN, FESTUS	Nigerian sculptor, trained at Yaba Technical Institute, Lagos.
IDUBOR, FELIX	Nigerian sculptor.
IGBESAMWA, INE	Traditional Benin woodcarver, Nigeria.
IHAMA, DAVID	Traditional Benin brass caster, Nigeria.
INNEH, CHIEF OMOREGBE	Traditional Benin brass caster, Nigeria.
KAKOOZA, GEORGE	Ugandan sculptor, trained at Makerere's School of Fine Arts and now head of its department of sculpture.

GLOSSARY OF
200 NAMES

NAME	ROLE
KAMBA, JEAN-BOSCO	Zaïrian painter, trained by Moonens, Lubumbashi.
KOFI, VINCENT AKWETE	Ghanaian sculptor, trained and now teaching at Kumasi University of Science and Technology.
LATTIER, CHRISTIAN	Ivory Coast sculptor. Instructor of sculpture, Institut National des Arts, Abidjan.
LODS, PIERRE	French painter. Founder of Poto-Poto School, Brazzaville, People's Republic of Congo. Teaching at École Nationale des Arts du Sénégal, Dakar.
LANMANDOUCELO, VINCENT	Traditional Fon brass caster, Dahomey.
MALANGATANA, VALENTE	Painter from Mozambique.
MALOBA, GREGORY	Kenyan sculptor trained at Makerere. Head of department of design, University College, Nairobi.
MARC-STANISLAS, FRÈRE	Belgian priest and artist. Founder of Académie des Beaux-Arts, Kinshasa, Republic of Zaïre.
MASSENGO, GRÉGOIRE	Souvenir carver, Brazzaville, People's Republic of Congo.
McEWEN, FRANK	Director, National Gallery of Rhodesia, Salisbury, and founder of workshop school.
MENSAH, BENJAMIN	Zaïrian sculptor trained and now teaching at Académie des Beaux-Arts, Kinshasa.
MEYEROWITZ, H. V.	Sculptor and designer. Former director of art department, Achimota College, Accra, Ghana.
MODE	Zaïrian painter trained by Moonens, Lubumbashi.
MOONENS, LAURENT	Belgian artist. Founder of school in Lubumbashi, Republic of Zaïre.
MOUNT, PAUL	English art teacher and sculptor. Former director, art department, Yaba Technical Institute, Lagos, Nigeria.
MUKAROBGWA, THOMAS	Rhodesian painter, trained in workshop school of National Gallery of Rhodesia.
MUNGE, MUTISYA	Souvenir carver and originator of Wakamba style, Kenya.
MURRAY, KENNETH	Former director, Antiquities Service, Nigeria.

NAME	ROLE
MUSOKE, TERESA	Ugandan painter and graphic artist, trained at Makerere and now teaching there.
MWENZE KIBWANGA	Zaïrian painter trained by Desfossés, Lubumbashi.
N'DIAYE, IBRAHIM	Senegalese painter and teacher.
NJAU, ELIMO	Tanzanian painter, trained at Makerere School of Fine Arts, Kampala, Uganda.
NJOYA, IBRAYIMA	Painter from Cameroun.
NTIRO, SAM	Tanzanian painter, trained at Makerere School of Fine Arts, Kampala, Uganda.
NWOKO, DEMAS	Nigerian painter, trained at Ahmadu Bello University, Zaria.
OKEKE, C. UCHE	Nigerian painter, trained at Ahmadu Bello University, Zaria.
OKEKE, SIMON	Nigerian painter, trained at Ahmadu Bello University, Zaria.
OLATUNDE, ASIRU	Nigerian metal sculptor working in Oshogbo.
O'MAHONEY, FATHER SEAN	Priest and a director of Catholic mission workshops in Nigeria.
OMODAMWVEN, J. N.	Traditional Benin brass caster, Nigeria.
ONDONGO	Congolese painter trained at Poto-Poto School, Brazzaville.
ONOBRAKPEYA, BRUCE	Nigerian painter and graphic artist, trained at Ahmadu Bello University, Zaria.
OSIFO, OSAGIE	Nigerian sculptor, trained at Yaba Technical Institute, Lagos.
OSSALI	Congolese painter, trained at Poto-Poto School, Brazzaville.
PATERSON, REV. EDWARD	Rector and former art instructor, Cyrene Mission, Bulawayo, Rhodesia.
PILIPILI	Zaïrian painter trained by Desfossés, Lubumbashi.
SALAHI, IBRAHIM EL	Sudanese painter, trained at the School of Fine and Applied Art in Khartoum and now head of department of painting and drawing there.
SEKOTO, GERARD	South African painter working in Paris.
SEVEN-SEVEN, TWINS (TAIWO OLANIYI)	Nigerian painter from Oshogbo workshop.

GLOSSARY OF
202   NAMES

NAME	ROLE
SHIBRAIN, AHMED MOHAMED	Sudanese painter and graphic artist trained at the School of Fine and Applied Art, Khartoum, and teacher of graphic art there.
SKUNDER BOGHOSSIAN	Ethiopian painter and teacher at the Fine Arts School, Addis Ababa.
SONGO, SAM	Painter and sculptor, trained and now teaching at Cyrene Mission, Bulawayo, Rhodesia.
TALL, PAPA IBRA	Senegalese painter and teacher. Founder of tapestry school, Thiès.
THANGO	Congolese painter, trained at Poto-Poto School, Brazzaville.
TIMMERMANS, PAUL	Belgian artist. Former director, Museum, Luluabourg, Republic of Zaïre.
TITABOHOU, IBRAYIMA	Cameroun painter.
TODD, CECIL	Painter. Director, School of Fine Arts, Makerere University College, Kampala, Uganda.
TROWELL, MARGARET	British teacher and painter. Founder of School of Fine Arts, Makerere University College, Kampala, Uganda.
WENGER, SUZANNE	Austrian-born painter and sculptor now resident in Oshogbo, Nigeria, where she is reconstructing important Yoruba shrines. Patron of several Nigerian artists.
WILLIAMS, DENIS	Artist from British Guiana. Director of design courses, Mbari, Oshogbo, Nigeria, and lecturer in art at various African universities.
YEMADJÊ CLAN	Traditional Fon appliqué cloth workers, Dahomey.
ZIGOMA	Congolese painter, trained at Poto-Poto School, Brazzaville.

BIBLIOGRAPHY

"L'Académie des Beaux-Arts et des Métiers d'Art." *Jeune Afrique,* IX, no. 23 (1956), 41–42.

Africa Hall. Addis Ababa: Administrative and Liaison Office, Africa Hall, 1963.

Allison, P. A. "A Yoruba Carver." *Nigeria Magazine,* no. 22, (1944), 49–50.

Ampofo, Oku. "Neo-African Art in the Gold Coast." *Africana, The Magazine of the West African Society,* 1, no. 3 (Summer 1949), 16–19.

"A New Carver (Felix Idubor of Nigeria)." *Nigeria Magazine,* no. 41 (1953), 22–27.

Antubam, Kofi. "Principles of Arts and Crafts." Unpublished manuscript, n.d. (typewritten).

———. "Ghanaian Art." *Catalogue of an Exhibition held at Accra Central Library* (1954).

———. "La peinture en Afrique Noire." *Présence Africaine,* n.s., no. 27–28 (Aout–Novembre 1959), 275–85.

———. "Arts of Ghana." *United Asia,* IX, no. 1 (1957), 61–70.

———. "From Ghana Folk Art to Kofi Antubam Art." *Catalog of an Exhibition Held at Accra Central Library,* December 20, 1961–January 20, 1962.

———. *Ghana's Heritage of Culture.* Leipzig: Koehler & Amelang, 1963.

Atcheson, Louise. "Skunder Boghossian." *Transition,* June 1963, 43–45.

Bascom, William R., and Gebauer, Paul. *Handbook of West African Art.* Popular Science Handbook Series, no. 5, Milwaukee Public Museum, 1954.

Beier, Ulli. "The Bochio." *Black Orpheus,* no. 3 (May 1958), 28–31.

———. "Carvers in Modern Architecture." *Nigeria Magazine,* no. 60 (1959), 60–75.

———. *Art in Nigeria 1960.* London: Cambridge University Press, 1960.

———. "Demas Nwoko." *Black Orpheus,* no. 8, n.d., 10–11.

———. "Complicated Carver: Lamidi Fakeye Exhibition in Ibadan." *West African Review,* XXXI, no. 391 (June 1960), 30–31.

———. "Three Zaria Artists." *West African Review,* XXXI, no. 395 (October 1960), 37–41.

———. *Uche Okeke: Drawings.* Ibadan: Mbari Publications, 1961.

———. "Contemporary Nigerian Art." *Nigeria Magazine,* no. 68 (March 1961), 27–51.

———. *Ibrahim el Salahi.* Ibadan: Mbari Publications, 1962.

———. "Experiment in Art Teaching." *Black Orpheus,* no. 12 (1963), 43–44.

———. *Asiru.* Oshogbo: Mbari Mbayo Publications, 1965.

———. "Seven-Seven." *Black Orpheus,* no. 22 (August 1967), 45–48.

———. *Contemporary Art in Africa.* New York: Frederick A. Praeger, 1968.

Beinart, Julian. "Malangatana." *Black Orpheus,* no. 10 (1962), 22–27.

"Bela, Mwenze, Pilipili, and Aroun." *Jeune Afrique,* IX, no. 23 (1956), 25–30.

Bohannan, Paul. *Africa and Africans.* Garden City, N.Y.: The Natural History Press, 1964.

Bradbury, R. E. *The Benin Kingdom and Edo-Speaking Peoples of South-Western Nigeria.* Ethnographic Survey of Africa, Western Africa, Part XIII. London: International African Institute, 1957.

Brausch, G. G. J-B. "La Crise de L'Artisanat Rural." *Brousse,* no. 1–2 (1949), 17–20.

Brokensha, David. "Ori Olokun, A New Art Center." *African Arts,* II, no. 3 (Spring 1969), 32–35.

Brown, Evelyn S. *Africa's Contemporary Art and Artists.* New York: Harmon Foundation, 1966.

Buraimoh, Jimoh. "Painting with Beads." *African Arts,* V, no. 1 (Autumn 1971), 16–19.

Caillens, Jean. "Prelude au II° congrès des écrivains et artistes noirs." *Présence Africaine,* no. 20 (Juin–Juillet 1958), 131–32.

Canaday, John. *Mainstreams of Modern Art.* New York: Holt, Rinehart and Winston, 1962.

Carroll, Reverend Kevin. "Yoruba Craft Work at Oye Ekiti, Ondo Province." *Nigeria Magazine,* no. 35 (1950), 344–54.

———. "Christian Art in Nigeria." *Liturgical Arts,* XXVI, no. 3 (May 1958), 91–94.

———. "The Carved Door of the University Catholic Chapel." *Ibadan,* no. 5 (February 1959), 18–19.

———. "Christian Art in Africa." *African Ecclesiastical Review,* III, no. 2 (April 1961), 141–44.

———. "Three Generations of Yoruba Carvers," *Ibadan,* no. 12 (June 1961), 21–24.

———. "Ekiti Yoruba Woodcarving." *Odu,* IV, no. 57, n.d., 3–10.

———. *Yoruba Religious Carving.* London: Geoffrey Chapman, 1967.

Chojnacki, S. "The Art of Gebre Kristos Desta." *Ethiopia Observer*, VII, no. 2 (1953), 104–13.

Critic. "Mbari Mbayo." *Nigeria Magazine*, no. 78 (September 1963), 223–28.

Crowder, Michael. "The Chase Manhattan Sculpture." *Nigeria Magazine*, no. 70 (September 1961), 285–89.

———. "Nigeria's Artists Emerge." *West African Review*, XXXIII, no. 417 (September 1962), 30–36, 59.

———. "Akolo." *Nigeria Magazine*, no. 74 (September 1962), 91.

de Deken, J. "Notre ami Pierre Romain-Desfossés." *Jeune Afrique*, IX, no. 23 (1956), 5–10.

Dick-Read, Robert. *Sanamu, Adventures in Searching African Art*. New York: E. P. Dutton, 1964.

Ducamp, P. "Willingly to School." *The Shell Magazine*, XLII, no. 672 (December 1962), 364–66.

Duckworth, Aidron. *Modern Makonde Sculpture*. Syracuse: Syracuse University Press, n.d.

Duerden, Dennis. "Is There a Nigerian Style of Painting?" *Nigeria Magazine*, no. 41 (1953), 51–59.

———. "Black Orpheus." *West African Review*, XXX, no. 385 (1959), 855–59.

Dugast, I., and Jeffreys, M. D. W. *L'Écriture des Bamum*. Memoirs de l'institut Français d'Afrique Noire, Centre de Cameroun, Serie: Populations, no. 4. Paris: Éditions L.D.L., 1950.

Earl, E. R. "African Enterprise (Kamba Woodcarvers)." *East African Annual* (1958–59), 145–47.

Elkan, Walter. "The East African Trade in Woodcarvings." *Africa*, XXVIII, no. 4 (October 1958), 314–23.

Enwonwu, Ben. "Modern Nigerian Artists' Work." *Illustrated London News*, CCXIII (1948), 12.

———. "Problems of the African Artist Today." *Présence Africaine*, no. 8–9–10 (June–November 1956), 174–79.

Fagg, William. "The Dilemma Which Faces African Art." *Listener* (1951), 413–15.

———. "African Christian Art and the Missionary's Influence." *Liturgical Arts*, XX (May 1952), 199.

———. *Afro-Portuguese Ivories*. London: Batchworth Press, 1959.

———. *Nigerian Images*. New York: Frederick A. Praeger, 1963.

———. *Divine Kingship in Africa*. London: The British Museum, 1970.

"Famous in Europe and America but Artist Returns to Find Inspiration." *South African Art News and Review*, I, no. 5 (June 22, 1961), 1–2.

"Felix Idubor." *African Arts*, II, no. 1 (Autumn 1968), 30–35.

Fleming, Daniel Johnson. *Each with his own Brush: Contemporary Christian Art in Asia and Africa*. New York: Friendship Press, 1952.

Frey, Roger. "Une Evolution de l'art Nègre—les pierres taillees de M'Bigou." *Bulletin de L'institut des Études Centraficaines,* I, no. 1 (1945), 97–104.

Glencross, B. "School with the Idea: Cyrene." *African World* (January 1949), 13–14.

Goldwater, Robert. *Bambara Sculpture from the Western Sudan.* New York: The Museum of Primitive Art, 1960.

———. *Senufo Sculpture from West Africa.* New York: The Museum of Primitive Art, 1964.

Goode, J. Paul, and Espenshade, Edward B., Jr. *World Atlas.* New York: Rand McNally, 1953.

Grebert, F. "Arts en Voie de Disparition au Gabon." *Africa,* VII, no. 1 (January 1934), 82–88.

Greenlaw, Jean-Pierre. "A Christian Approach to the Arts in Africa." *Liturgical Arts,* XXVI, no. 4 (1958), 108–10.

Guiart, Jean. *The Arts of the South Pacific.* New York: Golden Press, 1963.

Gunn, Harold D. *A Handbook of the African Collections of the Commercial Museum.* Philadelphia: Philadelphia Commercial Museum, n.d.

Hardy, G. "La Renaissance des Metiers d'art Indigène dans les Colonies Françaises." *Revue Économique Française* (1930), 8–20.

Head, Sydney W. "A Conversation with Gebre Kristos Desta." *African Arts,* II, no. 4 (Summer 1969), 20–25.

Henderson, R. "Artists from the Congo." *West African Review,* XXXIII, no. 412 (April 1962), 25–39.

Herskovits, M. J., and Bascom, W. R., eds. "The Problem of Stability and Change in African Culture." In *Continuity and Change in African Cultures.* Chicago: Phoenix Books, 1962, 1–14.

Highet, Juliet. "Five Nigerian Artists." *African Arts,* II, no. 2 (Winter 1969), 34–41.

Hobley, G. W. *Ethnology of A-Kamba and Other East African Tribes.* London: Cambridge University Press, 1910.

Howlett, Jacques. "Présence Africaine, 1947–1958." *The Journal of Negro History,* XLIII, no. 2 (April 1958), 140–50.

"Ibrahim N'Diaye, peintre sénégalais." *Afrique,* no. 14 (July 1962), 36–37.

Italiaander, Rolf. *Neue Kunst in Afrika.* Mannheim: Bibliographisches Institut AG, 1957.

———. "Introduction a l'Art Nouveau en Afrique." *Liaison,* LXIV–LXVII (1958 and 1959), 43–47.

———. *Kongo: Bilder und Verse.* Gutersloh: C. Bertelsmann Verlag, 1959.

Jahn, Janheinz. *Muntu.* London: Faber and Faber, 1961.

July, Robert W. *The Origins of Modern African Thought.* New York: Frederick A. Praeger, 1968.

Kennedy, Jean. "Two Nigerian Artists." *Nigeria Magazine,* no. 96 (March 1968), 2–11.

———. "Bruce Onobrakpeya." *African Arts,* V, no. 2 (Winter 1972), 48–49.

Kimble, George H. T. *Tropical Africa.* New York: Doubleday and Co., 1962.

Kochnitzky, Leon. *Shrines of Wonders.* New York: Clark and Fritts, 1952.

"Kofi Antubam, Painter and Sculptor." Information Release, Ghana-Information Services, no. CU/MI/9 (mimeographed).

Kofi, Vincent. *Sculpture in Ghana.* Accra: Ghana Information Service, 1964.

Lebeuf, Jean-Paul. "L'École des peintres de Poto-Poto." *Africa,* XXVI, no. 3 (July 1956), 277–80.

Legum, Colin. *Pan-Africanism: A Short Political Guide.* New York: Frederick A. Praeger, 1962.

Leuzinger, Elsy. *The Art of Africa.* New York: Crown, 1960.

Lindblom, G. *The Akamba.* Archives d'Études Orientales, XVII. Uppsala: Appelbergs Boktryckeri Aktiebolag, 1920.

Lods, Pierre. "Les Peintres de Poto-Poto." *Présence Africaine,* no. 24–25 (1959), 326–29.

Maloba, Gregory. "Petson Lombé." *Roho,* no. 2 (June 1962), 34.

Malangatana, Valente. "Two Poems." *Black Orpheus,* no. 10 (1962), 28–29.

Maquet, Emma. "L'Académie Officielle des Beaux-Arts d'Elisabethville." *Jeune Afrique,* XI, no. 29 (1958), 19–23.

"M'Bigou, tout un village qui sculpte." *Afrique,* no. 6 (Novembre 1961), 66–70.

McEwen, Frank. *New Art from Rhodesia.* London: Commonwealth Institute, 1963.

———. "Return to Origins: New Directions for African Arts." *African Arts,* I, no. 2 (Winter 1968), 18–25, 88.

Mead, M., Bird, J., and Himmelheber, H. *Technique and Personality.* New York: Museum of Primitive Art, 1963.

Mercier, P., and Lombard, J. *Guide du Musée d'Abomey.* Études Dahoméennes. Porto Novo: IFAN, 1959.

Meyerowitz, Eva L. R. "Woodcarving in the Yoruba Country Today." *Africa,* XIV, no. 2 (February 1943), 66–70.

Moonens, Laurent. "L'Oeuvre de Pierre Romain-Desfossés." *Jeune Afrique,* IX, no. 23 (1956), 33–36.

Murdock, George P. *Africa: Its Peoples and their Culture History.* New York: McGraw-Hill, 1959.

Murray, K. C. "Painting in Nigeria" *Nigeria Magazine,* no. 14 (1938), 112–13.

———. "Art Courses for Africans." *Oversea Education,* XXI, no. 2 (January 1950), 1020–21.

The Nigerian Hierarchy. *The Catholic Church in an Independent Nigeria.* A joint pastoral letter issued October 1, 1960.

NJau, Elimo. "Copying Puts God to Sleep." *Transition* (June 1963), 15–17.

Njoya, Sultan. *Histoire et Coutumes des Bamum.* Memoires de l'Institut Français d'Afrique Noire, Centre du Cameroun, Serie: Populations, no. 5. Paris: Éditions L.C.L., 1952.

Ntiro, Sam. "Kilimanjaro Gold Dust." *Roho*, no. 1 (June 1961), 9.

———. "East African Art." *Tanganyika Notes and Records*, no. 61 (September 1963), 121–34.

———. "The Future of East African Art." In *East Africa's Cultural Heritage*, Contemporary African Monographs Series no. 4. Nairobi: East African Institute of Social and Cultural Affairs, 1966, 55–69.

Odita, Emmanual. "Some Observations on Contemporary African Art." In *New African Literature and the Arts, I*. Joseph Okpaku, ed. New York: Thomas Y. Crowell, 1970.

Ogunwale, Titus A. "Lamidi Fakeye: Nigerian Traditional Sculptor." *African Arts*, IV, no. 2 (Winter 1971), 66–67.

"A Painter from the Sudan: el Salahi." *African Arts*, I, no. 1 (Autumn 1967), 16–26.

Pankhurst, Richard. "Afewerk Tekle." *Ethiopia Observer*, VI, no. 3 (1962), 189–240.

Pare, Isaac. "Un Artiste Camerounais peu Connu; Ibrahim Njoya." *Abbia*, VI (Août 1964), 173–85.

Paterson, Reverend Edward. "The Nature of Bantu Art and Some Suggestions for Its Encouragement." *Nada*, no 19 (1942), 41–50.

———. "Cyrene Art." *Nada*, no. 28 (1949), 45–50.

Perier, G. D. "The Evolution of Art in the Belgian Congo and Ruanda-Urundi under the Influence of Belgian Colonization." In *Arts in the Belgian Congo and Ruanda-Urundi*. Brussels: CID, 1950, 55–62.

"Portrait of an Artist (Ben Enwonwu)." *West African Review*, XXVIII, no. 352 (April 1957), 2–7.

"The Preservation and Development of Indigenous Arts." UNESCO Occasional Papers on Education, October 8, 1950.

Rattray, R. D. *Religion and Art in Ashanti*. London: Oxford University Press, 1927.

Rose, H. B. "Thorn Carvings of Shagamu." *West African Review*, XXXI (September 1960), 95.

Ryder, A. F. C. "A Note on the Afro-Portuguese Ivories." *Journal of African History*, v. 3 (1964), 363–65.

Schneider, Betty. "Malangatana of Mozambique." *African Arts*, V, no. 2 (Winter 1972), 40–45.

Schohy, André. "L'École Saint-Luc de Leopoldville et le Destin des Arts Congolais." *Congopresse* (Leopoldville), LXX (Août 1950), 1392–93.

Segy, Ladislas. "The Future of African Art." *Midwest Journal*, IV, no. 2 (Summer 1952), 11–25.

Sekoto, Gerard. "A South African Artist." *Présence Africaine*, no. 14–15 (Juin–Septembre 1957), 281–89.

Serumaga, Robert. "Conversation with Ibrahim el Salahi." *Topic*, no. 24 (1967), 14–15.

Shore-Bos, Megehelina. "Modern Makonde: A Discovery in East African Art." *African Arts,* III, no. 1 (Autumn 1969), 46–51.

Stevens, G. A. "The Future of African Art." *Africa,* III, no. 2 (February 1930), 150–60.

———. "African Art—The Next Phase." *Oversea Education,* X (1939), 171–76.

Stout, J. Anthony. *Modern Makonde Sculpture.* Nairobi: Kibo Art Gallery Publications, 1966.

Tangerman, E. J. *Whittling and Woodcarving.* New York: Dover Publications, 1962. Originally published by Whittlesey House and McGraw-Hill Book Company, 1936; cited by J. Anthony Stout, *Modern Makonde Sculpture,* Nairobi: Kibo Art Gallery Publications, 1966.

Tracey, Andrew. "Kamba Carvers." *African Music Society Journal,* II, no. 3 (1960), 55–58.

Tutuola, Amos. *The Brave African Huntress.* New York: Grove, 1958.

Trowell, Margaret. "Development of Art and Indigenous Crafts in Uganda." *Uganda Teachers' Journal,* II, no. 2 (May 1940), 76–81.

———. "Modern African Art in East Africa." *Man,* XLVII, no. 1 (January 1947), 1–7.

———. *African Tapestry.* London: Faber and Faber, 1957.

Vanden Bossche, Jean. "Pierre Romain-Desfossés et son Academie d'art Populaire." *Brousse,* n.s. 6 (1955), 17–25.

Van Herrewege, P. R. "Desfossés l'Homme, son oeuvre et sa Pensée." *Brousse,* no. 2 (1952), 12.

Von Sydow, Von Eckart. *Die Kunst der Naturvolker und der Vorzeit.* Berlin: Propylaen-Verlag, 1925.

Wannijn, Robert L. "Ancient Religious Insigniae in Bas-Congo." In *Arts in the Belgian Congo and Ruanda-Urundi.* Brussels: CID, 1950, 41–53.

Washington, Forrester B. "Contemporary Artists of Africa." New York: Harmon Foundation, 1960 (mimeographed).

Willett, Frank. *African Art.* New York: Praeger, 1971.

Williams, Denis. "A Sudanese Calligraphy." *Transition,* June 1963, 19–20.

———. "The Iconology of the Yoruba Edan Ogboni." *Africa Journal,* April 1964, 139–66.

Wingert, Paul S., and Linton, Ralph. *Arts of the South Seas.* New York: Museum of Modern Art, 1940.

Wingert, Paul S. *The Sculpture of Negro Africa.* New York: Columbia University Press, 1950.

———. *Primitive Art.* London: Oxford University Press, 1962.

"Wonderstone Wonders, Sculpture of Samuel Songo." *Time,* LXIV (August 2, 1954), 58.

Wood Sculptures of the Maconde People Album. Lourenço Marques: Instituto de Investigacao Cientifica de Mocambique, 1963.

NOTES

I. Survivals of Traditional Styles

1. Only in recent years have a few individuals within the church recognized the value of traditional art forms and tried to adapt them to Christian usage. See chapter 2.

2. The new "elite" is a term widely used both in Africa and in publications about Africa to describe the new group of professional and intellectual Africans. See George H. T. Kimble, *Tropical Africa,* II (New York: Doubleday and Co., 1962), pp. 364–408.

3. Kofi Antubam, "From Ghana Folk Art to Kofi Antubam Art," *Catalog of an Exhibition Held at Accra Central Library* (December 20, 1961–January 20, 1962), p. 6.

4. Outstanding among these commissions are the Yoruba-style doors carved by Koumouh Laniba for the Treasury in Porto-Novo, the capital of Dahomey, and the carvings by Lamidi Fakeye for government buildings in Western Nigeria (see p. 36). Also relevant is the door by the Benin carver Idah for the regional council headquarters in Benin City.

5. Museums having collections of traditional art were visited in the following places (wherever possible the date the museum was established is given):

English-speaking areas: Bulawayo, Rhodesia; Livingstone, Zambia; Lagos (1957), Jos (1952), Benin City, Ife, Ibadan, Oron, and Oshogbo (1966), all in Nigeria; Accra (1957) and the Asante Cultural Center, Kumasi, both in Ghana; Freetown, Sierra Leone (1957). There was also a museum in Monrovia, Liberia (1961).

French-speaking areas: museums established by the Institut Français d'Afrique

Noire (1938) at Douala and Foumban in Cameroun; Abidjan, Ivory Coast; Porto-Novo and Abomey (1944) in Dahomey; Bamako, Mali (1953); and Dakar, Senegal. Museums of traditional Cameroun art are also found in the palace at Foumban and in Maroua. In the Republic of Zaïre there were museums in Kinshasa (1935), Luluabourg (1959), and Lubumbashi (1942). In Rwanda there was a museum founded by the Institut pour la Récherche Scientifique en Afrique Centrale in Astrida and another museum in Kabgayi (1944).

6. Some of the problems African museums face in collecting were indicated by Ulli Beier, *Art in Nigeria, 1960* (London: Cambridge University Press, 1960), p. 6: "The great difficulty is that the [Nigerian] Antiquities Service itself can never be sure whether an object offered to them for sale has not been stolen from the rightful owner. Moreover, they find themselves in the most delicate situation of having to decide when to attempt to buy a certain object. The official collector may see, for example, a highly interesting mask in a village dance. Is he to leave things alone, because the object is still in use? If so, he may find, when he returns a year later, either that the object has been destroyed by white ants, or that it has been snatched by a private collector. Should he then, persuade the people to sell the object straight away? *In that case he preserves the object but he helps to destroy the culture that has produced it.*"

7. Examples of the former can be seen in William R. Bascom and Paul Gebauer, *Handbook of West African Art* (Popular Science Handbook Series, No. 5, Milwaukee Public Museum, 1954), Plates 45 and 67.

8. Another plaque of similar subject matter and quality is illustrated in Beier, Plate 9.

9. Two other Benin brass casters merit mention. J. N. Omodamwven, an outsider, joined the brass-workers guild in 1926, the first time in history someone unrelated to the guild members was accepted. Against his parents' wishes he insisted on becoming a brass caster and enrolled in the school for traditional crafts established by the late Oba Eweka II in his palace in the capital. Omodamwven has taught in the Arts and Crafts School in Benin City. David Ihama, like Omodamwven, is a pioneer, but of a different sort. He is the chief maker of imitation ancient Benin bronzes, burying his newly cast works until they acquire a deep green or brown crusty patina. Moreover, Ihama models imperfect and incomplete pieces or even deliberately mutilates the finished brasses to simulate the effects of age. They are then sold as genuine antiquities at prices up to $500 in Benin City and Lagos.

10. It was Bonsu who carved the models illustrating types of Ashanti wood carving reproduced in the authoritative work on the Ashanti by R. S. Rattray, *Religion and Art in Ashanti* (London: Oxford University Press, 1927).

11. There are a number of carvers who specialize exclusively in making the traditional stools. They are located in a small village, Ahwiaa, six miles from Kumasi. Most of their work is identical in style with the older examples. One distressing and recent innovation, however, is the occasional use of mahogany in

preference to the traditional ungrained white wood called sese. The carvers stated that Europeans preferred the mahogany stools.

12. Rattray, Plates 194 and 195.

13. Frank Willett, *African Art* (New York: Praeger, 1971), Plates 255, 256.

14. Beier, *Art in Nigeria*, p. 8.

15. Reverend Kevin Carroll, "Three Generations of Yoruba Carvers," *Ibadan*, no. 12 (June 1961), pp. 21–22.

16. Carroll, p. 22. See also below, pp. 31–33.

17. Reverend Kevin Carroll, *Yoruba Religious Carving* (London: Geoffrey Chapman, 1967), p. 99.

II. Mission-Inspired Art

1. In some areas copies of contemporary European mass-produced religious art are found. Such work may be seen in the workshops connected with many of the Catholic missions in Rwanda, Burundi, and the Republic of Zaïre.

2. Robert L. Wannijn, "Ancient Religious Insigniae in Bas-Congo," *Arts in the Belgian Congo and Ruanda-Urundi* (Brussels: CID, 1950), pp. 41–42.

3. Ibid., p. 45. Occasionally, small male and female figures or orants "are placed on the arms of the cross, above the head of Christ and at his feet. Their number varies from two to four and generally we find them kneeling or crouching, hands joined or arms crossed." Ibid.

4. B. Glencross, "School with the Idea: Cyrene," *African World* (January 1949), pp. 13–14.

5. Reverend Edward Paterson, "Cyrene Art," *Nada*, no. 28 (1949), pp. 48–49.

6. Some of those whose signatures appear are S. B. Katsande, B. P. Masibuko, J. V. Twala, Livingstone Sango, S. Chibaya, Lot Dugeni, James K. Ratumu, and K. Domech.

7. Other important Cyrene works are the large Bulawayo publicity office mural and the numerous paintings hung in the lounge of the airport terminal at Livingstone, Zambia.

8. Starting at the northwest corner and reading clockwise are the following subjects: St. Christopher, Crucifixion, St. Peter, Mary Magdalen, Madonna and Child, Adoration of the Shepherds, Adoration of the Magi, John the Baptist, Expulsion from Paradise, and the Drunkenness of Noah.

9. Starting at the northwest interior corner and reading clockwise are the following scenes: northwest corner, Spreading of the Faith; lower north wall, Zakeo, the Goodly Pearl, Christ and the Woman of Samaria, and The Stoning of St. Stephen; upper north wall, Parable of the Sower and the Seed and The Good Samaritan; apse, the martyrs Mqamusela, Bernard Midzeke, Simon of Cyrene, Manche Masomola, and Christ; lower south wall, Madonna and Child, Bethesda, and Parable of the Weeds; upper south wall, The Prodigal Son and The Lost Sheep; southwest corner, Parable of the Talents; and west wall, Last Judgment.

10. The figures of Christ and the martyrs are placed within Romanesque-style

arches. Furthermore, elongated and contorted seraphim, showing similarities with several Romanesque figures styles, are placed in the spandrels of the arches.

11. This decline was foreseen by Paterson: "There is to be no future for Cyrene art—it will perish when its teacher leaves, unless some encouragement is given to our artists to continue their art after leaving school and after entering their 20s and 30s when alone, I hold, finished art is to be expected of them. Cyrene art is merely a promise; its fruition depends upon help which must be given, either by the Government by means of organized shows of native crafts or by the demand of sympathetic Europeans. Unless there is demand and appreciation, there will be no incentive to create." Paterson, pp. 46–47.

12. The Nigerian Hierarchy, *The Catholic Church in an Independent Nigeria*, a joint pastoral letter issued October 1, 1960, pp. 26–27.

13. Reverend Kevin Carroll, "Christian Art in Africa," *African Ecclesiastical Review*, III, no. 2 (April 1961), p. 141. Another encyclical letter, *Musicae Sacrae Disciplina*, issued by Pope Pius XII, concerns the adaptation of traditional music to Christian uses. Ibid.

An even more specific proposal has been made by Jean-Pierre Greenlaw, a layman who taught art in Nigeria and who is very much interested in Church affairs. He proposes "a missionary arts and crafts center somewhere in Africa with contacts in other parts of the world and in Rome, with Propaganda Fide. . . . Priests and Fathers and Laymen with talent could study there and some might even specialize in native crafts and building methods or materials. Every mission area should have its own artist-craftsman-architect. His work would be in the nature of designing, guiding and organizing the local crafts in the interest not only of material requirements of building but through them of assuring the healthy development of the soul. Art forms could thus become a very powerful adjunct of the work of verbal teaching. . . ." (Then follow three specific steps for the formation of this center.) Jean-Pierre Greenlaw, "A Christian Approach to the Arts in Africa," *Liturgical Arts*, XXVI, no. 4 (1958), pp. 108–10.

14. Other subjects are the Temptation of St. Anthony, Flight into Egypt, Nativity, and Baptism of Christ.

15. Father Carroll was born in 1920 in Liverpool and went to Ghana in 1943, where he taught arts and crafts. In 1946 he did research on African art with Father O'Mahoney in London. He returned to Nigeria in 1947. He has published extensively on the problems of mission-inspired art as well as on traditional Yoruba carving.

16. Reverend Kevin Carroll, "Yoruba Craft Work at Oye-Ekiti, Ondo Province," *Nigeria Magazine*, no. 35 (1950), p. 347.

17. Ibid.

18. Among his father's works are a large equestrian house post in the Oba's palace at Illa and a head in the Lagos Museum.

19. Reverend Kevin Carroll, "The Carved Door of the University Catholic Chapel," *Ibadan*, no. 5 (February 1959), p. 18.

20. Reverend Kevin Carroll, *"Three Generations of Yoruba Carvers," Ibdan,* no. 12 (June 1961), p. 21.

21. For a detailed autobiography see Appendix.

22. The house posts at Ife were carved with the aid of another artist, Fayo. Reverend Kevin Carroll, *Yoruba Religious Carving* (London: Geoffrey Chapman, 1967), p. 6.

23. Regarding the latter commission Father Carroll writes: "In 1954 a telephone call came to Holy Cross Mission in Lagos from the Public Works Department. 'Could the Catholic Mission take on a carving job?' said a doubtful voice, 'You see, the Western Region Premier, the Honourable Awolowo, is insisting that we get a traditional carver to work on the furniture for the new House of Assembly. We heard the Mission might be able to help.' We heard later that the Department had advised the Premier that traditional carving would be too crude for decorating the ultra-modern furniture of the new House, but the Premier pressed his point. It was something new to see an African leader take such a stand." Reverend Kevin Carroll, "Christian Art in Nigeria," *Liturgical Arts,* XXVI, no. 3 (May 1958), p. 91.

24. Ulli Beier "Carvers in Modern Architecture," *Nigeria Magazine,* no. 60 (1959), p. 64.

III. Souvenir Art

1. J. Anthony Stout, *Modern Makonde Sculpture* (Nairobi: Kibo Art Gallery Publications, 1966), p. 16.

2. This practice gave rise to the term "airport art," coined by Frank McEwen, director of the Rhodesian National Gallery in Salisbury.

3. A.F.C. Ryder, "A Note on the Afro-Portuguese Ivories," *Journal of African History,* vol. 3 (1964), pp. 363–65.

4. This conclusion is based on several interesting points. First, with one exception, no Christian themes are represented on these cups. Moreover, blatant sexual themes, such as a woman openly displaying her sexual organs and a man's genitals being bitten by a crocodile, are depicted. Lastly, there are often fragile and awkward projections where the cup would normally be grasped. William Fagg, *Afro-Portuguese Ivories* (London: Batchworth Press, 1959), pp. x–xi.

5. Ibid., pp. xix–xx.

6. Ryder, pp. 363–65.

7. William Fagg, *Nigerian Images* (New York: Frederick A. Praeger, 1963), p. 39.

8. William Fagg, *Divine Kingship in Africa* (London: The British Museum, 1970) pp. 45–46.

9. Two such workshops were operated by the Catholic church in Lomé, Togo and Nyunda, Rwanda.

10. Desfossés, a French painter, founded an important art school in Lubumbashi, Republic of Zaïre, in the mid–1940s. See below pp. 74–79.

11. When the workshop was visited a craftsman was carving a Bateke figure illustrated in Paul S. Wingert, *The Sculpture of Negro Africa* (New York: Columbia University Press, 1950), Plate 77. For sale in Alhadeff's shop in Kinshasa was a copy of a Sepik River figure illustrated in P. S. Wingert and R. Linton, *Arts of the South Seas* (New York: Museum of Modern Art, 1946), p. 113, which had also been made in the workshop.

12. Heads, rather than busts, have appeared occasionally in traditional African sculpture, for example, the bronzes and terra cotta heads from Ife and Benin. Although a few clay busts, that is, heads with part of the upper torso included, have been found with traditional material in Africa, they are always fragments of full- or half-length figures.

13. In two areas realistic portrait busts are modeled in clay and later sun baked or kiln dried. N'tuli, a Zulu from Eshowe, South Africa, has achieved some fame in the souvenir shops of Johannesburg for his small, extremely realistic, dark-grey clay busts. Flora Avuaguto, a Teso working in the Elgon Nyanza area on the border between Kenya and Uganda, also produced busts in this medium.

Ebony was never used by traditional African sculptors, who preferred to work in softer woods. It was not until the influx of tourists after World War II and their fondness for the finish and permanency of ebony that its use became popular. A short history of the use of the wood elsewhere is recounted in Stout, p. 2, fn. 5, in which he cites E. J. Tangerman, *Whittling and Woodcarving* (New York: Dover Publications, 1962; originally published by Whittlesey House and McGraw-Hill, 1936).

14. "M'Bigou, tout un village qui sculpte," *Afrique,* no. 6 (Novembre 1961), pp. 66–70.

15. All M'Bigou carvings seen in Gabon in the early 1960s were small in size, usually only a few inches high. Carvings from that village seen for sale in Nigeria at the end of the decade were considerably larger, sometimes almost a foot tall.

16. Justus Akeredolu carved the first chess set in 1963 at the suggestion of Mrs. R. E. Bradbury, wife of the late British anthropologist who worked in Benin City.

17. Some of Akeredolu's followers, all of them working in Western Nigeria, are Joseph Lamuren of Shagamu, G. H. Aghara of Owo, and J. T. Otun of Lagos. Lamuren is probably the most successful. According to H. B. Rose, "Thorn Carving of Shagamu," *West African Review,* XXXI (September 1960), p. 95, Lamuren has about eight carvers in his workshop, with each man specializing in a different part of the body. One carves legs and arms while another does heads. The workshop turns out about thirty carvings a week that are sold for 75¢ to $2.10 each. The relatively new nativity scenes bring a premium price, selling for almost $10.

18. The CMS bookshops have handled these carvings for many years. The small size of these works and their popularity with Europeans have made them a desirable addition to the shops' merchandise.

19. For illustrations of the two types of traditional Fon seats see P. Mercier

and J. Lombard, *Guide du Musée* D'Abomey ("Études Dahoméenes," Porto-Novo: IFAN, 1959), Plate 1, Figures 1 and 2; and Plate 2, Figure 1.

20. A bochio is a carved standing figure placed by the Fon in a small thatched shrine before the house. It is always used in association with Legba, a large carved phallus. Both objects serve as protective deities for the house. For illustrations of bochio see Ulli Beier, "The Bochio," *Black Orpheus,* no. 3 (May 1958), Plate 1, Figures 1 and 2; Plate 2, Figure 1; Plate 3; and Plate 4.

21. According to Walter Elkan, "The East African Trade in Woodcarvings," *Africa,* XXVIII, no. 4 (October 1958), p. 321, the style, with Wakamba encouragement, has spread to the Zaramu, a people living near Dar es Salaam in Tanzania. The Zaramu specialize in Wakamba-style carvings made from black ebony, a material only recently used by the Wakamba. The finished products are then sold to Wakamba dealers through Dar.

22. In some cases Wakamba have traveled to areas such as Tanzania, where ebony is readily available. They remain there and carve or else take the wood back to Kenya. Sam Ntiro, "East African Art," *Tanganyika Notes and Records,* no. 61 (September 1961), p. 123.

23. Other, hardly "new" additions to the Wakamba repertoire have been reported by Stout. He recounts an exchange between himself and a dealer who had been very successful in asking his carvers to make accurate reproductions of West African art. Stout, pp. xvi–xvii.

24. This fault is partly a result of the learning process. A student begins by copying a single figure. When he has learned to reproduce it exactly he is given another figure, and this process continues until he learns the entire repertoire.

25. Ntiro, p. 123.

26. For example, Elkan, pp. 314–23; Ntiro, pp. 121–34; Andrew Tracey, "Kamba Carvers," *African Music Society Journal,* II, no. 3 (1960), pp. 55–58.

27. C. W. Hobley, *Ethnology of A-Kamba and Other East African Tribes* (London: Cambridge University Press, 1910), p. 29. G. Lindblom, *The Akamba* (Archives D'Études Orientales, XVII, Uppsala: Appelbergs Boktryokeri Aktiebolag, 1920), pp. 357 and 366.

28. See M. Leiris and J. Delange, *African Art* (New York: Golden Press, 1968), Plate 428, p. 365.

29. Elkan, p. 315.

30. Stout, p. 1.

31. Elkan, p. 315.

32. At one time it was suggested that an embargo be placed on the export of these carvings so that they could be purchased only in Kenya and would be "a little thing peculiar to Kenya." One New York firm reports that it imports between 200,000 and 250,000 souvenir carvings a year from Kenya, Tanzania, and Zambia, which it then sells nationally through some 1,500 retail outlets.

33. Elkan, p. 315.

34. For example, these workshops may be found in Kenya at Wamunyi, the Wakamba carving center ninety miles from Nairobi, in Nairobi itself, at Mombasa, and at Dar es Salaam.

35. Tracey, p. 57.

36. Elkan, p. 318.

37. Ibid., p. 322.

38. The Makonde are indigenous to a plateau of the same name in the district of Cabo Delgado in Mozambique, just south of the Rovuma River. The area inhabited by the tribe extends across the river into the district of Lindi in Tanzania. *Wood Sculptures of the Maconde People Album* (Lourenço Marques: Instituto de Investigacao Cientifica de Mocambique, 1963), p. 1.

There has been considerable migration to Tanzania because of the high cost of goods and scarcity of employment in Mozambique. Moreover, about 10,000 Makonde refugees entered Tanzania in 1964 as the result of fighting on the plateau between the Portuguese and Tanzania-based Rebels. Stout, p. 2, n.8 (p. 112).

39. Souvenir carvers working on the Makonde plateau carve figures and occasionally figure groups engaged in genre activities, such as an old woman carrying firewood and a crouching hunter with a bow. In style these figures are realistically proportioned and show a concern with descriptive details. In some heads there is even a relationship to the ebony portrait bust style. For examples of this style see *Wood Sculptures of the Maconde People Album*.

About 150 Makonde carvers work near Mtwara. Here they are under the close supervision of a European souvenir art exporter, who insists on good craftsmanship. Realism is stressed, and innovation is discouraged as presenting unnecessary marketing difficulties. Stout, p. 8.

40. Ibid., pp. 9–10.

41. Women or female spirits carrying water are a common subject among Makonde carvings probably because water carrying was a major occupation on the Makonde plateau. It was necessary to travel to the rim of the plateau to obtain it, and because of its scarcity water was a highly valued commodity. Stout, fn. 14, p. 113.

42. This remark does not mean to imply that the sculptor either knew or was influenced by Romanesque work.

43. See Stout, Plate IV, p. 22.

44. Ibid., Plate XLVI, p. 64.

45. Ibid., p. 30.

46. Ibid., p. 99.

47. Among the hallucinogens used in East Africa are marijuana and hyoscyamine. A stimulant with possible hallucinogenic properties known as miraa is used in Somalia and Kenya. Ibid., p. 101.

48. Ibid., pp. 8–9.

49. Recently, however, in an effort to heighten aesthetic interest, the Makonde have begun to give texture to the surfaces of a small number of pieces by leaving sections roughhewn.

IV. The Emergence of a New Art: Introduction

1. The majority of artists studying in Europe have been from the English-speaking areas of East Africa and Nigeria and Ghana. In most cases they traveled to England and studied there on government scholarships. The schools that seem to be favored, probably because they are the oldest and best known, are the Slade School of Fine Art of the University of London, the Royal College of Art, and Goldsmith's College of Art, all in London.

2. Only a few tribes traditionally made paintings. For example, paintings on walls were created by the Fon of Dahomey, the Yoruba and Ibo of Nigeria, the Dogon of Mali, the Mangbetu of Zaïre, and the N'debele of South Africa. These paintings, almost always executed by amateurs, were usually simple and crude.

3. In exceptional cases, however, prices are comparable to those asked in Europe and the United States: $2,000 to $3,000 for an oil painting. The educated African, however, has many demands on his salary that a Western wage earner does not have. For example, in addition to providing for his own immediate family, he usually partially supports his large extended family, and often pays for the education of the numerous children of his less fortunate brothers and sisters.

4. The Contemporaries and the Cape Coast Palette Group, both formed more recently, are also organizations interested in furthering Ghanaian art. The government-sponsored Ghana Arts Council is attempting to consolidate all three currently active groups into one organization.

5. The name is derived from Mbari shrines, houses filled with sculptured mud figures built by the Ibo peoples of southeastern Nigeria.

6. Beier is an important figure in both the traditional and the new African art. He has written widely on both arts and, in addition, has served as editor of two major African literary journals, *Black Orpheus* and *Odu*, magazines that have done much to promote high standards in contemporary African culture. Beier also taught contemporary literature at the University of Ibadan. He left Nigeria in 1967 for New Guinea, where he continued to encourage young artists. In 1968 he arranged an exhibition of the work of a new Papuan artist, Hape, which was shown at the Mbari center in Oshogbo. In 1971 he returned to Nigeria to teach at the University of Ife.

7. Other founders were Francis Ademola, D.C. Fagunwa, Yetunde Esan, and Mabe Imoukhuede.

8. For a history of the beginning of this center see below, pp. 147–56.

9. Njau also established the Kibo Gallery in Moshi, Tanzania, where he shows works of East African artists as well as art from other parts of Africa. The gallery also has a modern publishing program.

The Nommo Gallery in Kampala, Uganda also encourages artists to work by providing an outlet for their production. It has exhibited works by many new artists, particularly those trained at the School of Fine Arts at Makerere University College in Kampala. The Gallery Africa in Nairobi also shows the work of new artists working in East Africa.

10. Colin Legum, *Pan Africanism: A Short Political Guide* (New York: Frederick A. Praeger, 1962), p. 98. For a history of the journal's first decade see Jacques Howlett, "Présence Africaine, 1947–1958," *The Journal of Negro History*, XLIII, no. 2 (April 1958), pp. 140–50.

11. In addition to the museums interested chiefly in traditional art (listed in chapter 1, n. 5), all of which are at least partially government financed, the Rhodesian National Gallery receives a government subsidy. See below, pp. 117–23.

12. These schools have not only trained painters and sculptors, some of whom have become leaders of the new movement, but they have often dictated the aesthetic standards that these artists have followed thoughout their careers. Frequently government schools also further their graduates' careers by assigning them to positions either within the art school or in secondary schools. Occasionally government art school graduates are assigned to museum positions where they utilize their training both in the preservation and restoration of art works and in the preparation of exhibitions.

13. For dates of establishment of these museums see chapter 1, n. 5. In the years since achieving their independence from France African countries in which these museums are found have changed the names of these institutions in order to reflect their governments' independent status.

14. Margaret Trowell, *African Tapestry* (London: Faber and Faber, 1957), p. 103.

15. Both groups aid music, dance, literature, and theater as well.

16. Kofi Antubam, "Principles of Arts and Crafts," unpublished manuscript, n.d. (typewritten).

V. Art Schools in French-Speaking Africa

1. Pierre Romain-Desfossés, a French painter, settled in Zaïre in 1940. A member of one of France's oldest naval families, he was born at Brest in 1887. An exhibition of his work was held in Paris in 1938. After arriving in Zaïre, he stayed successively at Pointe-Noîre, Brazzaville, and in Kivu Province, finally settling in Lumumbashi, where he died in 1954.

2. After Desfossés' death an exhibition of works by several students of the school was held at the Brussels World's Fair in 1958, and one year later the Museum of Modern Art in New York acquired a number of the school's paintings.

3. The sculptor's name was Aroun Kabasia. Born in Munga, Zambia, he went to Zaïre in 1940, joining Desfossés in 1950. Several years after Desfossés' death he returned to Zambia and no further information is available concerning his activi-

NOTES
220

ties ("Bela, Mwenze, Pilipili and Aroun," *Jeune Afrique,* IX, no. 23 [1956], p. 28). His sculpture is dull and pedestrian and does not approach the originality found in the work of the school's painters.

4. Ibid., p. 25.

5. Feathers and sticks with frayed ends, which might be considered brushes of a kind, as well as fingers, are used in the techniques of traditional painting in Africa.

6. "Bela, Mwenze, Pilipili and Aroun," p. 27.

7. In addition to Bela, Mwenze, and Pilipili, other artists who worked with Desfossés include Lilima, Kabala, Ilunga, Kipinda, and N'Kulu.

8. "Bela, Mwenze, Pilipili and Aroun," p. 26. At the time that Mwenze was interviewed, a large one-man exhibition of his work was being held in Lubumbashi.

9. Mwenze has stated that he used this technique "so as to be different from other artists."

10. See Paul Wingert, *The Sculpture of Negro Africa* (New York: Columbia University Press, 1950), Plate 104.

11. Before going to Africa, Moonens studied at the Brussels Academy of Fine Arts and the Higher Institute of Decorative Arts. Following this training he was an instructor of drawing and painting at the Malenbeek Academy. From 1948 to 1951 he taught painting in Kinshasa, training Kabelua, Kayonbonga, and Mongita. Mongita has served as Minister of Culture in the independent Congolese government.

12. See V. E. Von Sydow, *Die Kunst der Naturvölker und der Vorzeit* (Berlin: Propylaen-Verlag, 1925), pp. 159–60 and Plate 7.

13. Born at Uden, Holland, in 1917, De Maegt studied at the Higher St. Luke's Institute at Schaerbeek, Brussels, at the Louvain Royal Academy, at the National Higher Institute of Fine Arts at Antwerp, and at the Academia Belgica in Rome.

14. It took its name from the similarly named École St. Luc art schools in Belgium. Frère Marc studied painting and sculpture at the École St. Luc at Liège before going to Zaïre in 1941.

15. Frère Marc left Kinshasa to teach art at a small school in Nyunda, Rwanda.

16. Entering students had to furnish proof of six years of primary school, and be tested on their drawing ability. About two hundred students applied each year, from which forty were chosen.

A seven-year painting course followed the practices of many European art schools. The students began by arranging points, lines, and triangles into compositions and, gradually, after they had learned some of the fundamentals of design, they were taught to sketch from nature. At this stage the Kinshasa Zoo was a favorite haunt. With this basic knowledge the students went on to create wallpaper designs, posters, and finally oil paintings. However, no graduates in painting have so far distinguished themselves.

The three-year architecture course was unusual, for at only a few other sub-Saharan schools and universities have full courses of study in the subject been offered to Africans.

17. Mensah's commissions include a relief and mask in the New Stanley Hotel in Kinshasa, a monument to Commander Hannsun in Matadi, a monument to Père van Hengethoven in Kisantu, and a relief at the Camp Militaire in Thysville.

18. Information prepared by Frère Denis on the school's history is particularly revealing. He states that Frère Marc "saw that Negro art was dead and that the African with his customs, the heritage of his belief in evil spirits, his religious conception based on a god infinitely transcendent, and the cult of protective ancestors was no longer thinkable before the influence of the new European ideas...."

19. There was also in Brazzaville the École des Arts, a school for crafts, at which bookbinding, textile and wallpaper design, ceramics, and souvenir carving were taught. Much of the work, however, was tasteless and uninspired. A number of graduates have gone into textile houses or have sold works through a local shop, Artisanat Artistique Africain. The school was founded by the noted musicologist M. Pepper in 1942. In 1954 its direction was taken on by a French painter, Jacques Pariot. One of Pariot's former ceramics instructors, Gabriel Sere, later headed the art section of the Lycée Technique in Libreville, Gabon.

20. The word poto-poto refers to mud recently churned by a herd of elephants.

21. P. Ducamp, "Willingly to School," *The Shell Magazine*, XLII, no. 672 (December 1962), p. 366.

22. Ibid, pp. 366–67.

23. Ibid., p. 366.

24. Other important painters associated with the school are Mounkala, Okola, Iloki, Ouassa, Ossali, Bandila, Oko, Ilunga, and Bokoko. In 1966, Ouassa (sometimes spelled Wassa) gained international fame by winning the graphic prize at the UNESCO-sponsored First World Festival of Negro Arts at Dakar.

25. One such work, seen in Libreville, Gabon, and much too poor to be an original Ondongo, was signed, unlike an authentic work, with backward Ns.

26. See Wingert, *The Sculpture of Negro Africa*, Plate 25; and Robert Goldwater, *Senufo Sculpture from West Africa* (New York: The Museum of Primitive Art, 1964), Plate 38.

27. A Kuyu-style head was observed at the school by the author. It was the only example of traditional art in evidence, which certainly explains its popularity.

28. Simultaneity is defined by John Canaday, *Mainstream of Modern Art* (New York: Holt, Rinehart and Winston, 1962), p. 458, as follows: "the simultaneous revelation of more than one aspect of an object in an effort to express the total image."

29. Papa Ibra Tall is sometimes also known as Tall Papa Ibra, following the

traditional Senegalese custom of putting the surname first. Recently, however, the Senegalese government decreed that citizens must place surnames last.

30. An example with the same designs may be seen in a Tuareg blanket illustrated in Plate V. no. 10, of Harold D. Gunn, *A Handbook of the African Collections of the Commercial Museum* (Philadelphia: Philadelphia Commercial Museum, n.d.), p. 47.

31. These artists are interested primarily in modern American jazz, particularly in instrumentalists such as Coleman Hawkins, Lester Young, and Cannonball Adderly.

VI. Art Schools in English-Speaking East and Central Africa

1. English-speaking East and Central Africa includes the Sudan, Ethiopia, Uganda, Kenya, Tanzania, Zambia, Malawi, and Rhodesia.

2. Makerere University College was founded as a technical college in 1921. The next year it changed its emphasis, adopting its present title from the name of the hill on which it is situated.

3. Mrs. Trowell studied at the Slade School in London from 1923 to 1927. Five years later she left for Africa. She was director of the art school from 1937 until her departure in the late 1950s, and also served as curator of the Uganda Museum during the war years.

4. Margaret Trowell, *African Tapestry* (London: Faber and Faber, 1957), pp. 103–17.

5. Mrs. Trowell writes: "They were, of course, very annoyed that I would not teach them the way. They have told me since that they felt that I was lazy because I would never take a brush and show them how." Ibid., p. 115.

6. The life of Christ was illustrated with reproductions of paintings from the School of Fine Arts and was published as *And Was Made Man* (London: Society for Promoting Christian Knowledge, 1956).

7. Trowell, p. 104.

8. Ham Mukasa has an important place in the modern history of Uganda. Born in 1872, he was the first Buganda to learn English. He played a major role as an adviser to political leaders until his death in 1956. He was also one of the founders of the Boy Scouts in Uganda.

9. Gregory Maloba, "Petson Lombé," *Roho,* no. 2 (June 1962), p. 34.

10. Sam Ntiro, "Kilimanjaro Gold Dust," *Roho,* no. 1 (June 1961), p. 9.

11. Njau's wife, Rebecca, a playwright, is a Kikuyu.

12. A smaller work, similar in style, was done four years earlier for the Uganda Technical College Library, Kampala.

13. Denis Williams, "A Sudanese Calligraphy," *Transition* (June 1963), p. 20.

14. Robert Serumaga, "Conversation with Ibrahim el Salahi," *Topic,* no. 24 (1967), pp. 14–15.

15. Ethiopia, independent throughout most of its long history and never a British colony like Uganda and the Sudan, nevertheless uses English as its second language.

16. Ethiopian artists are generally referred to by their first name or names.

17. Interview with Skunder Boghossian, September 1, 1968.

18. The subjects of these paintings indicate that Skunder may be familiar with the creation myths of the Dogon people of Mali as set forth in the works of French ethnologist Marcel Griaule.

19. Louise Atcheson, "Skunder Boghossian," *Transition* (June 1963), p. 43.

20. Selby Mvusi, a South African painter who had studied in the United States, experimented with abstraction in the early 1960s. Until his death in an automobile accident in late 1967, Mvusi taught painting in the design department at University College, Nairobi.

21. Sydney W. Head, "A Conversation with Gebre Kristos Desta," *African Arts,* II, no. 4 (Summer 1969), p. 22.

22. Ibid., p. 23.

23. Interview with Gebre Kristos Desta, August 31, 1968.

24. Frank McEwen, "Return to Origins: New Directions for African Art," *African Arts,* I, no. 2 (Winter 1968), pp. 18–25, 88.

25. Cf. Plate 332, Jean Guiart, *The Arts of the South Pacific* (New York: Golden Press, 1963).

VII. Art Schools in English-Speaking West Africa

1. English-speaking West Africa includes Gambia, Sierra Leone, Liberia, Ghana, and Nigeria.

2. Achimota College is now the University of Ghana and is located in Legon, outside of Accra.

3. As a young student at Achimota, Antubam was Eva Meyerowitz's field research assistant for her books *The Sacred State of Akan* and *Akan Traditions of Culture.*

4. *Oware* is the Ashanti name for the seed game played on a scooped-out game board found throughout Africa.

5. Antubam had decided ideas about European abstract art. In an interview on January 13, 1962, he stated: "One thing I don't do is abstract art. People who do those things are playing and at this stage of the development of my country, there's no need for it. All national galleries in Europe have a classical, serious art. This is no time for joker artists. My country must first establish that kind of art which will go into a museum to serve as an inspiration. The artist must help society to be less confused and more peaceful—abstract art does just the opposite. What the world needs is the artist who can see in chaos something likely to bring

less confusion. The artist who paints confusion and melancholy is not helping. . . . I don't like distortion. I like beautiful women, children, etc. I am interested in basic values. Every country must first establish their Renaissance, then they can fool around."

6. Two quotations which show Antubam's attitude toward traditional African art follow: "the art of a people changes and develops, passing through three main evolutionary stages if it is allowed to follow its natural course of growth. There is first a period of archaism featured by spontaneous expressions of disproportions and abstract symbolisms due to ill knowledge of the natural rules about things in their environment, distortions that spring from an almost fanatical belief in magic and superstition, crude execution resulting from the use of primitive implements and conservative attitudes in art. This is followed by a classical stage at which folk art gives way to creative art; a period of naturalism synthesized by serious research into and codification of existing native cultural conceptions, a search for and the use of natural rules with their resultant effect of a scientific and professional attitude in art. A third stage follows the particular people's full realization of themselves as a nation and the growth of their national pride. It is the time of dynamic movement and realism in art. Artists seek in all earnestness and expand in their means and method of expression by knowledge acquired from other lands. There is a general widening of scope of expression at this stage and artists become more and more conscious of the importance of perspective and the effects of romantic and atmospheric changes particularly in painting. And, the expression of three dimensions in drawing and painting ceases to be a mystery." Kofi Antubam, "Ghanaian Art," Catalog of an exhibition held at Accra Central Library (1954), p. 3.

"Art to the Primitive man must always have a purpose, and 'art for art's sake' as a slogan was unknown to him. In his drawings and paintings, if any, he only sees two dimensions. Sculpture, which becomes his principal form of expression, tends to be static and crude in execution, his tools being too simple in conception and setup for detail work. . . . In the later years of his history even the primitive man grows out of his shell of backwardness. . . . Nor can his art, which is not an isolated phenomenon, stand still. With the rebirth came fresh knowledge and consequently changes in concepts of good and evil, beauty and ugliness. All along, however, he makes sure that he has his eyes on the fact that every people develops a specific style of art by giving preferences to certain objects and forms of design." Kofi Antubam, "Principles of Arts and Crafts," unpublished manuscript, n.d. (typewritten), pp. 62–63.

7. Asihene was a student in the department in the early 1940s. Shortly thereafter he went to Goldsmith's College of Art in London to further his training. In 1950 he was elected a Fellow of the Royal Society of Arts and in 1952 was awarded the Art Teacher's Diploma from Kumasi.

8. Teacher-training colleges in English-speaking areas train teachers for pri-

mary and secondary schools. Most of those who specialize in art go on to teach in primary schools, however, as art is rarely taught in secondary school.

9. *Okyerema* means someone who, by sounding the drum, binds towns together.

10. In Kofi's wood sculpture he often seemingly shows a disrespect for the material. For example, he might carelessly use wood partially eaten by termites and might place his figures outdoors without applying any protective coating. But these circumstances both tend to show that Kofi is striving to reveal the true character of wood.

11. Eric Taylor, a leading English graphic artist, is one of the best-known artists to have taught in Africa. Born in England in 1909, he studied art at the William Ellis School, Hampstead, and the Royal College of Art, London. Formerly Head of the Design School at the Leeds College of Art, he has also traveled widely, lecturing to art students in Austria, Germany, Holland, Denmark, and Italy.

12. Blue is a traditionally popular color, particularly among Yoruba tribes of Western Nigeria. Yoruba women frequently dress in indigo-dyed cloth and much traditional Yoruba sculpture is colored with blue. The indigo dyeing of cloth is a major industry in Kano, the most important city of Northern Nigeria.

13. The specific influences Grillo mentions result from his tribal background and his acquaintance with European art history gained from his studies at Zaria. The last statement in this quotation seems rather naive. It is interesting that other Zaria graduates, when asked by the author about influences, replied similarly.

14. There has been continuing cultural contact between Nigeria and Brazil since the days of the slave trade, when many Nigerians served as slaves in the South American country. Some of these slaves, eventually freed, returned to Nigeria, and often became wealthy, building houses in the style that has since become known as "Brazilian."

15. Simon's specialization in sculpture while at Zaria probably explains in part his preference for rounded forms in painting.

16. Lino-cut is a shortened term for linoleum cut, a twentieth-century process whereby the surface of a piece of linoleum, mounted on a wood block, is cut exactly as for a wood block print. Although linoleum is more easily worked than wood, the lino-cut print usually lacks clarity and definition when compared to the wood block impression.

17. Akinola Lasekan, a Yoruba born in Owo in 1916, is one of the earliest of the new Nigerian painters. His paintings deal with genre subjects and are painted in a descriptive, academic style. Self-taught, he began his career in 1935 as a designer of textiles. In 1940 Lasekan and the sculptor Justus Akerodulu opened a studio in Lagos. Four years later Lasekan held his first major exhibition. He taught painting at the University of Nigeria at Nsukka and more recently served as administrator for the Nigerian Council for Advancement of Art in Lagos.

18. Nwoko thought about the scene for a year before starting to paint it. He

never paints a subject he has just seen as he believes the immediate stimulus of a scene is probably "too emotional."

19. Compare with the works of Otto Dix and George Grosz, for example, Dix's *Meeting a Madman at Night,* reproduced in John Canaday, *Mainstream of Modern Art* (New York: Holt, Rinehart and Winston, 1962), Plate 525. Nwoko has stated, however, that he was not familiar with the works of these painters.

20. Yusuf Grillo, the present department head, hopes to lengthen the program to four years.

21. Although Mount "kept control over the whole, it was strictly a fifty-fifty project." Interview with Paul Mount, June 26, 1961.

22. It is interesting that Idehen carved details on the relief, just as in the traditional Benin bronzes details were sometimes chased on the cast work.

23. Ulli Beier, "Experiment in Art Teaching," *Black Orpheus,* no. 12 (1963), pp. 43–44; and Ulli Beier, *Contemporary Art in Africa* (New York: Frederick A. Praeger, 1968) pp. 89–164.

24. Beier, "Experiment in Art Teaching," pp. 43–44.

25. Beier, *Contemporary Art in Africa,* p. 108.

26. Hezbon Owiti, a painter and printmaker from Kenya, also spent time at the Oshogbo workshop at Ulli Beier's invitation.

27. Seven-Seven gives several fanciful explanations for his rather bizarre name. Beier, *Contemporary Art in Africa,* p. 113. His real name is Taiwo Olaniyi.

28. Ibid.

29. Ibid.

30. This head has some resemblance, purely unintentional, to animal masks of the Ivory Coast and Cameroun.

31. Beier, *Contemporary Art in Africa,* p. 129.

32. There were earlier claims that similar methods were used in English-speaking Africa by Reverend Edward Paterson at the Cyrene Mission in Rhodesia and by Margaret Trowell at Makerere University College in Uganda. The "school styles" resulting from both these efforts, however, were clearly based on European prototypes.

33. Ulli Beier, "Three Zaria Artists," *West African Review,* XXXI, no. 395 (October 1960), p. 37.

VIII. Artists Independent of African Art Schools

1. Guedes' style is closely related to that of the early twentieth-century Spanish architect Gaudi in his conception of buildings as plastic, modeled forms.

2. Guedes has patronized other artists and craftsmen: for example, a bricklayer, Gonsalvos, who executes plaster murals from Guedes' designs; a woodcarver, Filippe, who carves lions and Nativities for tourists; and an embroiderer who copies works by native painters.

3. For a short autobiography of Malangatana see appendix, pp. 195–98.

4. Valente Malangatana, "Two Poems," *Black Orpheus,* no. 10 (1962), pp. 28–29.

5. Cameroun, at that time, was a German colony. Some members of the present Sultan's court still speak German. The old palace, although still standing, has been supplanted by a functional building nondescript in style.

6. Not only an architect and painter, Njoya has also been a musician and sculptor. He carved the entrance doors of Foumban's main mosque and decorated the palace of Mantum with sculpture.

7. Several books on the Bamoun tribe have been written using this alphabet. A handwritten volume on Bamoun history and customs was prepared under the direction of Sultan Njoya. This work has been translated into French and published as *Histoire et Coutumes des Bamun,* Memoires de L'Institut Français d'Afrique Noire, Centre du Cameroun, Serie: Populations, no. 5 (Paris: Éditions L.C.L., 1952). Two smaller volumes, one on religion and another on medicine, were also written.

8. I. Dugast and M. D. W. Jeffreys identify the foreground figures, numbered one through seven, in their description of this scene, which serves as a frontispiece to their publication *L'Écriture des Bamun,* Memoires de L'Institut Français d'Afrique Noire, Centre du Cameroun, Serie: Populations, no. 2 (Paris: Éditions L.C.L., 1950.

9. The term *primitive* is used in this sense to denote style elements such as lack of perspective and modeling and the kind of hierarchical scaling found in other so-called primitive painting, such as in thirteenth- and fourteenth-century Italian works. It is not to be confused with the word *primitive,* often used to describe traditional African art.

10. Dugast and Jeffreys, p. 66.

11. The intertwined snakes at the bottom of the painting *Sultan Njoya Teaches* is a traditional Bamoun motive and appears in the tribe's carved wooden stools. *The Battle* contains a few traditional motives; numerous designs borrowed from Islamic art, such as the star pattern; and several patterns of the artist's own creation.

12. Others in this group were Napper, Rebeyrolle, Simon Dat, and Taylor. In France the group has shown in the Musée d'art Moderne.

13. "Ibrahim N'Diaye, peintre sénégalais," *Afrique,* no. 14 (July 1962), p. 37.

14. "Location" is the term commonly used in South Africa to denote the large African settlements, often at considerable distances from the major cities, in which Africans are working in the cities are required to live.

15. Jean Caillens, "Prelude au IIe congrés des écrivains et artistes noirs," *Présence Africaine,* no. 20 (Juin–Juillet 1958), p. 132.

16. "Famous in Europe and America but Artist Returns to Find Inspiration," *South African Art News and Review,* I, no. 5 (June 22, 1961), p. 2. Although Sekoto asserts his style is "purely African," he rarely borrows style traits from

traditional African art. His style is, in fact, quite close to styles found in modern European painting.

17. Gerard Sekoto, "A South African Artist," *Présence Africaine,* no. 14–15 (Juin–Septembre 1957), p. 285.

18. Although Sekoto grew up in a rural environment, his father, a Christian preacher, forbade the youth to participate in local tribal festivals and rites.

19. More descriptive information concerning the symbolism of these windows may be found in a guidebook sold in Africa Hall: *"Left window;* . . . Above [the foreground group] a group of Africans is carrying a burden in the shape of the African continent, which is symbolic of ignorance and illiteracy; a huge dragon with a malignant face, a symbol of the colonial era, is sitting on it. On the left side of the window a skeleton clad with a red mantle is lashing the group of Africans: it is a symbol of the evil force which is pushing the continent into backwardness. At the top of the window, the rich and virgin forest of Africa appears in thunder and fire; this gives the work an atmosphere of horror, suffering and struggle. A huge, black unbroken chain framing the picture appears like a symbol of slavery. *Right window:* Higher up [above the foreground] a big sun is rising, and in it the various lands of Africa can be seen, as well as the different types of people who inhabit them and who seem to be watching the scene from within. At the top of the window the red skeleton, symbolizing the evil force, is flying away in despair, abandoning everything behind him. *Middle window:* The two [foreground] figures wear the Ethiopian national costume because the artist felt that Ethiopia should play a leading role in Africa for having untiringly endeavoured to reach this ideal. Behind them, a group of Africans in their different national costumes are standing as a symbol of the participation of the entire continent in this great struggle for freedom, and of the responsibility freedom entails, their seriousness being also the expression of their incessant search for knowledge. On the left side of the window, slightly beyond the foreground, a knight in armour holding the scale of Justice and a sword and bearing the United Nations emblem on his chest, symbolizes the principles and aspirations of the United Nations and Africa's faith in and support for them. At the top, a serene landscape and a rising sun are symbols of enlightenment and hope: this is the dawn of a constructive era in the life of the African nations." *Africa Hall* (Addis Ababa: Administrative and Liaison Office, Africa Hall, 1963).

20. Oku Ampofo, "Neo-African Art in the Gold Coast," *Africana* (The Magazine of the West African Society), I, no. 3 (Summer 1949), p. 18.

21. The use of the word *neo* here means simply *new,* without any of the implications of *pseudo* as often implied in contemporary usage.

22. The exhibition was brought by Mrs. Ruth Faux, wife of a former British official in Africa, and was held in the New York Public Library.

23. A traditional carver, Kwame Bediaku, aids by blocking out Ampofo's wood sculpture.

24. In the cement fondu method the figures are not cast, but rather are built up around an armature, bit by bit, with the sculptor modeling the cement as he works. When the basic form is completed, a final finish consisting of a coating of marble granules is applied.

25. The late Kenneth Murray, a British subject who lived in Nigeria for many years, was a director of the Department of Antiquities. He was instrumental in developing the Nigeria Museum, one of the best in Africa, and in acquiring its fine collection of traditional African sculpture.

26. Forrester B. Washington, *Contemporary Artists of Africa,* (New York: Harmon Foundation, 1960), p. 21. Many younger Nigerian artists feel, however, that because of his governmental position and his mesmeric effect upon state officials, Enwonwu has excessively dominated and occasionally stifled developments within the burgeoning art movement in Nigeria.

27. Ben Enwonwu, "Problems of the African Artist Today," *Présence Africaine,* nos. 8–10 (June–November 1956), pp. 174–79.

28. Ulli Beier, *Art in Nigeria 1960* (London: Cambridge University Press, 1960), p. 10.

29. Dennis Duerden, "African Art and Its Critics," *Ibadan,* no. 6 (June 1959), p. 17.

30. The overall narrative sequence in the scenes represented on the doors reads from left to right, beginning with the Bosch-like tree spirits, continuing through traditional Nigerian activities and the advent of the European, and ending with Independence. This sequential arrangement is not found in the doors traditional to Africa, for example, in those carved by the Dogon, Senufo, and Yoruba tribes. All but the last of the National Hall doors, however, like traditional examples, have no narrative sequence within the individual doors.

31. Emokpae did study for a while at Yaba Technical Institute in the mid-1960's but by this time his artistic style and career were already well established. He will, therefore, for the purpose of this study, be considered independent of art-school training.

INDEX

Abidjan art school, 83, 92
Abidjan museum, 45
abstract art: Antubam's views on, 224–25; of Ethiopian Gebre Kristos, 116–17
Académie des Beaux-Arts (Kinshasa), 74, 81–83
Académie des Beaux-Arts et des Métiers d'Art (Lubumbashi), 74, 77–79
Accra Museum, 72
Achimota College, 124
Addis Ababa's Fine Arts School, 95, 111–17
Adebisi. See Fabunmi
Afewerk Tekle, 73, 169–73, 186, 199
Afolabi, Jacob, 147–48
Africa Hall windows, 171, 229
African art: categories of, xvi; future of, 193; glossary of artists, 199–203; mission-inspired, xvi, 22–38; new, xvi, 62–73, 187-94; souvenir, xvi, 39–61; summarized, xvi, 187–93; support of, 63–72, 192; traditional, xvi, 3–21
"African Art," 68
African Forum, 67
African Studies Center, UCLA, 67
Afro-Portuguese ivories, 41–43
Ahmadu Bello University, 124, 132–42, 159
Aho, Justin, 51
Ainslie, William, 30
Akamba Industries Co-operative Society, 40, 55

Akanji, Adebisi, 153–57, 199
Akeredolu, Justus, 49, 199
Akintola, S. L., 41
Akolo, Jimo, 133–34, 199
Akwapim, 6, 65, 173, 174
Alhadeff, Leo, 40, 44–45, 76, 199
American encouragement of African art, 67–68
Ampofo, Oku, 65, 72, 173–75, 184, 190, 199
AMSAC (American Society of African Culture), 67
Antubam, Kofi, 5, 65, 67, 71, 72, 124–28, 171, 190, 199, 224–25
appliqué cloth, 15–17
Arabic art, 105–11
Areogun, 19–21, 199
Art et Louange, 31
art schools: Addis Ababa's Fine Arts School, 111–17; Ahmadu Bello University in Zaria, 132–43; artists independent of, 160; Cyrene Mission School in Rhodesia, 23–30; Desfossés', 74–79; in English-speaking East and Central Africa, 95–123; in English-speaking West Africa, 124–59; in French-speaking Africa, 74–94; Khartoum's School of Fine and Applied Arts, 105–11; Kinshasa's Académie des Beaux-Arts, 81–83; Lubumbashi's, 74–81; Makerere University College in

art schools: (*cont.*)

Uganda, 95–105; mission-run, 23–38; Moonens', 74, 79–81; Poto-Poto, 83–90; Rhodesia's National Gallery workshop, 117–23; summarized, 187–92; Western influence on, 62–63; Yaba Technical Institute in Lagos, 142–47; *see also* workshops

artists: art-school trained, 189–90; autobiographies of, 194–98; in English-speaking East and Central Africa, 95–123; in English-speaking West Africa, 124–59; in French-speaking Africa, 74–94; independent of art schools, 160–86; listed, 199–203; of "new art," summarized, 187–92; "untrained" group, 188–89

Ashanti art, 6, 12–15, 160
Asihene, S.V., 72, 127, 199
Asiru Olatunde. *See* Olatunde
autobiographies of artists, 194–98
Azikiwe, Nnamdi, 72, 176

Bakala, D., 82
Bakuba crafts, 9
Bamgboye, 19–21, 199
Bamoun art, 9, 161–65
Bandele, 19, 20, 33, 195, 199
Bantu Men's Social Centre, 73
Bapende masks, 7–8
Barranger, Marie, 31, 199
Bayaka masks, 7–8
Beier, Georgina Betts, 148–51
Beier, Ulli, 36, 65, 119–20, 147–58, 179, 195, 199
Beinart, Julian, 147, 200
Bela, 76–77, 200
Benin art, 9–13
Benin Carvers Association, 40
Betts, Georgina, 148–51
Bibi ivories, 43
Bisiri, Yemi, 17–21, 200
Bonsu, Osei, Jr., 15
Bonsu, Osei, Sr., 14–15, 200
Botbol, Albert, 92
brass work: Ashanti, 13–15; Bamoun, 9; Benin, 10–13; Christian-inspired, 31; Fon, 17; Yoruba, 19
Brazzaville's Poto-Poto School, 83–90
British colonies: art in, 70; art schools in former, 95–159
British Council, 71
Brown, Evelyn, 67

Buraimoh, Jimoh, 148–53, 156, 200
Burrell, Mrs. R., 123
busts made for souvenir sale, 46–48

calligraphy, Arabic, 105–6
Cameroun art, 7, 9
"canoe and palm tree" paintings, 46
Carroll, Father Kevin, 20, 31–33, 195, 200
carving. *See* sculpture; woodcarving
Castle, Robert, 167
categories of African art, xvi
Catholic Church's encouragement of African art, 30–38
cement fondu, 190
cement screens, 155–57
Central African art schools, 95–123
chapel decorations at Cyrene Mission, 28–29
Chemchemi center, 66
church art, 22–38
cire perdue technique, 12, 19, 31, 129–30
Clark, J. P., 65
cloth making, appliqué, 15–17
colonialism's effect on arts, 69
commercial art, 132–33
Congo: Christian art, 22–24; Poto-Poto art school, 83–90
contemporary art. *See* new art
copying traditional art for souvenir sales, 43–45
Crowder, Michael, 46, 158, 200
crucifixes, 23–24
cups: Afro-Portuguese, 42; effigy, 82
Cyrene Mission, 23–30, 123

Dahomey brasses, 31
Dakar's École des Arts, 83–84, 89
Dar es Salaam carvers, 56, 60–61
De Maegt, Jean, 81
Denis, Frére, 81
Desfossès, Pierre Romain-, 44, 69, 74–79, 83, 85, 89, 94, 200
Diop, Alioune, 67
Donvidé, Aqueminon, 51, 200
Donvidé family carvings, 49–51
doors, carved, 33–36, 129, 180–81
Dube, Denson, 120
Duerden, Dennis, 138, 200

East African art schools, 95–123
École des Arts du Sénégal, 70, 83–84, 89
École St. Luc, 81; *see also* Académie des Beaux-Arts

effigy cups, 82
Ekiti woodcarving, 19–21
Elizabeth II, Queen, 10, 11, 176
Elkan, Walter, 55
Emokpae, Erhabor, 184–86, 200
English-speaking Africa's art schools, 95–159
Enwonwu, Ben, 67, 72, 176–79, 184, 186, 190, 200
Epstein, Jacob, 97, 176, 190
Erguavo, Palmer, 10
Ethiopia: art in 73, 169–73; art schools in, 95, 111–17
European-African style, mission art's, 22–38

Fabunmi, Adebisi, 148
Fagg, William, 43
Fakeye, Lamidi, 19, 20, 33–38, 72, 194–95, 200
Farfield Foundation, 66
Fax, Elton, 67
Fine Arts School, Addis Ababa, 95, 111–17
Fon art, 15–17, 31, 51
Fraenkel, Peter, 179
French colonial areas: art in, 70; art schools in, 74–94
furniture carvings, 49–51
future of African art, 193

Galerie Labac, 41, 71
Gandelin, Edith, 84
Gebre Kristos Desta, 116–18, 171, 200
Ghana: art schools in, 124–34; government support of art in, 70–71; new art movement in, 65–66
Ghana Industrial Development Corporation, 41
Ghana Society of Artists, 65, 125
Glencross, B., 25, 29
Gluckman, Judith, 167
governmental encouragement of art, 68–73
Grillo, Yusuf, 72, 133–34, 200
Guedes, Amancio, 147, 160
Guedes, Dorothy, 198
Guedes, Miranda, 197

"Le Hangar," 74
Harmon Foundation, 67
Hausa dealers, 40
Honutondji, Étienne, 29, 31, 200
house posts, 19–21, 37

Ibadan Mbari Club, 65–66
IDC (Industrial Development Corporation), 41
Idehen, Ebomwoyi, 144
Idehen, Festus, 68, 72, 143–46, 200
Idubor, Felix, 146, 160, 179–83, 186
IFAN (Institut Français d'Afrique Noire), 70
Ife art center, 158
Igbesamwa, Ine, 9, 200
Ihama, David, 10, 200, 212
independent artists, 160–86
Industrial Development Corporation, 41
Inneh, Omoregbe, 10–13, 200
Inneh, Osdaye, 10, 13
Institut Français d'Afrique Noire, 70
Institut Nationale des Arts (Abidjan), 83, 92
Islamic art, 105–11
ivories, Afro-Portuguese, 41–43
Ivory Coast: art school in, 83, 92; museum of, 45

John XXIII, Pope, 30

Kabingo, 69
Kabongo, 69
Kakooza, George, 102–4, 200
Kamba, Jean-Bosco, 79, 80, 201
Kandinsky, Wassily, 116
Kelly, C., 149
Kelly, P. M., 31–32
Kennedy, President and Mrs. J. F., 41
Khartoum art school, 95, 105–11
Kibwanga. See Mwenze Kibwanga
Kingdon, Jonathan, 101
Kinshasa academy, 81–83
Kofi, Vincent, 66, 71, 129–32, 144, 201
Kumasi University art school, 124–32, 158–59
Kumalo, Lazarus, 24–26, 123

Lagos art school, 124, 142–47
Lam, Wilfredo, 114
Lanmandoucelo, Vincent, 17, 18, 201
Lasekan, Akinola, 138
Lattier, Christian, 92–94, 201
Lawrence, Jacob, 67
Lods, Pierre, 83–85, 89–90, 94, 201
Lower Congo, art of, 22–24
Lubumbashi art schools, 74-81

Lufwa, Andre, 81, 83
Luluabourg museum, 7–8

Mackendrick, J. M., 127
Maison des Artisanats, 45
Makerere University College art school, 70,
    95–105, 158
Makonde carvings, 56–61
Malangatana, Valente, 160–62, 186, 195–98,
    201
Maloba, Gregory, 96–98, 102, 190, 201
Mankana, Ignace, 82
Manyandure, Bernard, 120–23
Marc-Stanislas, Frère, 74, 81–83, 94, 201
Mariga, Joram, 120
masks: Poto-Poto school's stylized, 87–89;
    tribal, 7–8
Massengo, Grégoire, 46–48, 201
Matta, Roberto, 114
Mbari Clubs, 65–66, 147–58
M'Bigou carving, 48
McEwen, Frank, 70, 117–20, 201
Mensah, Benjamin, 81–82, 201
Meyerowitz, H. V., 124, 127, 201
mission art, 22–38: Catholic Church's aid
    to, 30–38; crucifixes, 23–24; Cyrene Mis-
    sion style, 23–30; souvenir styles created
    by?, 44; summarized, xvi
Mode, 79–81, 201
modern African art. See new art
Moonens, Laurent, 74, 79–81, 89, 201
Moore, Henry, 96
Moses, Lemon, 120
Mount, Paul, 68, 144–46, 201
Mphahlele, Ezekiel, 65, 66
Mteki, Boira, 120–23
Mteki, Richard, 120
Mukarobgwa, Thomas, 117, 120–21, 201
Mukasa, Ham, 96
Mukomberanwa, Nicholas, 120
Mulongoya, Pilipili. See Pilipili
Munge, Mutisya, 54, 201
Murray, Kenneth, 176, 201
Museum of Modern Art, New York, 119
museums: collecting problems of, 212; copy-
    ing of traditional art at, 45; government
    aid to, 68–69; and preservation of Afri-
    can heritage, 5–6; workshops at, 117–23
Muslim art, 105–11
Musoke, Teresa, 102–4, 202

Mwambetu, 55
Mwenze Kibwanga, 77–79, 202

National Gallery of Rhodesia, 95, 117–23
N'Diaye, Ibrahim, 90, 165–67, 186, 202
"Neo-African" art, 173
new art: artists of, 187-92; emergence of,
    62–73; in English-speaking Africa, 95–
    159; in French-speaking Africa, 74–93;
    future of, 193; by independent artists,
    160–86; media and techniques of, 191;
    patronage of, 63–72, 193; subject mat-
    ter of, 191; summarized, xvi, 187–94
Nigeria: art schools in, 124, 132–47; En-
    wonwu salaried by, 176; government sup-
    port of art in, 70–71, 176; Mbari Clubs'
    influence on intellectual life of, 65–66;
    mission-inspired art in, 31–38; new-art
    movement in, 65–66; thorn carving in,
    48–49
Nigeria Magazine, 71, 158
Njau, Elimo, 66, 96, 100–1, 202
Njoya, Ibrayima, 161–65, 186, 187, 202
Ntiro, Sam, 67, 96–101, 190, 202
Nwoko, Demas, 65, 133, 136, 140–43, 192,
    202

Oba Akenzua II, 12
Oba Eweka II, 10–13
Obo-Ekiti, 19
Ogboni brasses, 17
Ogundele, Rufus, 148
Okeke, C. Uche, 65–66, 133–40, 202
Okeke, Simon, 133–35, 202
Okigbo, Christopher, 65, 66, 140
Olaniyi, Taiwo. See Seven-Seven
Olatunde, Asiru, 153–56, 202
O'Mahoney, Father Sean, 31–33, 195, 202
Omodamwven, J. N., 10, 202, 212
Ondongo, 85–87, 202
Onobrakpeya, Bruce, 133–37, 147, 202
Oshogbo art school, 66, 124, 147–58
Osifo, Osagie, 144–47, 202
Ossali, 84, 202
Oye-Ekiti workshop, 31–38
Oyelami, Muriana, 148

Paa ya Paa Art Gallery, 66
Paterson, Edward, 23–30, 119–20, 123
patronage of art, 63–72, 192–93

People's Republic of Congo, 83–90
Pilipili Mulongoya, 76–78, 202
Pius XII, Pope, 30, 31
plaques, commemorative, 11–13
Pletinckx, M., 77
Pollaiuolo, Antonio del, 177
Portuguese colonies, 160
Poto-Poto school, 70, 81, 83–90
Preller, Alex, 167
Présence Africaine, 30, 67
Protestant mission art, 23–29

Rattray, R. D., 15
religion: function of in African art, 4; as influencing Arabic Shibrain, 105–6
Republic of South Africa, 72–73
Rhodesia: mission-inspired art in, 23–29; National Gallery's workshop school, 70, 95, 117–23
Rhodes-Livingstone Museum Craft Village, 45
rock art, 85–87
Romain-Desfossés. *See* Desfossés
Roman Catholic Church's encouragement of African art, 30–38
rope sculptures, 92–94
Roosevelt, Franklin D., 41
Rumsey, Mrs. Philippa, 198
Ryder, A. F. C., 43

Salahi, Ibrahim el, 108–12, 161, 202
Salisbury workshop, 117–23
schools, art. *See* art schools
School of Fine and Applied Art, Khartoum, 70, 95, 105–11
School of Fine Arts, Makerere College, 70, 95–105, 158
screens, cement, 155–57
sculpture: Afro-Portuguese ivories, 41–43; Ashanti woodcarvings, 15; Benin traditional, 9–10; busts, 46–48; carved doors, 33–36, 129, 180–81; copies of traditional for souvenir sales, 43–45; Ekiti carvings, 19–21; Makonde carvings, 56–61; Nigeria's sponsorship of Enwonwu's, 176–79; rope, 92–94; steatite, 48; thorn carving, 48–49; Wakamba, 51–56; wood as traditional, 3
Sekoto, Gerard, 67, 94, 160, 167–70, 184, 186, 190, 202
Sénégal's art schools, 70, 83–84, 89

Senghor, President, 84, 90
Seven-Seven, Twins, 148–51, 153, 156, 202
Sherbro ivories, 43
Shibrain, Ahmed Mohamed, 105–8, 203
Skunder Boghossian, 111–16, 171, 203
social function of African art, 4
Societé Africaine de Culture, 66–67
Songo, Sam, 26, 27, 30, 68, 203
South Africa, Republic of, 72–73
souvenir art, 39–61; Afro-Portuguese ivories, 41–43; copies of traditional art, 43–45; Makonde carvings, 56–61; success of, 61; summarized, xvi; in traditional style, 6; Wakamba carvings, 51–56
Soyinka, Wole, 65
spirit carving, 57–60
stained glass windows, 171–72, 229
steatite carving, 47–48
stick-figure style, 87
Stout, J. Anthony, 60
sub-Saharan art, 3
Sudan's School of Fine and Applied Art, 95, 105–11
support of new art, 63–72, 192–93

Tall, Papa Ibra, 90–92, 94, 203
tapestries, Senegalese, 90–92
Taylor, Eric, 132
Thango, 85, 88–89, 203
Thiès tapestry school, 89, 203
thorn carving, 48–49
Timmermans, Paul, 9, 203
Titabohou, Ibrayima, 163, 203
Todd, Cecil, 101–4, 203
tourist art. *See* souvenir art
traditional art, 3–21: Ashanti, 12–15; Benin, 9–13; copied for souvenir sales, 43–45; Fon, 15–17; museum preservation of, 5–6; summarized, xvi, 21; Yoruba, 17–19
Trowell, Margaret, 70, 95–98, 101, 203
Tutuola, Amos, 65, 177

Uganda's Makerere art school, 95–105
University of Science and Technology, Kumasi, 124–32
"untrained" artists, 188–89

Van Gogh, Vincent, 120

Wakamba art, 40, 52–56
Wambua, Josiah, 55

Washington, Forrester, 67
weights, cast brass, 13
Wenger, Suzanne, 151–56, 203
West African art schools, 124–59
Willett, Frank, 19
Williams, Denis, 106, 147–48, 151, 203
windows, stained-glass, 171–72, 229
Wingert, Paul, 129
Wolford, Mr. and Mrs. Richard F., 15
Wolof tribe, 40
woodcarving: Ashanti, 15; Benin traditional, 9–10; doors, 33–36, 129, 180–81; Ekiti, 19–21; furniture, 49–51; souvenir, 43–61; see also sculpture

workshops: Catholic, 31–38; Oshogbo, 147–58; Oye-Ekiti, 31–38; Salisbury, 117–23
World Crafts Council, 41

Yaba Technical Institute, 124, 142–47
Yèmadjê, 15–17, 203
Yoruba: Christian-inspired craftsmen, 31–38; traditional-style art of, 17–19

Zaïre: art schools in, 74–83; government support of arts in, 69; traditional art in, 7–8
Zaria's art school, 132–42
Zigoma, 85–88, 203

Other DACAPO titles of interest

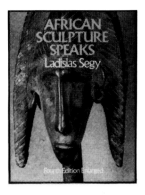

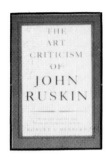
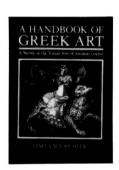
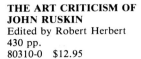